NEGOTIATING
DEVELOPMENT

NEGOTIATING DEVELOPMENT

Rationales and practice for development obligations and planning gain

Patsy Healey
Department of Town and Country Planning, University of Newcastle, UK

Michael Purdue
Newcastle Law School, University of Newcastle, UK

Frank Ennis
Centre for Planning, University of Strathclyde, UK

E & FN SPON
An Imprint of Chapman & Hall

London · Glasgow · Weinheim · New York · Tokyo · Melbourne · Madras

Published by
E & FN Spon, an imprint of Chapman & Hall, 2–6 Boundary Row,
London SE1 8HN, UK

Chapman & Hall, 2–6 Boundary Row, London SE1 8HN, UK

Blackie Academic & Professional, Wester Cleddens Road, Bishopbriggs, Glasgow G64 2NZ, UK

Chapman & Hall GmbH, Pappelallee 3, 69469 Weinheim, Germany

Chapman & Hall USA, 115 Fifth Avenue, New York, NY 10003, USA

Chapman & Hall Japan, ITP-Japan, Kyowa Building, 3F, 2-2-1 Hirakawacho, Chiyoda-ku, Tokyo 102, Japan

Chapman & Hall Australia, 102 Dodds Street, South Melbourne, Victoria 3205, Australia

Chapman & Hall India, R. Seshadri, 32 Second Main Road, CIT East, Madras 600 035, India

First edition 1995

© 1995 Patsy Healey, Michael Purdue and Frank Ennis

Typeset in 10pt Garamond by Saxon Graphics Ltd, Derby

Printed in Great Britain by St Edmundsbury Press, Bury St Edmunds, Suffolk

ISBN 0 419 19410 X

A catalogue record for this book is available from the British Library

♾ Printed on permanent acid-free text paper, manufactured in accordance with ANSI/NISO Z39.48-1992 and ANSI/NISO Z39.48-1984 (Permanence of Paper).

CONTENTS

PREFACE

This book provides an account of the interaction between land use planning regulation and development activity in Britain from the mid-1980s to the early 1990s. It focuses in particular on the negotiation of formal agreements, by which regulatory bodies and developers take on a negative or positive obligation, supplementing the regulatory requirements of the land use planning system. We refer to these as development obligations. Through this 'window' on land use planning and development practice, we provide an insight into the changing nature of the planning system itself. We also offer our own views on the way the system might evolve to meet the demands of a development context in which private interests, that is, those undertaking development, are expected both to provide and pay for most development investment, while at the same time being required to pay to mitigate the impacts of their projects on the wider community. In addition, the system must work in a political context where all concerned with a development project will expect their interests to be considered in the making of regulatory decisions.

The book is based on research undertaken for the Joseph Rowntree Foundation on Negotiating Environmental and Community Impacts: a changing role for planning gain (Healey *et al.,* 1993a; Ennis *et al.*, 1993). The research involved a general review of approaches to the negotiation of development, and particularly, the contentious matter of planning gain. This served to identify perspectives and alternative rationales being used to justify and set limits to the negotiation of development impacts. We also undertook five detailed case studies, in Harlow, Tewkesbury, Solihull, Wandsworth and Newcastle, in which we examined all the agreements negotiated between 1984 and 1991, through documentary research and interviews with planning officers, councillors, local groups and developers.

Part One provides a discussion of the context of planning and development practice in the 1980s/early 1990s in England. The first chapter examines how the planning system addresses the relation between development impacts and the community interest in the planning system. The second chapter reviews the way that current approaches to the negotiation of development obligations have evolved from earlier debates on the distribution of the value land gains from development and planning activity. Chapter 3 shifts perspective to examine the relationship from the point of view of development activity. It illustrates both the complexity and variety of such activity, and the consequent diversity in the ways it is affected by planning regulation. Chapter 4 examines the relationship from the point of view of legal argument. It examines the relation between agreements and other ways of securing development objectives, the range of legal bases for agreements, the role of development obligations as material considerations in planning law, and the legal role of the development plan, and its relation to obligations.

The empirical core of the book, Part Two, is based on our own research, set in the context of other recent research on the planning system, the development process and the negotiation of development. It also takes account of research and debate on the relations between land use regulation and the development process in the United States and in other European countries. It examines the scale and scope of the negotiation of agreements (Chapter 5), the way the practice is justified in national and local policy and how this affects the direction and limits of negotiation (Chapter 6) and the practical issues faced in managing the negotiation process (Chapter 7). In Part Three, we offer our own ideas as to future directions in the context of the development of the planning system itself. Chapter 8 puts forward the approach we advocate, considers its wider implications and the consequences for the practical management of the negotiation process. We also provide a bibliography, an appendix on research method, an index of legal cases cited and a general index.

We hope this book will be of interest to all those concerned with contemporary practice of the British planning system, its relation to the development process, and its future evolution. It is aimed in particular at practitioners interested in reflecting on current practice, at policy-makers considering changes to the system, at students of planning, planning law and development seeking to learn about the interaction between land use planning regulation and development activity, and at international scholars interested in the evolution of land use planning systems in general and the practice of negotiating with developers in particular.

We have tried to adopt a style which should be understandable to all such readers. Nevertheless, there are inevitably a number of specialist terms, evolved in policy debate, or in legal and planning practice. We have tried to clarify these as we go along.

We should like to express our thanks to the Joseph Rowntree Foundation for funding this research; particularly to members of the Project Advisory Group who guided the development of our work and Anne Baines, then of the Foundation, who was such a supportive research manager. We must also thank all those in our five case study authorities (Wandsworth, Solihull, Newcastle, Harlow and Tewkesbury) who helped us in our empirical work, as well as the various developers, planners, lawyers and interest groups we have discussed our work with, in interviews and seminars. Our particular thanks go to James Barlow, Andrew Skaburskis, Sarah Whatmore and Roddy MacDonald with whom we exchanged research reports and findings as fellow academics working on these questions. We should also like to thank David Warburton and Jules Brown for helping out with sub-editing. Finally, this project would have been impossible without the help of our project secretary, Jill Connolly, who has managed the production process of our collaboration in research and publication.

LIST OF FIGURES

LIST OF TABLES

AGREEMENT CASES

ABOUT THE AUTHORS

Patsy Healey is Professor of Town and Country Planning and Director of the Centre for Research in European Urban Environments at the University of Newcastle, UK. She is a specialist in the theory and practice of urban planning, and has made contributions to the communicative approach to planning theory and to the institutional analysis of planning systems and property development processes. Her publications include *Land Use Planning and the Mediation of Urban Change* (Healey *et al.*, 1988), *Dilemmas of Planning Practice* (with Thomas, Avebury, 1991), *Rebuilding the City: Property-led Urban Regeneration* (Healey *et al.* (eds), 1992), and *Managing Cities* (Healey *et al.* (eds), 1995). She is a Board Member of the Tyne and Wear Development Corporation, and was a member of the Joseph Rowntree Foundation's Inquiry into Planning and Housing (1994).

Michael Purdue is Professor of Law in the Newcastle Law School at the University of Newcastle. He is a specialist in planning and environmental law. He worked as a solicitor for the Greater London Council, representing them at planning inquiries, and has taught law at several universities. His publications include *Cases and Materials on Planning Law* (1978), *Sizewell B: An Anatomy of the Inquiry* (with O'Riordan, Kemp, 1988), *Planning Law and Procedure* (with Young, Rowan-Robinson, 1989) and *Planning Appeals: A Critique* (1991). He is case-editor of the *Journal of Planning and Environment Law*.

Frank Ennis is a lecturer in the Centre for Planning, University of Strathclyde. He has wide experience in the teaching of social science disciplines. His research interests include development appraisal, the operation of property markets and urban development processes with particular reference to questions related to infrastructure provision. Recent publications include 'Planning obligations in development plans', *Land Use Policy*, 1994.

SUPPLEMENT: NOTE ON A KEY LEGAL DECISION

On May 11 1995 the House of Lords gave judgement in the case of **Tesco (Witney) [1994]**. The facts of this case are set out in Figure 4.3 but the crucial issue was whether the Secretary of State, on appeal, had wrongly disregarded an offer by the developer to fund the construction of a relief road. The House of Lords upheld the Secretary of State's decision. It is the first time that the House of Lords has been called upon to rule on the scope of planning obligations and on the extent that such planning obligations are material considerations in the determination of a planning application. As the House of Lords is the highest court in the United Kingdom,[1] the judgements are the most authoritative statement of the law on such matters. Five Law Lords heard the appeal but only Lord Keith of Kinkel and Lord Hoffman gave reasoned judgements. As the other three Law Lords agreed with Lord Keith's judgement, it is this judgement which is binding but Lord Hoffman's views will still be very influential.

The decision reviews the legitimate purpose of planning obligations entered into under section 106 of the Town and Country Planning Act 1990, which is the normal provision under which developers bind themselves to make contributions. It considers the various aspects of the relationship between an obligation and a planning permission, and in particular the weight to be given to such an obligation in determining an application for planning permission. It lays down important principles with regard to the boundary between matters of law and matters of policy and adds a further interpretation to current policy and legal debate on how far to constrain the 'buying' of a planning permission with the offer of an obligation. The terms used below are defined in Chapter 4.

On the issue of the content of planning obligations, the decision settles the confusion over whether the same rules apply to the lawfulness of planning obligations as apply to the lawfulness of planning conditions. Lord Keith clearly accepted that the Court of Appeal was correct in the case of **Good [1994]** to hold that a planning obligation could be valid even if it did not fairly or reasonably relate to any development which was being sought by the person entering into the obligation. Lord Hoffman even more explicitly stated that:

> The vires of planning obligations depends entirely upon the terms of section 106. This does not require that the planning obligation should relate to any particular development. As the Court of Appeal held in Good v Epping Forest District Council [1994] 1 WLR 376, the only tests for the validity of a planning obligation outside the express terms of section 106 are that it must be for a planning purpose and not *Wednesbury*[2] unreasonable.

Lord Hoffman also rejected the argument, first suggested in **Bradford [1986]**, that, if a condition would be invalid as being manifestly unreasonable, it would automatically follow that the same requirement in a planning obligation would also be invalid. So it is now clear that there is very little legal restriction on what can be agreed or offered unilaterally by way of a planning obligation under section 106 of the Town and Country Planning Act 1990.

On the question of the relationship between a planning obligation and the determination of an application for planning permission, both Lord Keith and Lord Hoffman accepted that it would be unlawful for a planning authority to take into account the existence or absence of a planning obligation which had no connection whatsoever with the development which was being determined. Lord Hoffman in this regard specifically accepted that:

> A benefit unrelated to the development would not be a 'material consideration' and a refusal based upon the developer's unwillingness to provide such a benefit would therefore be unlawful.

However, neither Lord Keith nor Lord Hoffman give much guidance as to what constitutes a sufficient connection. Previously the Court of Appeal in a series of decisions (see Chapter 4) had held that to be a material consideration the planning obligation must fairly and reasonably relate to the development permitted. Lord Keith did not directly reject this test, which for many years has been used by the courts to test the lawfulness of planning conditions, but he said that the parallel between planning conditions and planning obligations could not be exact. Lord Hoffman agreed, and stated, that applying the words of section 70(2) of the Town and Country Planning Act, the principal questions must always be whether the planning obligation was 'material consideration', and whether the planning authority had regard to it. In this respect Lord Hoffman went on to hold that to be material, the obligation did not need to have the effect of rendering acceptable a development which would otherwise have been unacceptable. Therefore, as a matter of law, there was nothing in the 1990 Act which required a planning authority to adopt the tests of necessity and proportionality which were laid down in circular 16/91 (1991b). On the other hand, Lord Hoffman also accepted that, as a matter of policy, the Secretary of State could decide to give no weight whatsoever to a planning obligation, even if it was a material consideration.

So, where, as in the **Tesco (Witney) [1994]** case, there is some slight relationship between the offer to build the new road and the development of a new superstore (because the new foodstore would have made the traffic situation in Witney slightly worse), the planning authority, whether the local planning authority or the Secretary of State on appeal, can, as a matter of policy, either place great weight on the public interest in getting a new relief road or give it no weight at all on the grounds that it is not necessary to make the development of the superstore acceptable. This means that the law imposes very little restriction on the use of planning obligations. As long as they serve a planning purpose and have some connection to the development being granted, the planning authority can take their existence or absence into account whether or not they are needed to make the development acceptable and however disproportionate the relationship.

In adopting this relaxed approach, the House of Lords was clearly concerned that the courts should not get involved in matters of planning judgement and that these matters should be left to the relevant planning authorities. This is understandable but we would argue that there is an important distinction between the courts laying down clear principles as to how planning authorities should determine whether a planning obligation is material and the courts getting involved in the merits of the decision. The present 'deferential' approach means that planning authorities are not required to justify the link between planning applications and planning obligations in a clear systematic way. This leaves open a wide scope for completely divergent approaches. Such diversity is likely to have the effect of increasing the present confusion and doubts over when and what development obligations should be negotiated.

NOTES

1. When the House of Lords sits as a court it is composed only of judges specially appointed to the House of Lords as Lords of Appeal in Ordinary and other peers who hold or have held high judicial office.
2. By *Wednesbury* unreasonable the courts mean that the condition was totally irrational; see Chapter 4 (p. 89) for an explanation of the approach of the courts.

PART ONE

THE ISSUES

1

DEVELOPMENT IMPACTS, THE COMMUNITY INTEREST AND THE PLANNING SYSTEM

1.1 INTRODUCTION

1.1.1 From blueprints to contracts: changing approaches to land use planning

This chapter locates the practice of negotiating planning agreements in the context of the changing nature of the planning system in Britain today. In the early postwar period, planning agreements, like development control itself, were treated as a minor aspect of planning implementation. The primary emphasis in the discussion of planning was on determining the strategy and content of the plan. The plan was expected to provide the overall framework within which development activity, both public and private, would take place. Physical, environmental and social infrastructures, such as highways, water resources, urban green spaces and community facilities, were funded by the public sector, as a claim on national and local taxation.

The plan strategy was expected to embody an integrated conception of the urban structure of a town, within which economic efficiency, social welfare and environmental conservation objectives could be met (Healey, 1994a). The plan in effect embodied a comprehensive model of urban development strategy, providing **instructions** for public-sector investment programmes and **guidelines** for the private-sector developer. This approach has often been called a **blueprint** model of planning, an analogy drawn from engineering projects. It assumed that those in charge of the plan had the power to **command** resources for plan implementation and to **control** how implementation took place.

This top-down notion of planning was linked to other areas of public policy in early postwar Britain, encapsulated in the idea of a centrally planned welfare state. Land use planning was intended to realize the postwar objectives of providing reasonable living and working environments for ordinary people (Cullingworth, 1975). There was also a strong emphasis on both improving environmental quality and limiting the spread of development around cities. This derived from the strong cultural orientation in Britain towards the defence of the countryside and open land assets. Opportunities for development were restricted around villages, towns and cities by policies for containing urban growth (Cullingworth, 1975; Ravetz, 1980; Hall *et al.*, 1973). The result for those landowners and developers with sites within the urban **envelope** was a sheltered, relatively risk-free, environment within which to realize profits. It is in this context that the issue of betterment was debated, since it was argued that developers should return to the public exchequer the profits they made as a result of the planning regime (see Chapter 2).

This situation has changed fundamentally in Britain since the 1960s. Public-sector expenditure constraints mean that the private sector is increasingly expected to be responsible for funding physical and social infrastructure projects. Developers must now pay, often in advance, for necessary infrastructure for their schemes which they once expected to be provided by the public sector. This shift in responsibility has happened in parallel to the rise of environmentalism in national and local politics which has concentrated public attention on the impacts of development, their limitation and mitigation. Questions about land use change and development affect a wide range of people with diverse and often conflicting interests and concerns. Identifying and addressing these conflicts takes time. Tensions between national government and local authorities mean that planning policies are often controversial, with different views within the public sector as to what is appropriate. By the 1980s, the development plan, was no longer seen to provide a determining blueprint. Rather, it had become a collection of policy principles, more or less coherently connected into a framework (Healey, 1993). At times, and particularly in the 1980s, plans have even been sidelined, with decisions on projects made through the political and administrative processes of development control decisions and appeals, rather than through previously agreed policy principles.

The result has been a much more uncertain investment context for developers, with opportunities for very considerable gains for the skilled and well-placed developer in times of economic prosperity. But equally, there lies the danger of considerable losses when the swings of the property market turn downwards. During the 1980s in particular, developers were targeted by government as key agents in the physical transformation of Britain. They were presented in government rhetoric as being at the forefront of economic development, providing space for new lifestyles (e.g. new settlements) and commercial environments (e.g. the business park), and regenerating older industrial conurbations by producing space for new activities. **Levering in** private-sector development into areas with weak development prospects became a major policy preoccupation of both national and local government (Thornley, 1991; Healey, 1994a).

Yet in more prosperous regions, on the more affluent fringes of conurbations, and in rural areas, the concern for countryside protection remained strong. This has meant that land release for development has been strongly resisted, which in turn kept development values high (Gerald Eve *et al.*, 1992). To obtain planning permission in these situations, developers have been strongly motivated to negotiate their way into local community acceptability. The consequence of these pressures has been a planning system which has become more negotiative in form, with development relationships tending towards a collaborative or partnership arrangement. In this context, developers are encouraged to seek out profitable development opportunities. This may involve paying upfront for infrastructure requirements for projects and mitigating other potentially adverse local impacts. Such costs are worth paying where market conditions are buoyant and where community resistance to development limits supply. They may also be worth paying where subsidy is available to encourage development.

Within this new relationship between developers and planning authorities, planning agreements take on much greater significance than in the earlier **command and control** approach to land use regulation. They become a significant mechanism through which developer and planning authority express the balance of duties and obligations between them. The British planning system since the war has thus moved from a **directing and providing** regime, supplemented by the administrative regulation of private-sector development, to a negotiative form of regulation in which making contracts formalized as agreements has a much stronger place. This has implications both for practice and for law, as we will illustrate.

1.1.2 Bringing in the community interest

This shift in regulatory form has evolved in parallel to changes in the political community. The postwar planning system was founded on the notion of a consensual and unitary **public interest** in how land use change and development should be managed. Planning strategies could be articulated by local planning authorities, subject to overview by national government.

Conflict was at the margins. By the 1980s, however, this conception had given way to recognition of the diversity of interests in local environmental questions. The planning system has developed into a system for managing conflicts between different interests (Healey *et al.*, 1988; Brindley *et al.*, 1989). These include: land and property owners and developers; those adjacent to development; the infrastructure providers; various pressure groups concerned with the quality of local communities, with the protection and enhancement of environmental assets and with a whole range of social, economic and environmental issues. This has had the effect of overlaying upon the emerging negotiative practice between planning authority and developer with respect to infrastructure and local amenity issues the more complex political processes of mediation among competing environmental interests (Grove-White, 1991). By the mid-1980s, government policy had deliberately reduced the role of the plan (DoE, 1986). The mediation of conflicts thus took place around individual projects, in a **project-led** approach. The system of land use regulation was thus confronted with a political challenge, to find ways of accommodating the claims for attention of multiple interests, while enabling agreed development to proceed. Planning agreements appeared to offer a way of striking bargains which safeguarded the public interest.

One consequence of the project-led approach of the 1980s, therefore, was to raise the issue of planning agreements, commonly referred to under the term **planning gain**, to the forefront of public attention. The research upon which this book is based was stimulated by the cries for help from local councillors struggling to understand the practices in which they were engaged and searching for ways to work out legitimate ground rules. Their dilemmas were paralleled by a general confusion, among lawyers, planners and developers, as to whether or not it was appropriate to seek community benefits, in some form, in the negotiation of development projects. The frequently cited example was the retail firm which offered a swimming pool in a deal which allowed development of a superstore on the edge of town (see Figure 1.1).

Does this case represent a subversion of planning principles by the offer of a community benefit unrelated to the development? Was it an appropriate compensation to the community for loss of edge of town landscape? Was it a subversion of environmental sustainability principles by encouraging compensation for an adverse impact rather than reducing the level of impact? Was it an appropriate gain to the community in return for the benefit to the developer of the slight adjustment of a planning constraint, and the high land value this produced?

Since then other cases have been negotiated which seem to represent **buying planning permission**. In October 1994, proposals were made to extend the Merry Hill Shopping Centre in the Black Country by 650 000 sq. ft of retail space.

In October 1991, approval was granted for a twin Marks & Spencer and Tesco out of town superstore at Holmbush (Shoreham-by-Sea) in Adur District, West Sussex. The retail element of the scheme comprises 108 000 sq. ft for Marks & Spencer and 80 000 sq. ft for Tesco, together with a cafe/restaurant. The obligation allows for the transfer of a site for a 25 × 10 metre indoor swimming pool to the local authority. The development company will also pay the major part of the construction cost of the scheme, handing the pool over to the local authority on completion. *The obligation makes the opening of the superstore conditional on the completion of the swimming pool.*

The original scheme showed a site for a 'community development' and, using evidence in the South East Regional Recreation Strategy on swimming pool requirements (the District has no public indoor pool), agreement was reached. The District Council's own surveys showed a high level of support for the scheme among local people. This obligation appears to fit within the spirit of paragraph 2 of PPG 17 on Sport and Recreation, which states that sports and recreational facilities can form an important component of major retail developments.

Source: Elson and Payne, 1993, p. 24.

Figure 1.1   Swimming pool in conjunction with an edge of town retail development

A key factor is the developers' offer of a planning gain package equivalent to £6.75m for infrastructure and other capital projects in the borough (of Dudley), to be invested under the direction of the borough council following local consultation (Planning, 1091, 21.10.94, p. 24).

Is this compensation for adverse impacts on retail provision elsewhere in the borough, or a bribe to overcome local resistance?

1.1.3 Towards a new regulatory regime

In parallel with these concerns about planning gain, pressure was coming from various parties in the early 1990s, including the development industry itself, to make the planning system more predictable. The project-led approach gave confused signals to landowners and developers seeking to establish the value of their assets, while those concerned with environmental quality questioned the accountability of regulatory decisions made on an *ad hoc* basis. The very real problems of financing physical and social infrastructures added further dimensions of uncertainty. Since 1989, government has responded to the search for greater certainty by a re-assertion of the importance of the plan. Government *Planning Policy Guidance*, introduced in 1988 to provide greater clarity as to government policy on a range of topics, began to stress from 1989 the importance of the development plan as the basis of policy. In 1991, an amendment to the 1990 Planning and Compensation Act, Section 54A, gave greater weight to the plan. By 1992, the minister for planning, Sir George Young claimed:

> The Act will bring about one of the most intense periods of forward planning we have seen. Our target is to have full coverage of develop-ment plans, covering strategic and local policies, so that there is a plan to guide every development control decision. In this way decisions would be plan-led, as we said on a number of occasions when the new legislation was debated (Young, 1992, p. 4).

Since then, both government guidance (DoE, 1992a) and legal judge-ments (see Chapter 4) have reiterated the importance of the plan as the primary source of principles framing planning regulatory decisions.

This **plan-led** approach co-exists in the 1990s in Britain with a continu-ation of negotiative practice and with the increasing awareness of the implications of absorbing the new agenda of environmental considera-tions into the land use planning arena (Healey and Shaw, 1993). It was not at all clear how these tendencies were to be combined. Nevertheless, col-lectively these moves represent a search for a new regulatory form for the planning system (Healey, 1994a).

In this book, we seek to make a contribution to this search. Central to any new form for the planning system is the way the impacts of proposed development projects are considered. Whether impacts are identified in policy principles or on a case-by-case basis in relation to individual pro-jects, questions arise as to the range of impacts considered, their prioriti-zation, appropriate mitigating measures for adverse impacts and the consequences for developers of addressing impacts. Decisions on devel-opment projects may or may not need the mechanism of a planning agreement as such to conclude a negotiation. However, the practice of negotiating agreements provides a valuable window on arguments and negotiative practices about impacts and about obligations. We consider that such arguments and practices will become central within the plan-ning system of the later 1990s. The rest of this chapter examines the nature of development impacts, and the perspectives of developers and the general community in considering such impacts.

1.2 THE IMPACTS OF DEVELOPMENT

1.2.1 Development and its impacts

The regulation of land use may have several objectives. The purposes to which the British planning system has been directed have been a variable combination of environmental conservation, accommodating the space needs of economic activity, providing decent living environments for ordinary people and promoting and protecting property values. Such policy-oriented objectives are typically combined with the specific purpose of protecting existing activities from 'bad neighbours'. This was encapsulated in the notion of **amenity** (Cullingworth, 1988, p. 196). New development was expected to avoid loss of amenity – of light, views, sound quality, air quality and level of traffic – to immediate neighbours. Over time, this concept has been stretched to cover the impacts of development on the wider community. One objective of the new plan-led planning system is to relate the identification of impacts to explicit policy principles.

This requires the identification of the impacts of a development project. In the first case, the emphasis is on the link between a development project and specific planning policy objectives. Does a superstore project or a business park scheme in a specific location enhance or detract from a local economic development strategy? Does it meet local design principles? In the second case, the emphasis is on the potential adverse **externality** costs of a project, known in the language of economics as social costs. Will a housing scheme add to existing local traffic problems? How will it affect the patterns of footpaths giving access to the countryside? Will it upset wildlife habitats? Is it of such a scale that existing community services, such as schools and recreation facilities, will become overloaded? If there are such adverse social costs, who is to pay for putting them right? Should the landowner, the developer, or the occupants of the development pay, or should it be existing residents and if so, should they pay through national or local taxes?

Much of the literature on development impacts, planning agreements and **planning gain** makes relatively simple assumptions about projects: that development is profitable; that its impacts are easy to identify; that it is relatively simple to work out who should bear the cost. As a consequence, little attention has been given until recently to ways of expressing policies in plans which will guide the discussion of impacts and their mitigation on individual projects. However, the above are far from simple or uncontested assumptions, as Bailey (1990) shows in relation to infrastructure; and

Cowell (1993) with regard to impact mitigation. The expression of policy frameworks and principles to govern the negotiation process therefore requires a sensitive understanding of the development process and land and property market behaviour, as Loughlin argued in 1980.

Development involves transforming the natural features and physical structures of sites and buildings and the uses within them (Cadman and Austin-Crowe, 1978). It is in effect a production process. Development projects can be enormously varied. Obvious variations relate to scale (from a house extension to a major urban development project) and location (a greenfield site, a city centre renewal project, or an old industrial zone). Of less visible but fundamental significance are variations in the relations of production (from a single owner-occupier, to a nexus of landowners, financiers, developers, contractors and their various consultants). The development process involves accomplishing a set of events; for example, obtaining land for development; obtaining finance; designing the building project; organizing services; construction; and marketing the project to potential end-users. The number, nature, sequence and timescale of these events are also potentially highly variable. In producing development projects, private-sector agents may have a variety of objectives, and position themselves in relation to different market considerations. One firm may be building to an owner-occupier's specifications; another building into a speculative market segment ('executive housing'; 'high quality business park'); a third may be balancing a portfolio of business operations; and a fourth seeking a turnover of projects to beat the banker from the door. **Market conditions** also vary in complex cyclical ways, affecting land supply, the availability and costs of building capacity and the supply of finance, as well as the demand for completed projects. Planning regulation affects these variable development project proposals and objectives at a number of points in the transformation of a site from one use and built form to another (Gore and Nicholson, 1991; Healey, 1991a, 1992a). We discuss this variation further in Chapter 3.

Identifying the *impacts* of development involves examining the ways a particular project for development, redevelopment or refurbishment relates to its specific site, to the area around it, and to the wider environment. It requires tracing the relations between a project and the context within which it will exist, both during and after development. These relations could be economic, social, or ecological. They could relate to the site and the wider environment as a physical resource, or as a landscape feature, or as a symbolic space. A project to expand a quarry for building materials could be considered in terms of the balance of advantage between the need for building materials for economic development and the destruction of farmland and landscape assets. This might lead to agreements including obligations for restoration of these assets.

However, it may be that such assets cannot be recreated through restoration. A good example here is the argument over whether the M25 extension should be driven through Oxleas Wood in North Kent, an area of ancient woodland. Can ancient woodland be recreated? If the road is needed at all, should it not be put underground, despite the cost? In some cases, landscape assets or symbolic spaces are considered of such importance that any kind of development near them, whatever the restoration undertaken and compensation provided, is considered unacceptable, for example the vista of St Paul's Cathedral, or the open space around Stonehenge. In such cases, sites and environments take on the quality of the culturally 'sacred'. It sometimes happens that a project which starts off with a relatively ordinary set of impact problems, such as landscape restoration after mineral extraction, or accommodating traffic impacts, enters the realm of the sacred by the discovery of archaeological or palaeontological heritage underground. Examples of such situations include the Rose Theatre in Southwark, where Shakespere's theatre was discovered under the surface as the foundations for an office building were being dug, and the mammoth quarry in Oxfordshire, claimed now to be a site of international palaeontological significance, discovered during mineral extraction activities.

1.2.2 The developers' interests

One way to cut through the range and diversity of the impacts a project may generate for a community is to view these impacts from the perspectives of the developer and the community. The developer has a range of operational and market reasons to be concerned with the way a project relates to a site and its surroundings. A residential project of more than a few dwellings will need attention to the layout and future maintenance of the roads and pathways, the position of utility services (water/drainage/sewerage, electricity, gas, telecommunications), access to the main highway and other infrastructure networks, and the design and maintenance of landscaping. All these concerns will require the developer to negotiate with the various utility companies, the highway authorities and local authority departments dealing with landscape maintenance, to work out mutually acceptable arrangements. The developer needs to assure the future occupiers of the dwellings about current quality and future maintenance. The various utilities and other infrastructure agencies want reassurance about the quality of provision, about the impact on the general capacity of the infrastructure system in question and about the long-term maintenance implications.

A developer may also wish to improve the quality of a scheme by including environmental assets, such as a wildlife scheme or public art. These could be provided to make the scheme more attractive to potential purchasers. In a large scheme, the traffic generation and use of community facilities by the future residents could impose a significant impact on the local community. From a commercial point of view, a developer may consider that future occupants will be concerned about the resulting deficiencies. Realizing this, a developer may include in an application proposals to increase traffic capacity, for example, a new roundabout or traffic junction, or to contribute to community facilities (a recreation facility, for example). All the above elements could be included in the planning application.

The developer, the planning authority and the utility agencies may wish nevertheless to tie up the arrangements as to standards and responsibilities into a planning agreement, to bind the various parties contractually over the timescale of what may be a complex project over several years. These **developers' operational impacts** are thus one form of impact which may become development obligations in a planning agreement.

These operational impacts are ones which a developer actively seeks to have addressed in some way, because this makes sense from a commercial point of view. As Part Two shows, a great deal of the negotiation of planning agreements in the 1980s related to these sorts of impacts. Thus there may often be a mutual interest in alleviating impacts between developers and the planning authority, in its role as representative of the community interest.

1.2.3 Community interests and planning policies

The community interest is more difficult to identify because it is both institutionally fragmented and diverse. The local authority 'represents' the political community of its area, and has responsibility for local planning. It is also responsible for much highway maintenance, for landscape maintenance, and some community resources. Other infrastructures are provided by county or national government (highways) and by private companies (the regional water and electricity companies), British Gas, British Telecom, bus companies and by public agencies (e.g. British Rail).

However, neighbourhoods and village community organizations may campaign to have a formalized 'voice' in planning decisions. They may claim to represent their 'community' better than the local authority and seek status as representing community interests in negotiating with developers. Some parish councils in one of our case studies achieved this status (see Case 1).

A particular project may generate impacts which affect interests beyond the locality; for example in a neighbouring district; or in another part of the country linked to a project through the operation of a firm. The **Northumberland CC** case **[1989]** discussed in Chapter 4 is a case in point. Here a coal extraction proposal was linked to other activities of British Coal concerned in another part of the country. In the Oxfordshire

---

Case 1: Bishop's Cleeve, Tewkesbury

Development type: Residential

Developers: Bovis Homes Ltd, Robert Hitchins Ltd

Proposal: 1000 dwellings

The proposal, made in 1985, initially for 1000 dwellings later increased to 1700, was the outcome of an allocation under the Cheltenham Environs Local Plan.

The size of the development required major infrastructure provision viz.,

- on-site and off-site highways
- surface water and foul water drainage
- main foul and surface water sewer
- recreational and amenity open space (19.5 ha)
- commuted payments for open space maintenance
- landscaping
- primary school site (2.23 ha)
- playing field site (0.81 ha)

In addition, the developers 'made available' the sum of £500 000 to Bishop's Cleeve Parish Council for recreational and community purposes.

Highway obligations were secured by means of an agreement under section 33 of the Local Government (Miscellaneous Provisions) Act 1983, negotiated with Gloucestershire CC.

---

mammoth site just referred to, the link was made to nationally and internationally significant values and the groups who hold them. Establishing the community's interest in a development and its impacts is therefore a politically complex issue.

The planning system considers the impacts of development on the community through detailed guidance for development control and through planning policy objectives. Development control practice has built up over the years a wide-ranging list of considerations which are seen to be 'material' to a case (Davies *et al.*, 1986). This has grown by accretion, by custom and practice, as much as by deliberate policy. We discuss its content and status in more detail in Chapter 4.

Attempts have been made in the plan-making efforts of the late 1980s/early 1990s to edit these considerations and to identify the policy principles which underly them. Government advice in recent years, as already noted, has encouraged the incorporation of such principles into the development plan in order to provide legitimacy for these considerations (DoE, 1992a). Such considerations typically address aspects of development quality and spatially localized impacts, for example: building materials; building bulk and layout; visual, noise and air intrusion on neighbours; access for the disabled; safety and security matters. Recently under the influence of new environmental concerns, there has been increasing attention to ways of conserving energy and encouraging waste recycling in development projects.

The second direction is that of planning policy objectives, the planning authority's strategy for the management of land use and development in its area. This should be the primary focus of its development plan. The British planning system is distinctive in that the plan has a guidance role only. There is no equivalent in Britain to continental or US zoning ordinances. The development plan represents an attempt to identify a local authority's strategy, the range of its objectives, and how they interrelate. This is then expressed in specific policies and proposals, which embody ideas about fields of impact which a development might effect. For example, Birmingham's Unitary Development Plan (Birmigham City Council, 1990) seeks to promote economic development through supplying a range of industrial and commercial sites. However, it aims to ensure a balance between greenfield peripheral development and schemes in the city centre and older industrial zones by careful phasing policies. Newcastle's Unitary Development Plan (Newcastle City Council, 1993) aims to combine providing space for peripheral development to promote inward investment with a range of policies designed to reduce air pollution and promote energy conservation.

Table 1.1   Development plan preparation in five local authorities

	Deposit draft	Inquiry	Inquiry report	Adoption
LB Wandsworth (UDP)	1992	1993	1993	1994
Solihull MBC (UDP)	1990	1991	1992	*
Newcastle City Council (UDP)	1993	1994/5	n/a	n/a
Harlow BC (DDP)	1990	1991	1992	(1995)**
Tewkesbury–Ashchurch Local Plan	1990	1991	1992	(1995)***

*   Solihull is to have a second Local Plan Inquiry in 1995.
**   Harlow expects to adopt in 1995, but a Judicial Review is also expected.
*** awaiting outcome of Judicial Review on a planning permission.

However, drawing up a development plan is both technically and politically challenging. It may also be time-consuming. The procedures include requirements for consultation on content and a quasi-judicial inquiry into objections to a plan. The plans in our case study local authorities have taken several years to move through consultation stages to final approval (see Table 1.1).

The lack of a plan does not necessarily mean that there is no strategy. Authorities which have allowed their development plan to lapse into neglect through lack of revision, may nevertheless have very clear ideas about what is acceptable and what is not. In our case study authorities, we found that several were using the requirement to prepare a new plan as an opportunity to bring these ideas forward into formalized policies (e.g. Newcastle). Since such strategies are the result of local political evolution, they may be changed when local communities or national politics change sufficiently to overturn established councils, leading to policy change even when there is a recently agreed plan.

Development plans in Britain thus provide a useful but not necessarily comprehensive indication of the range of considerations which a planning authority, the utility agencies and the local political arena may bring to bear on a project. These considerations are expressed in statements which either take the form of site-specific proposals or more general performance criteria. In both cases, they are required by law to be accompanied by an explanation of the reasons for the policy, and this may include, an indication of whose actions the policy is supposed to affect. However, these statements do not necessarily indicate how the relation between a project and its impact is to be established.

Overarching a local community's efforts to articulate its planning policies are central government's various policy directives, embodied in circulars, planning policy guidance, regional guidance and ministerial statements. The authority of these statements derives from the role of the Secretary of State in modifying development plans, in calling in plans and applications for decision and in reviewing planning decisions on appeal (Rydin, 1993). The courts have given published policies a legal status by holding that they can be a material consideration in determining a planning application or appeal. The statements typically address specific topics and thus avoid the need to sort out the interconnections between topics. Yet they provide arguments for developers and local authorities to draw upon when discussing a proposed development project. Their content and the way this changes have significant effects on development opportunities. For example, government policy on out-of-town retail development has recently become much more restrictive, through revisions to Planning Policy Guidance 6 on Retail Development (DoE, 1993a); while the provision of affordable housing has now become a legitimate policy consideration in planning negotiations through Planning Policy Guidance 3 (DoE, 1992c).

Thus in identifying the potential impacts of a development proposal, a local planning authority will draw upon accumulated experience, precedents, awareness of local community concerns and of the concerns of the infrastructure companies and agencies, its development plans, government guidance and professional preoccupations (McLoughlin, 1973). To an extent, the whole system of development control, through which projects are judged in relation to the development plan and other material considerations, can be seen as a mechanism for addressing development impacts, although it is rarely conceptualized in these terms.

These considerations, along with the developers' commercial concerns, structure the identification of impacts and establish the relationship between a project and its impacts. Although some authorities have made valiant efforts to consolidate all their concerns into clear development plan policies, more precise development control guidance and development briefs for specific sites, there is still enormous interpretive leeway in the planning system, given its reliance upon judgement within the context of administrative discretion. Arguments as to the exact meaning of these policies often ended up in the courts for an authoritative determination. This is one reason why development control has been criticized in recent years (Davies *et al.*, 1986). Further, plans and planning officers, have until recently not been forthcoming in explaining, monitoring and reviewing the basis of the policy criteria used and the way these are applied to specific projects. This has been partly deliberate, to protect their power of discretionary judgement. But these days, interested parties and the courts demand more than this, creating pressures for clear and explicit reasoning.

1.2.4 Development impacts and betterment taxation

The consequence of the above range, diversity and ambiguity of community concerns with respect to a development project is that a large number of potential impacts of a development project may be identified. These may lead to refusal of a planning application, its modification to take account of community concerns (for example, the inclusion of an element of affordable housing, or a wildlife asset to replace environmental resources lost through the scheme), to the imposition of conditions on a development project (for example, requirements with respect to design and layout), or to the imposition of various obligations in the form of a planning agreement. These different alternatives are discussed in more detail in Chapter 4, and in Part Two. Agreements have particular value from the point of view of a community and developers, where the local authority seeks to bind the various parties to an agreed set of actions in a contractual rather than a regulatory form. For example, a developer may be required to make payments to, or contribute in kind to, the provision of landscape or traffic improvements to offset the loss of amenity and the congestion a project is likely to create.

Voluntary contracts in the form of an agreement are commonly seen as preferable to a **condition** under normal planning powers, because they appear more binding and have a wider scope (see Chapter 4).

There is one further objective which a community may have in negotiating over a development project. This relates to the claims a community may feel it is legitimate to impose on a project in view of the profits the developer will generate through building on a particular site. This is in effect a form of taxation. The traditional argument for such a tax is discussed in Chapter 2. It is sometimes considered that those developers who obtain planning permission should be required to pay for the 'betterment' generated by a planning system which limits land supply and thus concentrates land value. This value may then be captured by the lucky developer with planning permission. Since the abolition of Development Land Tax in 1986, and earlier mechanisms aimed at collecting betterment, some commentators consider that it is legitimate to seek **planning gain** for local communities as an *ad hoc* local approach to collecting betterment (Rodriguez-Bachiller *et al.*, 1992; Grant, 1991).

Extracting such 'gain' from developers is also attractive to local authorities and the infrastructure providers as a way of obtaining contributions to general and specific funds over and above those needed to cope with the specific impacts of projects. The pressure on local authorities and other public bodies to do this has been very strong in recent years. This is partly because of heavy cutbacks in public finance. It also arises from the ideological shift from public to private provision of many activities and services. This has the effect of making the search for private-sector contributions to investment and management a legitimate objective. By 1991, the Labour Party was advocating the use of planning gain for this purpose (Labour Party, 1994). Our research in Part Two illustrates this tendency in practice, with many agencies increasing the level of demands on developers for contributions for such provision. The difficult distinction here is between a development obligation to deal with a project impact and an obligation which is in effect a form of cross-subsidy from the development to wider community purposes, as the examples noted at the start of this chapter illustrate.

Calculating the incidence of betterment due to planning constraint alone, as opposed to that arising from the provision of some specific public investment, such as a highway or a school, is in any case by no means straightforward (see Chapter 3). To the extent that the negotiation of development obligations is being used to collect betterment, it has been primarily targeted at larger projects promoted by more affluent developers, notably the retail companies. It is also typically wrapped up in the language of contributions to community benefits and measures to mitigate development impacts. This reflects government opposition to the use of planning agreements as an *ad hoc* tax (see Chapter 2). Otherwise the recoupment of the profits of development only takes places through general taxes paid to the national exchequer, rather than earmarked, or 'hypothecated', for specific local purposes.

The argument over the justification for taxing betterment is complex and is explored further in Chapters 2 and 3. Suffice it to say at this point that such taxes are quite widespread in other countries, usually in the form of local development charges, which the community can use for the general enhancement of the community (Davies *et al.*, 1989; Lichfield and Darin-Drabkin, 1980). In Britain, since the mid-1980s, this option has been closed off. It is our view, and that of many of those we consulted within our research, that there would be considerable merit in local development charges of some kind. We discuss this issue further in Part Three. However, this is a different issue from the question of assessing and mitigating the adverse impacts of development.

Nevertheless, given the present climate of limited public-sector funds, it is not surprising to find the mechanism of planning agreements being considered as a form of *ad hoc* tax. Current government policy, while opposed to a general *ad hoc* tax, nevertheless encourages forms of cross-subsidy. This is most clearly evident in the discussion of private-sector contributions to affordable housing. Both Department of the Environment policy and many local authorities now encourage developers to include an element of social or affordable housing provision in residential schemes (DoE, 1991a, 1992c). This practice may be justified in terms of a relation to policy objectives (to promote mixed tenures, or more low-cost housing in a neighbourhood). It is possible in large schemes to argue for its provision in terms of a scheme's potential effects on the balance of housing provision in an area. But at the level of individual schemes, it is difficult not to see such policies as a requirement that developers subsidize social housing provision in return for the permission to develop, i.e. in taxation terms. Other comparable instances include encouraging developers to contribute to public art, to community facilities and to ecological resources.

Such practices are also to be found in other countries, most notably in the US, where **linkage** programmes have evolved to encourage developer contributions to social needs (Alterman, 1988; Wakeford, 1990; Nicholas *et al.*, 1991; Bailey, 1990). It is cases of this type which have produced most public concern over the use of planning agreements. Concern arises on two counts. The first relates to the potential subversion of agreed planning policies by the attraction of financial gain. This concern is particularly acute as agreements are voluntary and are rarely publically scrutinized. Such scrutiny only takes place in a formal way when challenged in the courts. Such legal challenges may be made by an aggrieved applicant, or, with much less opportunity, by 'third parties' who are able to convince the court that they have sufficient interest in the decision. We discuss these issues further in Chapters 2 and 4.

The second concern over such practices arises from the fear that encouraging developers to offer extras, over and beyond the impacts of their project, will discourage developers and local communities from seeking ways of alleviating impacts. The *ad hoc* tax approach in effect encourages **compensation plus**, rather than alleviation. It thus encourages **paying off** environmental losses, rather than preventing them arising. There is the further concern that compensation measures themselves may generate adverse impacts, which do not get adequate consideration.

This suggests that conflating developer contributions to deal with social needs and community benefits together with contributions to address social costs, that is the adverse impacts of development, can lead to situations where neither social needs nor social costs are adequately addressed, and where environmental losses are inadequately identified and addressed. We are thus in agreement with government policy (DoE, 1983, 1991b) that the two should not be combined and that the taxation of the profits of development projects should proceed separately from the requirement that developers mitigate the social costs they impose on a community. Although from the point of view of the developer, the result may be the same in terms of a 'burden' on project costs, the justification for them in policy terms is different. In Parts One and Two, we explain the basis for our conclusions, and return to the implications in Part Three.

To conclude, development obligations formalized in planning agreements may arise in three ways:

1. as an operational requirement from the point of view of the developer;
2. as a requirement necessary to meet planning policy objectives and/or to address the social costs (adverse impacts) of a project;
3. as an *ad hoc* tax or cross-subsidy to the community out of developers' profits.

We argue that these may be encapsulated in three *rationales* for the negotiation of development obligations. The first rationale emphasizes the *implementation of planned development*. Developers would be encouraged to contribute to the provision of planned infrastructure to enable their development schemes to proceed. Such contributions would directly relate to the proposed development but need not necessarily be part of, or on the site of, the development itself. The second rationale focuses on the *impact of the development* and the need to mitigate any social costs of that impact. In contrast to the first rationale it is not so much concerned with making the development work on its own terms but with accommodating that development within a wider area. This approach lends itself to negotiation. By stretching the link between the development and the social costs it generates, this rationale can be used to obtain all kinds of community benefits. The third rationale focuses on the benefit created by the community for the developer through both the regulation of development and the provision of infrastructure through public investment. In this rationale, the developer is seen as having a duty to return some of this benefit to the community, through a *local charge or tax*.

Examples of all of these could be found in planning practice in the late 1980s/early 1990s. Much public debate assumed that the dominant category was the third. The term 'planning gain' was commonly used to express this conception. In practice, however, the first and second were the predominant reasons for the obligations found in agreements, as we illustrate in Chapters 5 and 6.

The next three chapters now develop the context for our discussion of negotiating development with community interests in mind. Chapter 2 reviews the evolution of government policy, with respect to regulating and negotiating with developers. Chapter 3 examines the nature of development activity and how it is likely to be affected by different regulatory actions. Chapter 4 reviews the issues which have preoccupied legal debate and judicial decisions with respect to development regulation.

2

FROM BETTERMENT
TO DEVELOPMENT
OBLIGATIONS

2.1 THE PROFITS AND COSTS OF DEVELOPMENT

Historically, in British planning debate, the discussion of the impacts of development has been closely linked to the question of **betterment**. Both the granting of planning permission and the subsequent implementation of a development project produce benefits and costs. In the case of benefits, the most obvious and direct is the increase in the value of the land where planning permission is granted for a higher value use. Since the abolition of the Development Land Tax in 1985, there has existed no overt legal mechanism by which the state extracts specifically the increase in value of land caused by the granting of planning permission in a situation where planning policy limits land supply. As many commentators have pointed out (Davies, 1984; Rowan-Robinson and Lloyd, 1988), the making of an application for planning permission is akin to pulling the lever of a one-armed bandit. A grant of permission will normally increase the value of the land, provided there is a demand for the proposed use. A refusal will mean that the applicant has lost both the costs of making the application and the potential increase in value.

Of course, as discussed in the previous chapter, the decision to refuse or grant permission is made in accordance with what is seen to be the public interest or the good of the community and not on chance as with a gambling machine. While the owner or the developer may be seen to win when permission is granted, others may be seen to lose, as most developments impose costs as well as creating benefits. The state only shares in any of the profits which result from the grant of permission through taxes. At present in Britain, the taxes involved are the general taxes of capital gains tax and income and corporation tax. Capital gains tax will be imposed when land and property is sold and income tax and corporation tax will have to be paid on any profits which are made in exploiting the development. Even with a rate of capital gains tax of 40%, a land and property holding can be substantially enriched by selling land for which planning permission has just been granted. In times of a boom in land values such **windfalls**[1] can arouse social resentment and controversy.

As discussed in Chapter 1, the practice of negotiating development obligations in connection with the grant of planning permission is primarily aimed at ensuring that the adverse social and environmental costs from the development are limited. This can be done by imposing conditions on the grant itself, but doubts about the legal scope of conditions and practical difficulties in enforcement have meant that in the last three decades there has been increasing resort to legally separate agreements. There is an important legal distinction between conditions and agreements. A planning condition is imposed by the local planning authority as part of the public system for the regulation of development projects. Agreements are negotiated in private and are based on separate statutory provisions. Therefore the scope and legal consequences can be very different from those arising from a condition. This is further explained in Chapter 4. As Grant in particular has pointed out (Grant, 1991), the use of agreements to impose obligations on those carrying out a development could be seen as a substitute for a betterment levy or development tax. Clearly the knowledge that large profits can be made in connection with the development of land has encouraged local planning authorities to seek such obligations, especially when they perceive that the costs of the development will fall on the inhabitants they represent. Such costs include the provision of the infrastructure needed to service the development or the adverse environmental effects that the development will cause.

The arguments over development obligations in Britain in the 1980s and 1990s have striking similarities to those which bedeviled earlier schemes for the recoupment of betterment by the state. All three of these schemes failed. Indeed the practice of looking for 'planning gain' has often been condemned as an unconstitutional tax (e.g. Heap and Ward, 1980).

The ugly words **betterment** and **worsenment** are normally used to describe changes in the value of land produced by planning, either through limiting land supply or undertaking development. Changes in the value of land can be caused by a wide range of disparate factors. Both betterment and worsenment are used to refer to changes in land and property value caused by public actions. Betterment refers to changes which increase value, while worsenment covers actions which decrease the value. The most exhaustive attempt at defining betterment was made by the Uthwatt Committee which was set up during the Second World War under the chairmanship of Lord Justice Uthwatt to look at compensation and betterment.[2]

The report took betterment to mean:

> any increase in the value of land (including the buildings thereon) arising from central or local government action, whether positive e.g. by the execution of public works or improvement, or negative, e.g. by the imposition of restrictions on other land (Uthwatt Committee, 1942, para. 260).

This definition included first the most obvious form of betterment, whereby private land benefits by public improvements which take place on other land. As the report pointed out, in this first category of case there is a strong justification for requiring the owner of the land to give back to the state the increase in value, as not only has the value of the land been increased without any action by the owner or occupier but the state has borne the cost of the public improvements.

In the second category of case, where the state's action is negative in restricting some other person's activities, the increase is caused at least theoretically at the expense of those restricted. The restriction in supply of land on which particular activities can be carried out is the cause of the increase in value. The report argued that such restrictions had the effect of redistributing the potential development value from one land parcel to another; the shifting value theory.[3]

In this regard the report had in mind the system of town planning schemes imposed under the Town and Country Planning Act 1932. Such schemes only covered relatively small areas of land which had been judged ripe for development. They did not cover land which had already been developed and land which was thought not to be likely to be developed. Indeed, as the report pointed out, such schemes also provided examples of the first class of case since the schemes provided for public improvements in the form of planned roads and other amenities such as public spaces.

The implications of the shifting value theory were to be radically increased by the extension of local planning authority powers to restrict all development everywhere. Sometimes called the nationalization of development rights, this policy innovation was proposed by the Uthwatt report and implemented by the Town and Country Act 1947. Logically, if the increase in value to land was caused by decreasing the value of other land which was restricted, then any increase recouped by the state should be used to compensate those restricted. The solution was to nationalize development rights. The scheme introduced by the 1947 Act, but never fully implemented, provided for the once and for all nationalization of prospective development values at the fairly arbitrary sum of £300 million. No further compensation was payable for loss of value due to refusal of planning permission. Betterment was returned to the state through the betterment levy. However, the betterment levy was to be subjected to strong challenge, land and property owners and developers arguing that they needed an incentive to bring their land forward for development (Cullingworth, 1980). The levy was abolished by the Town and Country Planning Act 1954. This one-sided dismantling of the scheme did much to create the present situation in which, while it is generally accepted that there is no need to compensate for refusal to allow development,[4] there is an equal hostility to the state taking the whole of the increase caused by the operation of the regulatory system.

This hostility may be related to the fact that all the post-Second World War legislative schemes that have been created to recoup betterment have not been limited to taxing the increase in value caused by state actions but have included all increases in the value of land however caused. As Davies (1984) has pointed out, even the Uthwatt Committee, having defined betterment as set out above, then went on to propose betterment charges which covered an increase in value from any cause whatsoever. This approach had the very important practical advantage that it avoided the difficulty of precisely identifying the cause of the increase in the value of the land. This difficulty had made the collection of betterment under previous schemes impractical. However, in overcoming that practical difficulty, any charge which extracts the total increase in value, however caused, undermines its own legitimacy. This is because, as Grant points out, there is no particular reason why increases in land values should be treated differently from increases in the value of other commodities (Grant, 1991, p. 75).

This same problem arises with regard to development obligations. Just as Uthwatt thought it only fair and just that the state should take back the increase in land value caused by public improvements, local planning authorities justify the use of development obligations to require developers to pay for, or to provide the infrastructure necessary for, the development. This is not quite the same as the public authority itself paying for the works and then the state collecting the subsequent increase in value in the development land. Apart from the fact that, in the latter case, one public authority may have to pay for the costs and another authority recoup the betterment, the costs of the works and the increase in value caused will not necessarily be the same amount. However, where the public improvement is exclusively needed for the private development, as is the case of a new roundabout which feeds the traffic to and from a supermarket, the case for the cost falling on the private developer rather than the public purse is very strong. As Grant (1991) argues, this is merely simple 'cost recovery'. The statute book has always contained several provisions whereby the private sector can require roads, drains, sewers and water supplies to be built by statutory undertakers, on the condition that the person doing the requisitioning pays the cost.

By its nature, however, much of the infrastructure which is necessary for a development is used in common with other users. The further the services are from the site of the development, the more difficult it is to determine the proportion of use caused by the development never mind the increase in value to the development site caused by the improvements. Nevertheless developers have often been prepared to enter into planning agreements to pay for all or a proportion of such improvement, in order to unlock the grant of planning permission, even if by doing so they are allowing later developers to freeload on their investment.

In the case of increases in value caused by the restriction of other developments, while local planning authorities have not openly sought to extract such increases *per se*, the prospective increase has provided the context in which authorities have argued for the provision of community benefits to offset the social costs of a development. Where this has resulted in planning agreements, there is generally no precise identification of the increase in value or any attempt to put a price tag on the social costs.

The close relationship between betterment and development obligations extends to the objectives and consequences of their implementation. Most of the betterment schemes have not been merely revenue collection exercises but have been designed to affect the use and development of land, by either keeping down land prices and/or bringing forward land for development. However, as Grant (1991, p. 70) argues, revenue collection and land policies are often incompatible even if the actual consequences of the implementation of the scheme can be accurately predicted, which is rarely the case. In the case of development obligations, theoretically the obligation negotiated should always be planning-led, as it should be designed to solve the particular planning problems of the proposed development. Yet here again there is a danger that the local planning authority may be encouraged to breach sound policies because of the immediate desirability of the obligations on offer. There is also the difficult question of the extent to which particularly needed developments should be indirectly subsidized by not requiring obligations.

An analysis of the history of the state's three failed attempts at taxing betterment would seem to justify Grant's claim that:

> Some of the vacuum in national policy in this country is presently filled at local level by an alternative taxing system, that goes by the name of planning gain (Grant, 1991, p. 77).

Yet, as we assert in Chapter 1, the focus of the two processes is different. In the case of betterment, the emphasis is on the increase in the value of the land, while in the case of development obligations the focus is on the external costs caused by the development. In the latter case the objective is to ensure that these costs are internalized in the overall cost of the development. Thus Lichfield (1989) argued that

> Left to the market, the allocation of resources in any development pro-

ject (in amount, kind of use, form of use, activity) necessarily implies a particular distribution of costs and benefits from the development. It could be unfortunate in social terms. If unfettered, the market tends to overload utility services and transportation systems to the detriment of the established community, and could lead to adverse natural, social and economic environmental impacts on the current and potential population. From this it follows that the planning intervention results in a different distribution of the costs and benefits; its aims include, for example, making the polluter pay, internalizing the social costs mitigating impacts, etc. (Lichfield, 1989, p. 73).

Whether these costs are borne by the landowner, the developer or the ultimate consumers of the services provided will vary with the particular circumstances.

What has happened is that, over the years, the scope and nature of the costs for which it is thought legitimate to seek redress have radically increased, as the above quotation from Lichfield would suggest. It has become commonplace for local planning authorities to expect private developers to pay for the cost of highway improvements. The practice of seeking this and other public facilities has now received both judicial and Governmental approval as we discuss in Chapters 4 and 6. Attention has now moved to more remote and indirect social and environmental costs, both in policy and legal debate and in practice, as we show in Chapter 4 and Part Two.

Of course this redistribution of costs and benefits is heavily influenced by the potential profits from the sale of the land or the development and there is often an element of straightforward betterment recoupment. Loughlin (1981, p. 75) makes a distinction between internalization of social costs and the redistribution of resources in favour of disadvantaged groups which he terms **social needs**. However, the broader the definition of social costs, the harder it is to disentangle the two concepts or processes. Nevertheless it would seem to be an advantage of the practice of negotiating obligations that the focus is at least theoretically not on the increase in value caused by the grant of permission but on the costs and benefits that may be caused by the development. This should help to ensure that the process is planning-led and not tax-led, though as will be seen there is still the problem of how far the benefits proposed should indeed cancel out or solve the costs.

2.2 THE ATTEMPTS AT RECOUPING BETTERMENT

2.2.1 The pre-1947 mechanisms for betterment recovery

According to the Uthwatt report, the earliest legislative example of betterment was a statute of Henry VI in 1427 which empowered the Commissioners of Sewers to impose a levy on landowners for the increase in value of their land due to the erection of sea defences by the Commissioners (para. 276). Since that date there are various examples of Acts authorizing the recovery of the costs of public improvements from the owners of land who directly benefited from those improvements.[5] Indeed it would seem that by the turn of the nineteenth century, the principle that the betterment resulting from state activities should go to the state was generally accepted by Parliament,[6] as between 1895 and 1902 the London County Council successfully petitioned Parliament for nine Improvement Acts which allowed for betterment recovery. As Davies (1984, p.266) sets out, the London County Council in fact tried three different methods: (a) a direct charge or levy; (b) a set-off against compensation for compulsory purchase and (c) recoupment.

The term **recoupment** is used to describe the process by which land which has been compulsorily purchased in connection with a proposed development is then sold at a value which reflects the development. A good example described by Davies is the construction of Kingsway and Aldwych by the London County Council where two-thirds of the total cost was recovered by selling off the land adjoining the new works for building. Such mechanisms were used in the US and elsewhere to raise the finance for the construction of railways in the nineteenth century and have been widely used to finance urban insfrastructure improvements (Bailey, 1990; Wakeford, 1990; Kirwan, 1989). Such a method can be used to obtain the betterment derived not only from public works but also from development restrictions by buying land at existing use value and then selling it at a value which reflects the grant of planning permission. This mechanism was to be adopted by the Community Land Act 1975 under which it was envisaged that all major development could only take place on land which had been acquired by the local planning authority.

While it seems that set-offs and recoupment, which applied where land was being compulsory purchased, did result in significant amounts of betterment being collected, the mechanism of the direct levy was both unpopular and ineffective. The Uthwatt Committee states that the London County Council gave up trying to collect it when it was found that the administrative costs by far exceeded the amounts recovered (para. 269). It is therefore perhaps surprising that the first series of public Acts, which gave local authorities the power – later the duty – to plan for new development by way of Town Planning Schemes, adopted the same mechanism. In the Housing, Town Planning, etc. Act 1909, there was a 50% levy on any site value increments due to the scheme. This was raised to 75% in the Town and Country Planning Act 1932. Again very little betterment was ever collected (para. 292) and the fact that landowners were entitled to full compensation for decrease in value caused by the scheme made town planning a very expensive exercise for the authorities. As McKay and Cox (1979) conclude

It is not surprising, therefore, that commentators have argued that the protection of owners rights in this fashion was enough to make sound planning by local authorities unworkable because of the exorbitant compensation bill likely as a result of any local authority scheme (p. 76).

By the beginning of the Second World War, only 4% of the land in Great Britain was the subject of an operative Town Planning Scheme, yet owners of land had obtained 'interim development permission' for a very large area of land.

2.2.2 Betterment under the Town and Country Planning Act 1947

The 1947 Act imposed a **development charge** of 100% on the difference between the existing value of land and any increase in value caused by the grant of planning permission. As all significant development required planning permission under the Act, the application for planning permission after the appointed day became the trigger which set off the liability to pay the charge. Thus landowners still decided on whether or not land should be brought forward for development, though the Central Land Board (which was given the job of collecting the charge) was also given compulsory purchase powers. It was also envisaged that the public sector would play a major role in the development of new housing. The scheme therefore assumed that land sales in the private sector would take place at existing use values and so land would be brought forward into development by builders buying land from owners at those prices and then paying a charge for the right to develop the land. Lewis Silkin, the Minister, who piloted the Bill through Parliament, explained the process as follows:

> When the Bill becomes law, a developer will acquire his land at the existing use value. This will, of course, be lower than today's market price, which will include the development value. On getting consent from the local authority to build, he will then negotiate the development charge with the Central Land Board. As I have explained, this charge will be a sum which will not exceed the actual development value. In other words for his land and for the right to build, he will pay an aggregate which will not exceed and may well be substantially less than today's market price. He cannot, therefore, be worse off; he may be better off (Heap, 1975, p. 13).

In fact landowners, encouraged by pledges from the Conservative opposition to repeal the charge, held out for prices in excess of existing use value. As a result, land was either held back from development or builders found that they had to pay for the development value twice; first to the landowner and secondly to the Central Land Board. Heap (1975) has argued that the scheme might have worked if the Central Land Board had been prepared to give builders an incentive by dropping the rate of the charge. Indeed it seems that Lewis Silkin envisaged that the Bill would give the Board a discretion to drop the rate when they considered this expedient. Silkin considered that:

> there might be circumstances in which it would be important to encourage development by reducing the charge, either on account of economic conditions in the country generally, or in particular areas where unemployment is above average. The importance of securing a particular piece of development on a particular site now, instead of in, say, 20 years, may also lead to a reduction in the development charge, well below full development value (Heap, 1975, p. 11).

In the event the Bill, as enacted, gave no such flexibility to the Central Land Board; presumably on the grounds that it is constitutionally wrong to allow for the negotiation of a discount on taxes. Silkin's stress on the importance of *negotiating* the level of the charge to take into account different economic contexts is significant in the light of the wide flexibility which local planning authorities now have to negotiate development obligations and the wide variation in practice from region to region.

The betterment charge was repealed by the Town and Country Planning Act 1954 but the development value in land was still indirectly taken from landowners when their land was compulsorily purchased, as they received in compensation only the existing use value rather the price they could have sold the land for development on the private market. This could perhaps be defended in the public interest, when the owner had inherited or bought the land at existing use values, as the owner only lost a potential profit. It was completely indefensible on equity grounds when the owner had already paid a price which reflected the development value. It was just such a case (which resulted in the suicide of a Mr Pilgrim)[7] which provided the impetus for the Town and Country Planning Act 1959. This reverted to full market value as the basis for compulsory purchase.

As McKay and Cox (1979) conclude, the 1959 Act

> marked the lowest point to which state's role in controlling land values and development planning had fallen since before the 1919 Act (p. 82).

Owners of land were now allowed to keep all the betterment, whoever created it. The increase in urban growth and the accompanying need for new infrastructure in the 1960s, highlighted the contrast between public costs and private profits. The Labour Government which came to power after the 1964 election was ideologically committed to recouping development values to the state.

2.2.3 The Land Commission Act 1967

The new Government's first step on the betterment issue was by way of a purely fiscal mechanism: the capital gains tax created by the Finance Act 1965. However the Land Commission Act 1967 soon supplemented this by the introduction of a **betterment levy** (originally set at 40%). This, like the **development charge**, was exacted directly on the development value of land. It was similar to the capital gains tax in that in most cases liability only arose when the development value was actually realized through a sale or a granting of a tenancy. The exception was when the land value increased through the owner carrying out development even though no monies were received. As with the 1947 approach, as well as the collection of revenue, the objective was also to keep down land prices, which had recently gone through one of their periodic booms. A body – the Land Commission, similar to the Central Land Board – was set up to collect the levy and like the Central Land Board was also given the power to compulsorily purchase land which in its opinion was suitable for development.

The life of the Land Commission was even shorter than that of the Central Land Board and it was to receive substantial criticism. Grant has observed that:

> it faced a hostile reception both by many government departments whose senior civil servants thought it unnecessary, and by local authorities who found it too remote and clumsy and saw its land assembly activities as a potential threat to local government's own positive planning. On paper, its record was unimpressive. It had hired 10,000 staff and acquired only 2,800 acres of land at the time of its dissolution (Grant, 1979, p. 359).

This last criticism was rather unfair. As Grant himself has since pointed out, the bulk of the staff were engaged in the assessment and collection of betterment and not in the acquisition of land.[7,8] Nevertheless there does seem to have been general agreement even in the Labour party that the scheme was over bureaucratic and too complex to succeed in its objectives (McKay and Cox, 1979).

2.2.4 The Community Land Scheme and Development Land Tax

Although the incoming Conservative administration quickly scrapped the Land Commission and the levy,[9] by the end of its term of office in 1974 it was itself to propose a specific charge on increases in land values: the development land tax. This proposal evolved in the context of rapidly rising land prices and the correspondingly inflated profits that were often made by land speculation. A particular concern of the time was **land hoarding** where owners of land with planning permission hung on to the land without developing it, as the value continued to rise. A notorious example was 'Centre Point', a tall office block in central London built in the 1960s. The office block was built but remained unlet and unused for many years. Ironically Centre Point could be seen as an early example of 'planning gain' as, in return for the grant of permission for the office building, the local planning authority required part of the surrounding land to be dedicated for public highways. Certainly at this time there was concern about the high public costs of providing infrastructure. The Sheaf Committee which reported in 1972 stated that:

> Local authorities who buy sites in developing areas for services as and when required normally have to pay a price which reflects the value of that land for some sort of development and the value will normally have been enhanced by the provision or the prospect of provision of those and other public services ... Thus local authoritities may have to make 'double payment' for land required for statutory purposes in the sense that they are paying a price which reflects the benefits of services which they themselves or some other public authority are providing (DoE, 1972, para. 39).

In response the Government produced two White Papers which announced that the Government proposed to legislate to require developers to contribute to the costs of services provided by authorities in connection with new development.[10] This was in fact never implemented but the Government accepted the Sheaf Committee's view that planning agreements should be used by local authorities to secure private contributions to infrastructure costs.[11] This did eventually result in increased powers to enter into such agreements.[12] The main result of this rethinking on the land market was a proposal by the Chancellor to tax development gains as income. This proposal was taken up by the incoming Labour administration and enacted in the Finance Act 1974. The Development Land Tax, which was to be an essential first stage of the Community Land Scheme and which was introduced by the Development Land Tax Act 1976, essentially built upon this Conservative-inspired tax. It therefore had the rare advantage of cross-party support. As a result, it lasted much longer than previous attempts at recovering betterment.

Development Land Tax, like the betterment levy before it, was charged when either the owner actually sold the land or was deemed to sell it. The tax was therefore either on the actual profit from the sale (where planning permission had been granted this would therefore be the **realized development value**) or the deemed realized development value when the owner was taken to have made a disposal by carrying out development. It was levied initially at high rate of 80%, though there was a reduced rate for the first £150 000 of development value to encourage owners to bring forward land for development. In a way, the Development Land Tax was only an interim method whereby the state obtained betterment. This was because the Community Land Act 1975 envisaged that eventually all major development would have to be channelled through the ownership of the relevent local planning authority. As this land would be acquired at current use value, the authority could then recoup the development value by selling or leasing it for development. The authorities were not subject to Development Land Tax. In this way the scheme envisaged that the local planning authorities would be able to move away from negative planning control to positive planning, while at the same time recouping the betterment for the state.

The White Paper *Land*[13] summed up the arguments thus:

Public ownership of development land puts control of our scarcest resource in the hands of the community, and enables it thereby to take an overall perspective. In addition, by having this land available at the value of its current use, rather than at a value based on speculation as to its possible development, the community will be able to provide, in the places that it needs them, the public facilities it needs, but cannot now afford because of the inflated price it has to pay to the private owner (para. 20).

However the White Paper was not just concerned with the costs of providing public facilities. It was also concerned with the more indirect effects of private development, what it described as the side effects, 'the breakdown of old established communities and the increasing desertion of city centres'. It went on

there are costs involved – the cost of providing more roads, more trains and buses for example; and there are stresses, too, on the individual who has to spend time and money, probably in crowded conditions, travelling to and from work. These costs and stresses are not taken into account by the market but they should by planning authorities (para. 21).

This concern with the impacts of development and the way the private market tends to externalize the costs of such impacts, was to provide much of the impetus and justification for the negotiation of development obligations.

The initial high hopes about what the Community Land Scheme would achieve proved false and once again a Conservative victory at the 1979 election resulted in the repeal of the legislation.[14] However, as Grant (1979) has documented, even before this happened there was general dis-illusionment with how it was working. In contrast to the two previous schemes, except in the case of Wales where a special agency was created, local authorities were chosen to carry out the work of purchasing develop-ment land. The aim was to harness the land development skills which many local authorities had already developed (including experience in negotiating planning gain through planning agreements) and to avoid the hostility that many authorities had shown to the Land Commission. There was of course the problem that Conservative-controlled authorities were ideologically opposed to the concept of public ownership but a majority of authorities failed to acquire any land whatsoever mainly because of insuffi-cient government financial support for the scheme, the lack of financial incentives and flexibility for local authorities taking part (Barrett et al., 1978; Grant, 1979, p. 363). In the last regard the authority was only allowed to keep 30% of any profits itself and the whole accounting process was heavily supervised by central government. This can be usefully contrasted with the financial benefits which may be received under planning agree-ments, where there is no government control and the monies received can in practice be used for general expenditure. Grant (1979, p. 367) has pointed out how the government was concerned that the scheme should be self-supporting as quickly as possible. Local authorities were advised to concentrate on acquiring sites which would result in profits within two or three years. This had the consequence of discouraging authorities who wished to be involved in more substantial and long-term acquisition and development of land. It also underlined the potential conflict between the two objectives of recovering the increase in value for the community and the increased control over the planning of land; a potential conflict which equally applies to the practice of negotiating development obligations.

Consistent with the political consensus surrounding its birth, the Development Land Tax survived the repeal of the Community Land Act 1975 and lasted until 1985. One reason for its eventual repeal was that it, too, had a low rate of return in relation to the costs of collection, as landowners and developers evolved tax avoidance practices. Also in the meantime the scope of the exceptions to both the payment and the rate of the tax were extended. This made it relatively easy to organize land devel-opment in a way that minimized or totally avoided payment. Such was the extent of this avoidance that Grant (1991, p. 76) has described it as 'essen-tially a voluntary tax which produced remarkably little revenue'. Despite the relatively small amounts collected, the very existence of the tax must have affected the manner and pace in which land was brought forward for devel-opment; though it is difficult to decide whether its effects were benign or detrimental.[15] It seems at least to have given some positive encouragement to the negotiation of planning agreements as both on-site and off-site costs (which a developer undertook to incur as the price of obtaining planning permission) could be allowable in calculating the liability for Development Land Tax. Indeed in extreme cases the terms were so advantageous that the developer only in fact paid 6% of the cost of the obligations (Grant, 1986, p. 1002).The only party that really lost was central government who otherwise would have received more revenues; though sections of central government such as the Department of Highways also negotiated agreements in relation to highway improvements needed for development to go ahead. So paradoxically the existence of one system of recouping betterment through national taxation in fact encouraged the evolution of a practice of negotiating a form of betterment recoupment which varied in content and form from site to site.

The repeal of the Development Land Tax in 1985 coincided with the beginning of another boom in land prices. So, while Grant, writing in 1986, thought that the repeal would reduce the willingness of developers to enter into development obligations, all the evidence suggests that developers, during this boom period, became even more willing than before to play the 'planning gain' game if it would result in a quick grant of permission.

2.3 THE SHIFTING POLICY TOWARDS DEVELOPMENT OBLIGATIONS

In contrast to the deliberate and carefully worked out schemes for the recoupment of benefit, the practice and the policy for negotiating planning agreements have evolved in a pragmatic and *ad hoc* way. Instead of Government policy initiating practice, it has tended to react to the arrangements developed between developers and local planning authorities. In 1947, the Lord Chancellor, commenting on the power to enter into such agreements contained in the Town and Country Planning Bill,[16] said that the agreements contemplated would include:

> gifts of land in consideration of permission to develop other land; for permitting public right of access to private lands in consideration of permission to develop other land.[17]

This might be taken to suggest that as early as 1947 the Government was encouraging local planning authorities to sell planning permissions. It seems that the previous power in the Town and Country Planning Act 1932 has been used essentially as a bargaining tool; the developer undertaking not to develop one piece of land and foregoing the rights to compensation in return for obtaining the right to develop another piece of land and not to have to pay betterment (Wood, 1947; Jowell, 1977). However it is clear that such planning agreements were not intended to play an important role in the new comprehensive system of planning control contained in the 1947

Act. Jowell (1977) has suggested that until the late 1960s the powers were little used. Even before the dropping in 1968 of the need for ministerial approval many local authorities used local Acts to negotiate obligations. The property boom in the late 1960s which led to a demand for development in areas without adequate infrastructure accelerated this trend. It has already been pointed out that the 1970–74 Conservative Government's concern about the cost of providing infrastructure at this time almost resulted in a statutory requirement for developers to contribute to the cost. Instead the Government adopted a policy of encouraging the use of agreements as a means of obtaining financial contributions from developers.[18] In proposing a clause in the Housing and Planning Bill which which was under discussion in 1974 and strengthened the effectiveness of agreements, the Government minister involved expressed a very broad view of their scope. He stated:

> Local authorities are already able to make voluntary agreements with the developer for him to provide the necessary facilities to enable him to do the work or contribute towards the costs. I have in mind, for example, the provision of roads, public open space, land for schools and so on. I hope that local authorities will take advantage of this.[19]

Yet when the Conservative party returned to power in 1979, its first concern was to restrict the use of planning agreements. The increase in the use of these agreements had generated strong concern from legal commentators such as Heap (1975) that they were being abused. The Government asked the Property Advisory Group in 1980 to consider the question of 'planning gain'. Their report roundly condemned 'planning gain' and concluded that:

> we are unable to accept that, as a matter of general practice, planning gain has any place in our system of planning control (Property Advisory Group, 1981, para. 6.02).

The report defined planning gain as the obtaining of rights and benefits in connection with the grant of permission, which could not, or arguably could not, be embodied in a valid planning permission. This by itself would have outlawed all use of planning agreements and the report went on to make two special exceptions to this general rule. However, as Loughlin (1982) has argued, the scope and operation of these exceptions was hopelessly vague and really amounted to stating that planning gain was acceptable when it related to a legitimate planning concern. This in turn provokes the fundamental question of what is the scope and purpose of planning.

These shortcomings were carried through to circular 22/83 on *Planning Gain* (DoE, 1983) which set out the Government's policy on the use of planning agreements. In the case of infrastructure, the circular was prepared to countenance obligations to secure such facilities where they were either needed to enable the development to go ahead or were so directly related to the proposed development that the development ought not to be allowed to be permitted without them. This appeared to exclude obligations to contribute towards facilities which were not either part of the development itself or within its immediate vicinity. This was strengthened by two further tests of reasonableness. These required the contributions both to be related in scale and kind to the benefit which the development would receive from the facilities and that the need for the public facilities should arise wholly or substantially from the new development. While the circular's approach to permissible contributions to infrastructure was very restrictive, the only other category of permissible planning gain which it approved was the extremely vague category of mixed development. Here the obligation was acceptable if it was designed to secure an acceptable balance of uses. This was clearly related to the practice by which an application for office development might be approved subject to an obligation to provide an element of housing or commercial uses.

While the circular did provide at least some guidance by which developers could judge the propriety of the demands or expectations of local planning authorities, the only mechanism for enforcing this policy was the right of appeal against an unreasonable refusal. As Jowell and Grant (1983) argued at the time, this provides no remedy for cases where the authority has been induced to grant permission in return for obligations outside the guidelines. It equally neglected the reality that, in times of boom, developers may be prepared to agree to obligations outside the guidelines to save the costs and time of going to appeal.

The property boom of the late 1980s resulted in a growing suspicion that developers were doing just that and that the parameters of circular 22/83 were frequently being violated. The Department of the Environment therefore commissioned research into the use of planning agreements and in particular into whether 'the scope, contents and terms of those agreements are consistent with the Department's published policy and the reasons for any divergence'. This report (Grimley J.R. Eve *et al.*, 1992), to which we will refer extensively in Part Two, was published in Febuary 1992. While it concluded that the use of agreements had increased, it also found that:

> There is almost no evidence that agreements are used to secure wider planning or non-planning objectives such as local employment, affordable housing or payments to local authorities for no specific purpose (para. 7.9).

While our own research equally found little evidence of development obligations which were completely extraneous to the proposed development or which had nothing to do with planning purposes, this finding does appear to disguise the increase in the scope and kind of development obligations. Indeed the report itself goes on to find that, whether by agreement or as part of the proposed development, contributions are often negotiated 'which go beyond the regulation of the development proposed and the infrastructure necessary for it'. This the report distinguished as 'community gain' (para. 7.10, 7.11).

Indeed by the time the report appeared it was clear that Government policy towards the use of planning agreements had significantly changed. The Government began to discover the value of stable frameworks for property markets and realized that developers could usefully be made to pay for more of the costs they were imposing on the public purse. This coincided with the adoption of an environmental agenda. The government's report, *This Common Inheritance* (Secretaries of State, 1990), emphasized the appraisal and alleviation of adverse environmental impacts by those creating the impacts (see Chapter 1). It would appear to be these developments which led to the statutory and policy changes embodied in the Planning and Compensation Act 1991 and the new circular 16/91 (DoE, 1991b) on *Planning Obligations* which replaced circular 22/83 (DoE, 1983).

The research report came out very soon after these changes had been implemented. It was therefore reporting on the extent that there had been compliance with guidelines that had already been jettisoned. The statutory changes made, while they created new mechanisms to protect developers in the form of unilateral undertakings and rights of discharge and modification, also expanded considerably the scope of the legality and legitimacy of obligations by agreement or undertaking. The Act signalled a change in policy by clarifying and extending the kinds of obligations that can legally be created by agreement or undertaking, including the payment of money. Circular 16/91 built on these changes by rewriting the tests as to when such planning obligations should be sought. We examine these tests in detail in Chapter 6. While the circular affirms the general principle that they should only be sought 'where they are necessary to the granting of the permission, relevant to planning and relevant to the development to be permitted (para. B7, Annex B), the definition of such necessity and relevance is significantly widened. Thus in the case of infrastructure, the examples of community provisions, which can be sought where the need arises from the development, are expanded to include 'social, educational, recreational, sporting or other community provision' (para. B8(3), Annex B). This phrase implicitly accepts that the provision of such facilities is the concern of planning and that permission should be refused if those facilities are not available. The circular also drops the third test as to whether it is reasonable that the developer should have to bear the cost rather than be covered by national or local taxation or other means. This endorses the principle that developers should pay towards the capital costs of public facilities which service their developments even when those facilities are not wholly or substantially caused by the development. Also while the old policy was clearly intended to limit obligations to those on or very close to, the site of the development, the new policy expressly accepts that:

> Planning obligations can therefore relate to land, roads or buildings other than those covered by the planning permission, provided that there is a direct relationship between the two (DoE, 1991b, para. B8, Annex B).

The principle of allowing the requirement of mixed development is retained but is expanded by extending the objective 'to secure the implementation of local plan policies for a particular area or type of development'; the example of the inclusion of an element of affordable housing in a larger residential development is given (DoE, 1991b, para. B8(4)). The intention of this change is rather obscure but it would appear to be claiming that the implementation of local plan policies is in itself a good reason for seeking an obligation. The circular also endorses the use of obligations to offset damage to the environment caused by the development, though crucially the wording of the policy is limited to amenities and resources *on-site* and does not extend to the environmental impacts of the development *off-site* (DoE, 1991b, para. B8 (5)).

While the circular marks an important change in the government's policy towards the negotiation of development obligations by local planning authorities, the government would also seem to be moving back to the concept of statutory infrastructure charges, first floated by a Conservative administration in 1973. The Water Act 1989 (now the Water Industry Act 1991) enacted a system of **impact fees** under which there are obligatory charges for the connection of new houses to sewerage and water facilities: the charge is not imposed on commercial and industrial developments. These charges are aimed at covering the extra burden that is being imposed on those facilities. Similarly the consultation paper *Developers' Contributions to Highway Works* (DTp, 1992) proposed that developers should generally pay for highway improvements which are necessary as a result of the increase in the traffic which will flow onto trunk roads and motorways. This would be implemented by using the existing power to enter into agreements under section 278 of the Highways Act but the comprehensive and systematic nature of the proposals suggests that there would be little room for flexibility and negotiation and that it would essentially be an obligatory charge.[20]

2.4 CONCLUSIONS

There is thus a close link between policy debate and planning practice with respect to the recoupment of betterment and the negotiation of development obligations. While it is not surprising that local planning authorities should use development obligations as a means of obtaining for the community a portion of the increase in the value of land caused by the regulation of development, we would argue that the two should be kept distinct. The purposes of, and justification for, the two mechanisms are essentially different, as we have outlined in Chapter 1. In the case of development obligations the fundamental aim is to make the development acceptable in planning terms. In contrast, any betterment tax is concerned with claiming back for the state a share in the profits that flow from development as a result of increases in land values produced by planning regulation. The two have become confused as both are concerned with the need for and the consequences of the provision of infrastructure such as roads and sewerage. With betterment, the public cost of providing such facilities is one cause of the increase in value of the land. With development obligations the concern is with the impact of development projects on overburdened facilities. There has been much confusion on these issues in government policy. Circular 22/83 (DoE, 1983) generally condemned obligations as an unconstitutional tax, while before this, and again in circular 16/91 (DoE, 1991b), the requirement that developers should pay for facilities (the need for which was caused by the development) was clearly acknowledged. Of course there will always be an indirect link between the recoupment of betterment and paying for impacts. The more public facilities are financed by private money, the less need there is for taxation to pay for public expenditure. Nevertheless it is still important to distinguish between impact mitigation and taxation.

However, if the emphasis switches to impacts, it is necessary to know in advance what impact development obligations will have on the activities of developers. We have seen that many of the attempts to deal with the betterment issues foundered on incomplete knowledge of the workings of the development process and the strategies of developers. We tackle this subject in the next chapter.

NOTES

1. 'Windfalls' is the term for betterment in the US.
2. The final report was published September 1942 (Uthwatt Committee, 1942) Cmnd 6386.
3. See ibid., para. 22.
4. Any rights to the £300 million fund were gradually eroded in value by inflation and were eventually abolished by the Planning and Compensation Act 1991.
5. There were such acts in 1669 and 1677, for example.
6. Also note the endorsement of the principle by the special House of Lords Select Committee on Betterment in 1894.

7. For a colourful account of Harold Macmillan as the Minister responsible being taken to task by Churchill for the political storm that was aroused, see Macmillan (1979), pp. 428–9.

8. See Grant, 1991, p. 76, footnote 31.

9. See Land Commission Dissolution Act 1971.

10. See *Widening the Choice: The Next Steps in Housing*, Cmnd 5280 at para. 23 and *Better Homes Next Priorities*, Cmnd 5339.

11. See 867 HC Deb 3745 (27 Jan. 1974). See also circular 102/72 (DoE, 1972).

12. This was done not by extending section 52 in the Town and Country Planning Act 1971 but by creating a new housing power to enter into agreement to carry out works; see section 126 of the Housing Act 1974.

13. Cmnd 5730 (1974).

14. It was repealed by the Local Government Planning and Land Act 1980 but even before then the scheme had been wound up by the Government using powers under the 1975 Act itself.

15. For an analysis of the effects of the tax see Grant (1986), pp. 4 and 88.

16. This became section 25 of the Town and Country Planning Act 1947 but it was based on a previous power in section 34 of the Town and Country Planning Act 1932. For an acccount of the legislative history see Chapter 4.

17. House of Lords, vol. 149, col. 636.

18. There were repeated recommendations by the Department of the Environment that infrastructure obstacles to land release might be overcome by developers' contributions.

19. House of Commons, vol. 868, col. 1072, 5 Febuary 1974.

20. There is little sign at the moment that the government intends to go ahead with this proposal.

3

DEVELOPMENT IMPACTS AND THE DEVELOPER

3.1 THE ROLE OF THE LAND AND PROPERTY DEVELOPMENT SECTOR

The British land and property development sector has many distinctive characteristics. It is well-organized at national level, with bodies to represent the interests of land and property owners (the Country Landowners Association, the British Property Federation), a profession of property advisers (the Royal Institute of Chartered Surveyors), and a range of long-established substantial property investment and development companies. It has evolved from the traditional British patterns of landownership, with rural land held typically in medium to large holdings, and there are significant historic links between landowners and the financial sector (Massey and Catalano, 1978). Compared to many European countries, the development industry is highly oligopolistic, dominated by relatively few, large, regional and national companies and landowners. One result in the nineteenth century was that a key role was played by large landowners in urban development, building residential, industrial and commercial property for rent, on long leases and for sale (Dyos, 1961; Clarke, 1992). In some respects, the development of the planning system has built on this tradition of estate management and development, particularly in the new town programmes and the approach to comprehensive redevelopment.

Yet the conception behind the 1947 Town and Country Planning Act and related legislation represented a significant break with this tradition. As discussed in Chapters 1 and 2, it was anticipated that the state would become the major developer, with the private sector operating to implement state-defined programmes. At the margins, a system for regulating private-sector development activity, through the development control machinery, was established. Historians argue over why the once-powerful land and property sector was prepared to accept such a limitation on its role. One reason suggested is that it was seriously weakened by both the inter-war recession and the subsequent war, which had seen the destruction of property value as well as actual buildings. Others suggest that the post-war planning legislation brought many potential benefits to the sector. The development effort by the public sector served to reconstruct the assets of urban areas which created property value, while the planning frameworks and the firm regulation of development served both to stabilize and to enhance property values (Ambrose, 1986; Backwell and Dickens, 1978). As discussed in the previous chapter, it was relatively easy to argue that the planning system would, in such circumstances, create secure values for many urban and peri-urban land and property owners. The concept of betterment was therefore reasonably well-understood, if contested.

As the land and property sector recovered after the Second World War, fierce challenges developed to this accommodation between the interests of the state and the property sector, with the legislative and policy consequences outlined in the previous chapter (Cullingworth, 1980). The sector grew in scale and complexity in the fields of residential, retail and office development (Ball, 1983; Marriott, 1967). Industrial development, by contrast, was dominated by public agencies – local authorities and English Estates (Fothergill et al., 1987), with only a very few private industrial estates being developed (for example, the Slough Industrial Estate). Property development and investment became increasingly linked to the financial sector, partly through the role of property as an investment medium, and partly through the disjunctions between economic cycles and cycles of property investment (Barras, 1987; Harvey, 1985). In the past 20 years, the British land and property sector has been through two major boom–bust cycles. Typically during boom periods, developer-entrepreneurs have pushed for the planning system to be more flexible. In such situations, they offer contributions to extend infrastructure or overcome environmental hostility to development. In times of slump, land and property investors have sought more certainty from planning frameworks, while developers have looked to the public sector for subsidy. Such subsidy has taken the form of programmes of infrastructure development, as well as 'gap' funding to help make projects viable (for example, Urban Development Grant and City Grant introduced in the 1980s). The provision of clear planning frameworks to limit land release and maintain land values has helped to provide certainty.

The planning system has been slow to recognize explicitly the significance of the land and property development sector and its changing nature. Despite occasional comment on the relations between planning and property markets (Hall et al., 1973; Loughlin, 1980), planning debate until the 1980s tended to focus on social needs and environmental quality. One reason for this neglect was the heritage of the **command and control** model (see Chapter 1). It was assumed in the early post-war period that developers would *fit into* plans and frameworks. Another reason was the concern for equity in the regulatory role. If the planning system was making regulatory decisions about development projects, which might have huge land and property value consequences, it was seen to be important to be fair as possible between different landowners and developers. This discouraged understanding the diversity of development interests.

By the end of the 1970s, however, this situation was changing. Even before the Conservative administrations came to power in 1979, there had been encouragement to local authorities, in their land development and planning role, to pay more attention to market conditions (DoE, 1978). This pressure accelerated through the 1980s. The land and property sector is now seen as the primary agent in undertaking development. Public policy in Britain since then has been driven by the objective of reducing public expenditure and freeing up market activity. As a result, direct development by the public sector and tight regulatory control of the conditions of development are not favoured. Instead, public policy objectives are to be pursued either through partnership (where the public sector has a development interest, for example as landowner or end-user), or through flexible regulation. In line with regulatory policy in the financial, utilities and environmental arena, such regulation is now seen as providing a framework of rules which *enter into* and *frame* rather than *direct* the decisions and strategies of a regulated industry (Francis, 1993; see Chapter 1). It thus becomes critical to understand the character and dynamics of the industry subject to regulation. For land use planning, that industry is 'the development industry'.

In this context, the purpose of this chapter is to review how the increasing pressure within the planning system to negotiate contributions from developers to infrastructure costs, impact mitigation measures and community benefits affects developer costs and behaviour. Can developers afford to pay for impact mitigation? Can development projects bear the full social costs of projects? Who actually bears such costs? How variable is the ability to absorb them? Does the systematic imposition of requirements to make contributions significantly alter land and property development markets? Does the way in which policy is expressed in plans make a difference?

To address these questions, this chapter draws on the literature on the development industry and development obligations, supplemented by our research material. It is organized into three sections. The first reviews the relation between public policy and development activity at a general level. The second examines the question of the incidence of the costs of making contributions and meeting obligations. The third explores the issue of variability in the capacity to make contributions, in relation to projects, sites, sectors, local economies and development agents. In conclusion, we consider the implications of the variability in the development industry for the practice of negotiating development obligations.

3.2 PUBLIC POLICY AND DEVELOPMENT ACTIVITY

3.2.1 Development activity

One of the problems in understanding development activity is the enormous variability in the nature of development projects and the types of firms involved (see Chapter 1). Projects may vary from house extensions and the building of single houses on standard plots to multi-million urban redevelopment projects, such as Battery Park, New York or Canary Wharf in London. Those initiating development range from householders, to companies building for their own purposes, to property investors and property developers and traders. Property investors and developers may be specialist companies, or may be offshoots of corporate conglomerates or financial institutions diversifying into property to extend their portfolio of activities and investments. Land and property itself, as an economic commodity, is a highly varied product. It is also peculiar in that it is normally **spatially fixed** to particular places.[1] It is often said that property investment and dealing has relatively low entry costs for would-be developers, investors and traders (Fainstein, 1994). It thus provides opportunities for small-scale entrepreneurs and an investment source for local capital (such as, investment from small shopkeepers, restaurateurs, etc.), particularly at times when property values are secure or rising. Property **development** however requires access to capital on which a return cannot be achieved until development is completed and the project sold on or rented out. The larger the project, the longer the time period. Access to capital is therefore a significant constraint on entry to development activity on any significant scale. Further, expectations of stagnant or falling land and property values may depress property investment, property dealing and development.

Rather than address this variety, much of the literature on property development assumes a standardized model of development projects and of the development process. **Developers** are commonly referred to as a homogeneous category (e.g. Cadman and Austin-Crowe, 1978). More recently, attempts have been made both to analyse the variable forms which development activity can take and the factors shaping both the industry generally and local land and property markets. This work has focused on analysing the development process in terms of its social relations. It is commonly referred to as an institutional approach. It provides a vocabulary with which to examine the potential effects of public policy on development activity (Ball, 1986; Healey and Barrett, 1990; Krabben and Lambooy, 1993).

At the most specific level, development activity involves undertaking specific **development projects**. Any project involves accomplishing a series of **events**, or tasks, through which a site or property is transformed from one configuration to another. These events may include:

- identification of development opportunities;
- land assembly;
- project development;
- site clearance;
- acquisition of finance;
- organization of construction;
- organization of infrastructure;
- marketing and managing the end product.

This constitutes the **development process**. The sequence of events may vary in the order in which it is undertaken and who undertakes it. There is now a considerable literature which seeks to describe the various forms the development process can take and what 'drives' the process (Ball, 1986; Gore and Nicholson, 1991; Healey 1991a, 1992b). These analyses emphasize the role of the different players and networks in activating the various events in the process, and link these relations to wider forces shaping the strategies and interests of those involved. Figure 3.1 provides a typical example.

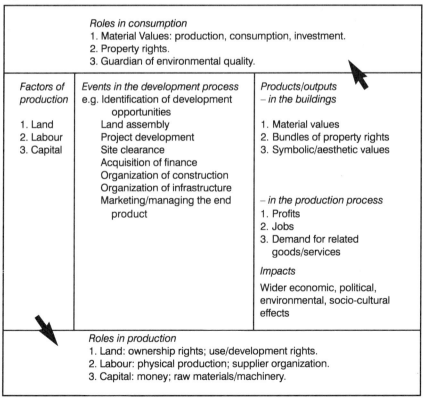

Figure 3.1 An institutional model of the development process (Harley, 1992a)

This kind of analysis helps to identify the diversity of ways of undertaking development and the potential for variation in the relations between actors in the development process. As we discuss in section 3.3, how the process of development is accomplished has a significant effect on who bears the cost of any planning requirements.

The way in which a development project is undertaken, that is, the form of the development process, depends on the nexus of agencies involved in the various events of the process. This nexus may be constant throughout the process, or may vary. In Canada, the US, Australia and France, for example, it is common for the agencies who are involved in the servicing and subdivision of residential sites to be different from those involved in building on sites (Barlow and King, 1992; Booth, 1991; Delaney and Hayward, 1994). In Britain, in contrast, residential developers typically undertake both tasks. In Sweden and the Netherlands, the state still has a key role in supplying urbanized land. Private-sector companies undertake the building and marketing work (Barlow and Duncan, 1994; Needham *et al.*, 1993). In Britain, large residential development firms negotiate options with landowners, or buy up long-term land banks. Capital tends to come from internal profits produced by sales to subsidized mortgaged owner-occupiers. (The residential developers in our Tewkesbury case study provide good examples.) For business park development projects, the relations between a development company and a financial institution may be critical. In the retail field, the development process is often driven by the interests of a few major retail companies. It is these companies which have contributed significantly to raising the offer stakes in the planning obligations game in recent years. This leads to the recognition that development activity varies between market sectors. Ball describes these different types of relationships in his concept of the **structures of provision** of property in different sectors (Ball, 1986).

The various firms involved in these relationships develop their strategies and make their decisions in response to a range of **signals**. We discuss these further in section 3.4 in terms of their impact on the variable incidence of the burden of development obligations. There are major debates in the development literature as to which signals are the most significant in driving development activity (Healey and Barrett, 1990). The old **command and control** models for the planning system assumed the development plan was the key factor. The models favoured by actors within the industry tend to focus on **demand** (Cadman and Austin-Crowe, 1978; Harvey, 1987). However, this demand may be expressed in various ways – the demand from occupiers is not necessarily equivalent to, nor responding to, the same economic conditions, as the demand from investors. The tension between the needs of occupiers and those of investors in the non-residential field in Britain is now widely recognized and analysed (Nabarro and Key, 1992; Rydin, 1993; Healey, 1994b). Other factors which may shape company strategies include the search for diversification, for increased market share, or specialization in a particular product type. Recent work on development activity thus suggests that there may be several factors structuring the strategies and interests of the various actors in the development process, and the range and mix of such 'driving forces' may vary over time and between stages of a development project.

The **development industry** as a term has come to be used to describe the collection of firms and agencies involved in development activity in one form or another. Critical to an understanding of the nature of the industry, and of its various sectors and networks, is an awareness of the types of firms involved and the forces driving their various strategies. The consequence of the activities of all these agents is a particular level of development activity. The activities of the industry in turn constitute land and property development markets, which then provide signals to individual firms as to market conditions and opportunities. The spatial spread and the segmentation of land and property markets will vary with the characteristics of the industry and the factors acting on it. One of the economic characteristics of the present period is the differentiation of types of product in both industrial and service sectors and the opening up of local and regional economies to diverse relations with national, European and global economic activity (Amin and Dietrich, 1991). A consequence for the property field is an equivalent tendency for differentiation and segmentation within land and property markets. In the Tyne and Wear conurbation, for example, some housing markets reflect demand from managers and professionals whose careers involve movements across the country. Others are extremely localized, to neighbourhoods within a district.

A fine-grained understanding of local development industry dynamics and local land and property markets is thus critical to assessing the way planning regulation, and consequently the negotiation of planning agreements, may interlock with local development activity. In exploring the way the state regulates development, it is therefore important to consider the relationships and consequences of planning systems as these affect development projects and process; the nexus of firms involved and their relationships; the level of development activity; the characteristics of land and property development markets; and the overall shape and capacity of the development industry.

3.2.2 The state and the development process

There are four ways in which public policy could affect land and property development through the development process. Governments can:

- undertake development;

- control the right to develop;
- provide financial measures to affect a firm's decisions;
- inform and persuade firms to act in certain ways.[2]

In British land policy, there has been a general shift away from the first type of action towards the other three (Healey, 1988). Nevertheless, all four types of action may be present in actual development projects.

The state as developer

Very little building is now undertaken as such by local authorities and other public-sector development promotion agencies (such as Urban Development Corporations, or English Partnership), for the reasons given earlier. Exceptions may be found, for example where a building is required for a public-sector function. In such cases, the state is in a similar situation to any other private developer. On the housing front, where the local authority used to be a major developer, housing associations, a form of non-governmental (NGO) agency, have now taken on most of the task of social housing production. Development activity by the public sector in the past had a significant impact on the development industry, through providing building and development opportunities which helped companies expand. Several firms grew to prominence as a result of the new town programme (Ball, 1983), and the town centre renewal programme, for example, office and retail developers in the 1960s (Marriott, 1967). In the 1980s, the strategy of property-led urban regeneration, notably Enterprise Zones and the work of the Urban Development Corporations, also provided sheltered opportunities which fostered the growth and expansion of some firms (Healey, 1994b).

State involvement may also open up new market opportunities, by demonstrating the viability of new types of product (for example, small factory units in the 1970s) (Fothergill *et al.*, 1987) or new areas (for example, older industrial zones in the 1980s), or refurbishment projects, through the promotion of **gentrification** common in the 1960s and 1980s. The public sector has powers of compulsory purchase and its efforts in the reclamation and servicing of derelict sites still play a key role in much urban redevelopment work. Where the public sector undertakes these tasks through acting as landowner, if only for a short while, it is able to impose obligations on subsequent development through restrictive covenants on the conveyance of the land. Private land law rather than the regulatory power of the planning system provides an effective means of control over subsequent use and development of a site. One of our case study authorities, Harlow, had used covenants included in land sales in the past to achieve what they now seek to negotiate through developers' contributions.

As a result of previous high levels of land purchase, for public housing, for road programmes and through land assembly for planning purposes or through the short-lived Community Land Act (see Chapter 2), many large urban authorities were substantial landowners by the end of the 1970s (Burrows, 1978). Negotiating planning obligations was relatively unimportant for them. However, government policy and local authority self-interest throughout the 1980s encouraged the sale of publicly-owned land. These public land sales provided a valuable source of sites for land-hungry developers in the boom years. Conflicts of interest could also build up between a local authority's development interest and its planning regulation interest. In addition land was transferred from local authorities to the Urban Development Corporations, reducing the local authority stock. One factor which has increased the use of agreements in these authorities recently has therefore been the reduced leverage which authorities have over development projects through their landownership powers. Again, among our case study authorities, it was in Harlow where the conflicts were most intense. A development offering substantial contributions to a cash-strapped council may be difficult to resist even if it goes against planning policy.

The state as controller of the right to develop

The impact of development control, i.e. planning's regulatory power, on the development process depends critically on the form which such control takes. As discussed in Chapter 1, one source of variation lies in the purposes of planning control. Regulation could focus at the level of building details, in the form of a building and simple land use zoning code. This provides ground rules for development activity. Such an approach is common in Europe and the US (Davies *et al.*, 1989; Wakeford, 1990; Cullingworth, 1993). Alternatively, regulation could be intended to achieve wider policy objectives. In the first case, all a developer needs to ensure is that code provisions have been met. In the second case, more care may be needed to work out exactly what a policy is likely to imply for a project. While a simple zoning code offers clarity and apparent certainty, problems arise when projects do not fit neatly into zoning categories. In policy-driven regulatory systems, there is always an uncertainty as to the way policies will be interpreted with respect to a site. If the uncertainty is large, then it may be difficult to predict what will be the costs of meeting regulatory requirements. This invites the gambling metaphor which some commentators use to describe planning regulation (see the start of Chapter 2). This could lead to the attribution of these costs falling later rather than earlier in the development process.

A second variable in regulatory systems is the way they are specified. There is a key difference between well-specified and stable regimes, with clear codes and plans which are then followed, and project-based systems where what is required is negotiated as the control decision is made. The latter has advantages for those developers interested in risk-taking and opening up opportunities speculatively. As Willis (1980) and Evans (1982) argue, such a situation generates 'rent-seeking' behaviour by developers aiming to maximize the chance of capturing the land value increment created by a variance in planning policy (see section 3.3). But it has disadvantages for the those developers without local knowledge and for the risk-averse firm.[3]

A third variable relates to the control of location and building form. A relaxed regime favours the entrepreneurial developer but creates problems for the risk-averse. A tight regime creates substantial values on some sites and holds up land and property values throughout the urban area. This raises **entry costs** to developers but also increases potential returns. It is helpful for risk-averse developers and existing owners, and creates highly-prized opportunities for the skilled developer-entrepreneur. Given the power of knowledgeable landowners, investors and developers in Britain, it is perhaps not surprising that tight regulatory regimes have been the norm. The small owner or developer is often at a disadvantage in the British context (Healey et al., 1988; Healey, 1994b).

Finally, systems of control can vary in the way they generate costs of getting a permit. The more discretionary and unpredictable the system is in practice, the more time is likely to be taken up in discussion and negotiation about a project, both between developer and planning authority and between developers, planning authorities and other parties. Other time factors include the timescale of the administrative decision process and the timescale of any challenges to decisions which may arise. One factor encouraging developers to negotiate agreements in the 1980s was the timescale between planning authority decision and appeal judgement. Offering obligations, in a period when timing was critical because of the property cycle, was seen as less costly than waiting and incurring the expenditure of an appeal.

The regulation of development through planning control thus does more than merely restrict opportunities for developers and landowners. It actively creates opportunities and values as it limits locations and forms of development. Further, the process of obtaining necessary permits enters into the financial calculations of a scheme as a cost.

The state's financial role

There has been an increasing tendency in British land policy in recent years to shift from direct development by the state to the promotion and regulation of development by financial measures. This parallels trends elsewhere in the environmental field (for example, road pricing to reduce congestion; differential pricing of petrol, etc.). The merit of a financial approach is, in theory, that a tax or incentive can be built into development costs at an early stage, and that it is left to the developer to work out how to adjust to the measure. In practice, different kinds of measures affect developers' financial calculations in different ways.

All those involved in development activity currently pay taxes as in the case of any other business (the Uniform Business Rate (UBR)(the replacement of local property rates), VAT, Corporation Tax and Capital Gains Tax). Most of these taxes currently accrue to central government. This results from the characteristic centralization of the British taxation system. One consequence is that variation in tax regimes to encourage particular types of development in particular places is unusual, in contrast, for example, to the US (Fainstein, 1994). Yet in the 1980s several measures were created to promote land and property development. One of these, the Enterprise Zone, provided incentives by withdrawing the requirement for property taxes (UBR), and Corporation and Income Tax for capital investment in industrial and commercial premises. The total amount of these subsidies to developers is substantial in terms of tax foregone. This measure applied to all firms within an Enterprise Zone area. As a result, highly profitable companies, such as Marks & Spencer and Texas Homecare, received the benefit of subsidy, as did industrial companies moving into a region and creating 'new' jobs. Occupiers, developers and end-users could negotiate to determine exactly where the capital investment benefits would fall, but developers derived substantial benefits via both the avoidance of Corporation and Income Tax and the attraction of the subsidies to end-users. Other incentives were provided through grant – Derelict Land Grant, Urban Development Grant and City Grant, and the various financial contributions the Urban Development Corporations could use to attract companies. The former were linked to particular projects; the latter to projects within Urban Development Corporation Areas.

All these incentives have had a major effect on the location of development in older industrial conurbations and on the structure of the development industry itself (Healey, 1994b; Kennedy-Skipton, 1994). Occupier firms have often moved within conurbations to obtain the benefits, while development firms have clustered around the subsidy regimes. A number of development firms were created specifically to take advantage of Enterprise Zone benefits, building for purchase by investment firms or end-users, though few have survived the property slump (for example, the demise of the firm Enterprise Zone Developments).

However, financial measures vary in their predictability and their point of incidence. Well-established taxation requirements are likely to become routinized within developers' and landowners' calculations. The only variable item may be the taxation level. In contrast, financial incentives may vary not only in their predictability (whether a site will be inside or outside an Enterprise Zone or Urban Development Corporations area or whether a project will attract grant), but in the time in the development process when the availability of an incentive is known. Urban Development Grant and City Grant are never certain until complex negotiations over a project have been completed. Enterprise Zone benefits are available for a defined time period once the zone has been declared. In response to this uncertainty, developer firms often engage in complex negotiations with other parties as to the distribution of the costs and benefits of a project, should grant become available. There are also variations in what the benefit is linked to. Enterprise Zone benefits are automatic, and linked to taxes calculated on notional property value (Uniform Business Rate) and the capital gains made. City Grant offers **gap finance** between the costs and returns on a project. If higher than expected returns are achieved, there is a clawback clause. In addition, grant regimes require a contractual relationship between the grant giver and the developer. Obligations may be imposed on developers through this mechanism. However, most grants are now channelled directly through central government offices. This makes it difficult to co-ordinate obligations arising through planning powers with those linked to grant regimes. One factor underlying this difficulty is the reluctance of British central government to allow local authorities significant tax raising powers.

Many commentators have argued that development obligations should be considered as a form of financial measure, as we discussed in Chapters 1 and 2. They have the advantage, it is claimed, that local authorities can use them as a 'proxy' for a variable local development tax. This is an attractive option for local authorities with few other income-generating options, but it leads to confusions between revenue-raising measures and impact mitigation measures, as we have stressed in previous chapters. For developers, they are either a direct financial cost (in money transfers or work undertaken) or a restriction on options. Several of the development interests in our survey argued for the extension of the practice into a more coherent system of local development taxation.

Two issues underlie these debates. Firstly, developers were concerned about predictability. The negotiation of obligations was like the negotiation of a grant. It was not clear until late in the stage of project development what the type and scale of obligations would be. This affects who pays for them and how. The second concern relates to the way the scale of an obligation is calculated. Here the critical issue in debate is whether an obligation relates to what is needed for the project, or to the need to mitigate an adverse impact; and whether the obligation is required pro rata according to the scale of a project, or whether it relates to the project's profitability.

The type and cost of meeting obligations are likely to be different in each case. Under the influence of US practice (Nicholas *et al.*, 1991; Delafons, 1991a, 1991b), there has been increasing interest in the early 1990s in the introduction of impact fees in Britain (Callies and Grant, 1991; Goodchild and Henneberry, 1994). There are also debates on whether 'quotas' for particular types of obligation should be established. These attempts at standardization in the interests of predictability, however, sit uneasily with the interests of some developers. Some may seek to negotiate minimal obligations and/or to trade off obligations with relaxation of regulatory requirements. It is also unclear whether such standardization should relate to project scale (as in impact fees) or project profits (as in betterment taxes). We return to these questions in Parts Two and Three.

The state's role as provider of information

The ideal market is a well-informed market. Poor information is a common reason for market failure, and this is frequently evident in the development field. In the oligopolistic conditions of Britain's development industry, much property information is managed and controlled by key companies and consultancy firms. Yet their failure to predict the scale of the property slump, and the divergence in the industry's estimates of property value, has raised serious questions about the quality of this information role. In Britain, the well-established planning framework also provides an information role. Through the development plan, the national Planning Policy Guidance notes, and other statements of planning policy and development briefs, landowners and developers are provided with information about the likely attitude a planning authority and the DoE may take to a project. Plans also provide information about what other project ideas may be around, where infrastructure investment is proposed, etc. Such information has a useful role for developers in reducing risk and providing project ideas to respond to. The effective planning authority may well use this informational role to encourage and persuade landowners and developers to act in certain ways.

The value of this informational role in stabilizing market conditions and co-ordinating the actions of one developer with another is widely acknowledged (Healey *et al.*, 1988; Keogh, 1981). It was one reason for the pressure from developers in the early 1990s for a more policy- and plan-driven planning system than in the project-driven 1980s. Planning systems have been introduced in several places for this purpose (Weiss, 1987; Stach, 1987, referring to the US). This suggests that clear policies as to the kinds of obligations local authorities expect may play both a helpful role in creating greater certainty for developers, and may encourage them to mould their projects in line with such regulatory requirements.

3.2.3 Development obligations and the development process

The state's impact on the development process in Britain thus remains broad-based and substantial, despite the general shift from an active public-sector development role to a framing and enabling role through planning regulation. Through this impact, the state has affected not only the level, location and type of development activity. It has influenced the nature of the firms operating in the industry and the characteristics of local land and property markets. It influences decisions about the various stages of the development process, through its role as landowner, land developer and end-user; through its role in controlling development rights; its various financial measures; and in the way information about policy is provided.

The negotiation of development obligations through planning and related agreements is thus only one of the several ways in which the public sector influences private-sector development decisions. Through awareness of plans and policies, developers may be persuaded to conform to planning policy before any discussion with a planning authority occurs (Grimley J. R. Eve *et al.*, 1992; Healey *et al.*, 1988).

Through negotiations with the local authority as landowner, or with the DoE with respect to a grant, a developer may take on a contractual obligation to provide a community benefit (see Chapter 4). Within the arena of planning regulation, a developer may accept a regulatory *condition* with respect to a particular benefit. So specific development obligations are only in theory likely to arise if none of these channels is available or they are seen as insufficient.

Other research shows that agreements were often used even if conditions could, legally speaking, do just as well. Local authorities and developers often favoured a 'belt and braces' approach, combining conditions and agreements. We examine further why this is so in Chapters 4 and 7.

Although many developers have been prepared to negotiate obligations under planning powers in recent years, there was by 1990 considerable concern among developers about the escalation in the scale and type of local authority demands. Developers also questioned the legitimacy of demands for obligations and criticized the lack of clarity about what was required. The concern with legitimacy related to the rationale for obligation requirements. If an obligation was seen as a requirement to pay for what was needed if a project was to go ahead, it was needed by the developer as much as the planning authority. However, if the purpose was to mitigate impact, there could be other parties involved and several ways to reduce an impact. Or the justification could be some kind of charge on project profitability. For a developer, a particular obligation could have elements of all three.

The concern with predictability is related to the incidence of costs. Within the nexus of relationships through which development projects are accomplished, each party will seek to push the costs onto another party. Where the nature and scale of obligations are appreciated late in the day, it is difficult for a developer to pass back the costs onto landowners. In addition, some kinds of obligations (e.g. ongoing maintenance claims) may create problems for project funders, future occupiers and the local authority itself.

However, the land and property sector has no consistent view on these questions, as our interviews showed. This variability is partly a reflection of the confused and ideological debate which linked the negotiation of obligations with planning gain and the betterment debate, as we have discussed in previous chapters. Another reason for the variability is that development projects, the development process, and the strategies and interests of firms in different sectors and segments of the development industry are all very different. What will benefit one firm at one time may adversely affect another. This raises two critical questions. Firstly, where development obligations are negotiated, who actually bears the cost? Secondly, how does the incidence of this cost vary between types of project and types of firm?

3.3 PAYING FOR OBLIGATIONS: WHO BEARS THE COST?

3.3.1 The policy debates

The development industry has divided views on who does and should bear the cost of development obligations. Some argue that the cost is a charge on developers' costs and potentially eats into profitability. Others believe the costs are a charge on the land price and can therefore be passed back to the landowner. Another argument considers that costs may be passed forward to the purchaser or occupier in sale prices or rents.

These issues are echoed in the wider policy debate. On the one hand, central and local government is increasingly concerned to make developers pay the full cost of the services needed to support increased development. This leads to an interest in keeping land and property values up. On the other hand, governments have a policy interest in keeping costs down where the concern is with low-cost housing, or attracting companies to locations.

This is acutely evident in the debates on housing affordability. Here government policy has encouraged negotiation with developers to provide some amount of affordable housing. Those developers who claim that obligations will be passed forward to consumers in house prices argue that this will make housing less affordable. If the cost of obligations eats into developers' profits, then there may be less profit to use to cross-subsidize the provision of social housing quotas. The solution seems to be to build any costs back into the land price. But can landowners be persuaded to accept this? Will the result merely be that landowners will hold land off the market, reducing supply and forcing up prices? Another difficult policy issue is the question of equity as between existing and new residents in an area. If new development brings in new people to a community, why should these new people 'freeload' on the facilities existing residents have built up? If a development project contributes a new community facility and passes the costs onto purchasers of the houses, why should these residents have to pay for a facility which is generally useful for all residents?

How commentators have thought about these questions has been influenced by their experience and their approach to conceptualizing the development process and the impacts on it of planning intervention. We consider two approaches used in the analytical literature, that of welfare economics and that of institutional analysis.

3.3.2 Welfare economics

The most commonly used theoretical tools employed in examining who pays for development obligations are derived from the welfare tradition in neo-classical economics. The presumption of the predictive models used is that, if markets work well, they are the most efficient way to allocate resources and thereby contribute to general human welfare. Public intervention should only be justified if, on balance, it produces a greater general welfare outcome than the market processes in question would otherwise produce.

There have been few British contributions to urban welfare economics which have given attention to the negotiation of obligations, although there is a more substantial American literature around the question of impact fees. Most British analysts start from the assumption that the regulation of land supply through development of itself generates an **economic rent**. This has some parallels with the concept of **betterment** discussed in the previous chapter. This arises from the difference in value of a site in its highest and best use from a market point of view and that generated by the existence of a restriction on supply. Public infrastructure investment also creates locational advantages which add to this rent. This leads to two levels of distributional question. The first concerns who 'captures' the economic rent. The second concerns whether the rent-seeking behaviour generated by the existence of the rent makes land allocation and development processes more or less efficient. If the former, then they are a contribution to general welfare and hence the general tax payer. If the latter, they represent a loss of general welfare.

Willis (1980) and Bowers (1992) both interpret the negotiation of developers' obligations as a struggle to capture the increment of economic rent generated when a local authority marginally modifies a planning policy to allow a development. Their focus is thus not on the case for betterment relating to the general restriction of land supply by planning regulation, but on the increment of value generated by marginal adjustments to established regulatory policy. They assume that planning policy generally has the effect of restricting land supply and thus creating economic rents. The marginal adjustment generates an increment of rent, given the overall restriction on supply maintained by planning regulation. This increment, argues Willis, could be captured by future users (in a rise in the value of their properties), by landowners (in a rise in the value of sites), or by the community, through the negotiation of obligations which provide benefits for the community. However, this last possibility has the effect of removing the opportunity for investment capture by future users and focusing its use on particular community projects, rather than contributing, via general taxation, to general welfare.

Keogh (1982) does not expect the benefits of the appreciation of land values to be passed on to the consumers of properties. He argues that house prices are controlled by the market in existing houses. This means that the costs of obligations cannot easily be passed forward to consumers. Therefore these must fall on developers or landowners. He argues that the practice of negotiating agreements could actually increase general efficiency by reducing the scale of windfall benefits to developers and landowners. In contrast, Evans (1982) (quoted by Bowers, 1992) has argued that the behaviours which develop around the practice of seeking out these increments in economic rent serve to make the process of negotiated obligations an overall cost to society at large, and hence to general welfare.

There is no agreement among economists as to general patterns in the distribution of the costs and benefits of the negotiation of obligations. Both Willis and Bowers argue that how the distribution works out is ultimately an empirical question, depending on particular market conditions and planning policies. A recent study by Bramley (1993), which draws on a substantial data set, builds a model which is more sensitive to such empirical variation. He has examined the effects of the imposition of infrastructure charges and social housing quotas on development obligations in the light of this model. He concluded that, generally, both types of obligation would tend to raise prices and/or lower output, depending on the buoyancy of markets. However, he emphasizes an important caveat, in that his study was undertaken in Britain in the mid-1980s, during a booming housing market and considerable relaxation of planning policies. So the study may only indicate what would happen in conditions of uncertain planning policy and hyperactive markets.

These British debates have been paralleled in the US and Canada focused in particular on the incidence of impact fees (Ryan, 1991). Once again, the state of local markets emerges as a key variable. If a location is very desirable or demand is high, the costs of obligations can be absorbed in prices demanded from purchasers. But if local housing markets are very price-sensitive, then this cannot happen and costs have to be absorbed by developers or owners. This could, of course, lead to subsidy if existing prices were lower than the costs of production of land and property for development. In this case, the costs would be borne by the public exchequer. An interesting study by Ferguson (1991), drawing on surveys in three US states, brings in further dimensions of variation, namely the type of developer and the predictability of the planning regime.

Of particular interest in this context is a series of papers by Skaburskis (1988, 1990, 1991). He uses empirical evidence to construct an econometric model based on developers' rational expectations. He stresses the importance of the stability of the policy regime in shaping developers' expectations. The more stable the regime, the more the costs of obligations will be built back into the land price. But his context is the residential development process in Canada, where the subdivision of sites into lots is separated from the construction of houses on lots. There are thus more actors in the development process who could capture the **economic rent** generated by a planning permit. He concludes:

> Impact fees are shifted forward to new home buyers and renters in stable markets that allow the free entry and exit of firms. When land supply is constrained, impact fees can have a greater delaying effect on development, and when the demand for housing continues to grow, the price increase induced by the fees is greater than the size of the impact fee. The secondary effect causes inner-city housing prices to increase more than those of suburban houses. In hot markets, in the kind of situations that policy concerns regarding housing affordability and impact fees arise, the burdens of the fees are shifted back to land and housing suppliers. The need for infrastructure expansion is also the highest at these times. The introduction of impact fees or, at least, the maintenance of existing fees can help municipalities share the windfalls due to rapid urban growth (Skaburskis, 1990, p. 181).

In other situations, land prices may be low as a result of substantial state ownership of development land and/or 'hidden' infrastructure subsidies. In such situations, especially where there is substantial new development, purchasers may have the opportunity to capture a significant share of the 'economic rent' or development gain resulting from urban growth. This situation has long prevailed in Australia where government policy has sought to keep housing affordable by keeping land and infrastructure costs low. In such situations, the introduction of developers' obligations may well either raise prices, or lead to developers switching to more affluent market segments (see discussion in Delaney and Hayward, 1994). Ferguson also reports such **upscaling** from his US studies (1991). This suggests that much more attention should be focused on the particular institutional conditions of local land and property development situations before conclusions can be made as to how the costs of developers' contributions are distributed.

3.3.3 Institutional approaches

An alternative route to the conceptualization of the distribution of costs and benefits from the negotiation of development obligations is provided by the institutionalist approach referred to earlier (see Rydin, 1993; Healey *et al.*, 1995). This emphasizes the way the organization of the development process in particular cases varies with the relation between the actors at various stages of the process and how this links to the factors which shape the strategies of actors. It stresses the diversity of conditions and relations within which development takes place.

In section 3.2, the range of events that might need to be accomplished in a development project was noted. How the costs of obligations are borne will in part depend on the sequence in which the events take place. If land purchase occurs early on, then it will not be possible to include development obligation costs in the land price unless these are clearly known in advance. If a developer has an option arrangement with a landowner, then the price can be finalized once all the planning negotiation has been completed. Many developers these days enter into such option arrangements and the costs of obligations may be included in the option contract.

However, the relationship through which the various events take place may change over time. Planning policies prevailing at the time of land sale may be superseded at a later period, and a quite different developer may have to negotiate obligation claims. Developers may also have to shift market sectors and segments as land and property market conditions change and/or as building costs rise. The result may then be a renegotiation of obligations. Some obligations entered into at one period may not be achievable in another. As we show in Part Two, some developers were unable to deliver the obligations agreed in the heady days of the 1980s development boom, for example the Harlow Business Park case (see Chapter 5 (Case 17)).

Fainstein (1994) illustrates how British Rail refused to reduce the land price at Kings Cross despite the property market slump, thus rendering unviable the complex package of community benefits negotiated in a major mixed use project around the station.

This suggests that the institutional relations of the development process and how these shift over time is a critical factor in explaining the variable incidence of the costs of obligations. Institutional analysts focus on the **power relations** of the various actors in the development process and how this affects what is negotiated when. Property interests have commonly been close to local government, seeking to influence both planning, development and investment policies to further their interests. In the US, Logan and Molotch (1987), Feagin (1983) and others argue that local government has been driven primarily by development interests. In Britain, with its greater centralization of both planning policy and the development industry, this influence has focused on both central and local government. General tendencies in the incidence of costs are explained in this approach by the economic, political and cultural forces shaping patterns of relations. This would suggest that, in times when demand, generated by economic growth and/or investment capital, is strongly switching into property and values are therefore rising, obligation costs can be passed forward in the increment of land value accruing in the time from land purchase to development purchase. These are the 'hot' markets to which Skaburskis (1990) refers. Political regimes which are successful in maintaining an upward movement in property values also facilitate such an outcome.

Where land and property relations are dominated by large owners and companies, with sophisticated and specialist advisers, it may also be possible to manage markets through oligopolistic practices to achieve such an outcome. Such economic, political and cultural conditions seemed to apply to the British development context until the 1980s. But the past 15 years have seen significant changes, with economic restructuring producing major changes in patterns of property demand, both in terms of location and type. Property development and investment are now even more closely tied to the financial sector than before and are driven as much by the relative attractions of different investment outlets as they are by demand from users for sites and buildings. Meanwhile, neo-liberal political philosophy has sought to break old oligopolies and reduce the extent to which markets are managed. Finally the London-based club-like culture at the prestigious core of the British development industry has been energetically challenged both by an influx of new firms, encouraged by the heady development opportunities of the 1980s, and the challenge of investment and economic analysts to the expertise of the traditional British surveyor. How this shift in culture affected development activity in the City of London has been well-described by Pryke (1991), and Fainstein (1994). The consequence is that the institutional relations of the development industry are now much less stable than in the past. As a result, just as the pressure from both the community and the development industry to negotiate more obligations has increased, so the ability to predict the incidence of obligations has decreased. It is in this context that the pressure for more clarity and certainty in practice and the discussion of impact fees must be placed.

3.3.4 The contingency of the distribution of costs

These academic debates lead to a number of conclusions which help to put the comments of developers and the strategies of policy-makers in perspective. One clear message is that there is no easy way to predict the incidence of the cost of obligations among the parties involved. How these costs work out is contingent on a number of variables. We turn to this variability in the next section. Secondly, most arguments suggest the costs should be borne in the land price. Whether this is likely to happen or not depends on:

1. the stability and clarity of the policy requirements;
2. the power relations among the various agents in the nexus of relationships; and
3. price movements in local property markets.

It is also clear that some firms are much more able to bear the costs of obligations and to push these costs backwards and forwards. The most favourably placed firms appear to be large well-capitalized companies, who can spread risks, across projects and over time.

Many commentators also stress that obligations are not necessarily a net cost to developers. They may bring benefits over and above access to the permit; for example, the design of a better project which is more attractive to purchasers, or publicity for a developer, or better relations between a developer and the community, which could reduce transaction costs for future projects. Such benefits may accrue to individual firms and to the 'general welfare'. But commentators also stress that this will only happen if the public sector adopts a systematic and predictable approach to the negotiation of obligations. As we show in Part Two, this does not yet exist in Britain, although there are signs of a move towards it.

3.4 VARIATION IN THE BURDEN OF OBLIGATIONS

3.4.1 The distributional consequences of planning regulation for development interests

There has been a long-standing interest in distributional issues in planning debate. This has focused primarily on the role of the system in improving the welfare of citizens generally and the disadvantaged in particular (Hall *et al.*, 1973; Ambrose, 1986). A different view is taken in legal debate. Here it is assumed that all interests of a particular type, an 'applicant' or a 'third party' for instance, are equivalent and should be treated equitably. There is therefore a concern in law and planning procedure that all applicants, and hence all developers, are treated fairly by the planning system, that is, with procedural equity.

As discussed earlier, the system has substantial distributive consequences for land and property owners. It creates very valuable opportunities for some by concentrating value on their sites, through restrictions elsewhere. These restrictions constrain the opportunities for others. This inherent 'unfairness' provided part of the justification for the taxation of betterment, as discussed in Chapter 2. Many countries currently tax development in some form or provide for compensation to disadvantaged land and property owners on the basis of this argument.

However, raising taxes to even out this unfairness between landowner interests assumes that substantial profits are obtained through development. During periods of property boom and in certain very favourable locations, this is of course the case. However, in situations where many projects are complex and undertaken over a considerable time period within which market fluctuations may occur, and where projects incur costs in site reclamation and costly property refurbishments, profits are often neither high nor secure. Thus inflexible taxation regimes could render some projects unprofitable. Some, as discussed earlier, may only go ahead with some form of subsidy.

This is why it is important, as we have already stressed, to separate out the argument for taxing development because of the existence of economic rent or development gain, available to some landowners only as a result of planning policy, from the case for requiring obligations to cover the social costs of a development project, whether physical, environmental or community-based. These latter are more appropriately seen as a project cost, rather than a tax on returns. Consequently, they should be treated as a **first charge** on a project budget, before any taxes are calculated.

A second distributive question concerns how fairly these costs are distributed among developers (Rodriguez-Bachiller *et al.*, 1992). It is clear from emerging planning policies on obligations that not all developers are treated alike. Obligation requirements are often targeted at developers of larger sites, or at more profitable projects The formalization of requirements in terms of quotas, fees or infrastructure charges is, in contrast, an attempt at more equal treatment across all types of project. The most developed approach of this kind is perhaps Berkshire's Infrastructure Schedule (Berkshire CC, 1989).

Size and likely profitability of a project are not the only variables affecting the distribution of obligation costs as between developers. A further factor is the clarity of policy. Planning regimes which demand considerable developer–planner negotiation, but say little about the ground rules for this, are likely to favour the developer with good local knowledge and contacts. Would-be developers from outside a region, or local interests without the right contacts, may be seriously disadvantaged in this context. As Rodriguez-Bachiller *et al.* (1992) argue, standardized taxation or fee regimes are much fairer as between developers in this regard.

3.4.2 Sources of variability in development projects

It is clear from the discussion in this chapter so far that development projects and development agencies are highly varied and that this is increasingly recognized in public policy. Drawing on the dimensions of development activity outlined in section 3.2 above, such variation can be considered at the level of the project type; its site and location; its market sector and segment; its local economy; and the developer. There are very many *types* of development project. One of the characteristics of British property development activity is that new build is predominantly in the form of large and hence relatively complex projects. Small projects relate primarily to the refurbishment and extension of properties, or individual dwellings. Development projects are thus unlikely to have standard dimensions. This is one reason why the discretionary, judgmental nature of the British planning system has proved so useful. Zoning systems, providing precise and hence predictable ground rules for development and rights to develop projects which fit these rules, have continued in countries where planning systems regulate urban extension and land subdivision, producing standard sized plots on which purchasers would themselves organize the building process.[4] Project variability means, however, that it is difficult to predict what physical, social and environmental requirements and impacts a particular project will have. If projects are variable so are their impacts. As a result, standardized fee regimes are likely to be unfair as between developers, since a project with limited impacts could have to pay for more than the cost of mitigating actual impacts while a project with many impacts could pay less.

Projects also vary in their *site and location*. On some sites, high value already exists because of the surroundings. On others, development activity may transform an area, helping to create value within it. This raises the issue of the balance between the positive and negative impacts of a project. If a project creates value in an area, through environmental transformation, producing community assets (for example, a leisure facility), or generating jobs, should it have to meet obligations to mitigate any adverse impacts? And how should projects which come forward within an area as a result of the first project be treated? Should they have to bear any of the costs of obligations entered into by the developers of the first projects? Consortium arrangements among developers are often set up to address this problem. In such consortia, contracts are entered into to distribute the costs of infrastructure and obligations among the various parties. An early example of a consortia to develop a large tract of land is that of Lower Earley, in Berkshire (Davis and Healey, 1983; Henry, 1984). This has parallels with the practice of land readjustment, now popular in Asia. As an alternative, where developers are unable to agree among themselves, a development brief may be prepared by the planning authority, specifying requirements. This happened in one of our case study authorities, Solihull, in the Cranmore–Widney Area (Case 2).

Project costs will also vary in relation to the particular market in which a project is positioned. This involves not merely variation within market *sectors*; residential projects are different from industrial ones; office

Case 2: Cranmore–Widney Area, Solihull

Developer: various

Proposal: 5000 dwellings

The site was originally identified as suitable for industrial and residential development in the West Midlands County Structure Plan in 1975. The major part of the development was residential involving the construction of 5000 dwellings. On this development, Solihull acted as co-ordinator.

1. Setting the framework for the development which involved phasing of the 37 sites which constituted the development and the determining requirements for area development (e.g. physical infrastructure, open space, social and community facilities). This was formalized in the Cranmore–Widney Local Policy Plan where Solihull stated that it would act to ensure or encourage such provision.
2. A section 52 agreement was negotiated for each site application to secure contributions from the developer. Each agreement follows a standard format. Developers were to:
   (a) lay out such land within the site as public open space and footpaths at their own expense;
   (b) transfer to the Council or to the Highway Authority all land laid out as public open space and footpaths at a total consideration of £1 only;
   (c) contribute to the maintenance of the land at the rate of £50 per 100 sq. m;
   (d) make provision for off-site sewers;
   (e) make contributions towards highway improvements; the increased capacity of the sewer; the cost of laying out playing fields; construction of a balancing lake; the cost of an off-site distributor road.

schemes differ from retail ones. There is variation also by market **segment**. Within the residential sector, projects can range from schemes for 500 or more dwellings undertaken by major regional or national housebuilding firms, to social housing projects by housing associations and schemes by small local builders, and to householder extensions. Within the retail sector, projects may be for the expansion of a small neighbourhood shop, to a group of shops in a district centre, or a major hypermarket or mega-retail complex. These variations involve both differences in returns due to property market conditions and a different nexus of property development relations.

The larger residential developers and the big retail multiples are enormously more powerful, both financially and politically, than those operating in other market sectors and segments. These powerful players have had a major influence not merely in negotiating **entry** into particular localities through **trading off** obligations for planning permission. They have also been able to affect both the content of *Planning Policy Guidance* and of local planning policy. The Plymouth case, where three retail companies were in competition to obtain planning permission for major schemes, is a case in point (see Chapter 4). Smaller firms and those in weaker markets find themselves in a less advantageous position when negotiating with planning authorities.

Projects will only come forward if there is a market opportunity (i.e. actual or potential demand at a cost which makes a project commercially profitable), or some other funding source. Market opportunities may arise from actual occupier demand; or from developer perception of potential occupier demand, as discussed earlier. The greater the demand, the higher the potential returns. Clearly, the scale and pattern of demand for property is related, if not necessarily directly, to the 'health' of *local economies*. Among our case studies, Tewkesbury and Solihull had much stronger local economies than Newcastle, Wandsworth and Harlow. Assumptions about property market conditions were one reason why Newcastle had rarely required development obligations until the mid-1980s. In Harlow, the opportunity for achieving positive obligations negotiated with developers was compromised when both occupier demand and developer confidence sagged at the end of the 1980s.

This raises the question as to whether contracts relating to obligations are allowed to lapse while the development itself goes ahead; or whether the development itself is stalled if obligations are not honoured. In politically highly charged situations such as the Kings Cross Station site, this may well happen (Fainstein, 1994). If a development does proceed without its associated obligations, then the social costs of the project will fall on the community. The community is in effect subsidizing the developer. Such a subsidy could of course be deliberate, as in a case we found in Newcastle (Case 3).

Finally, projects will vary with the particular characteristics of the *developer*. Some of these link to the context set by the relations of a property sector and segment, and are encouraged or limited by the characteristics of local economies and local land and property markets. Yet these do not determine the specific interests, strategies, financial and other resources of a developer. One of the critical capacities of the skilled planning authority negotiator is the ability to work out the specific interests and resources of a project developer. Some may be involved in development only on one occasion in their lifetime. For many applicants, development is an occasional activity, linked to the alteration or expansion of company premises. Some

Case 3: Fenkle Street/Low Friar Street, Newcastle

Development type: mixed

Developer: Blackfriars Properties

Proposal: conversion of buildings to form shop units and 29 maisonettes/flats

According to Newcastle's policy for car-parking standards, Blackfriars had to provide 29 car-parking spaces for the residents of the development.

As they were unable to make such provision on-site, the City Council offered contract car-parking spaces. Those spaces were to cost the tenants at 25% of the annual rate in the first year of occupancy and increasing to 45% by the sixth year. The cost of contract car-parking space was to remain at 50% for the next 19 years.

What is significant here is that in car-parking agreements, Newcastle normally expects the developer to pay the 50% or more of the cost of contract car-parking permits as a commuted sum. In this instance the developer made no payment and hence the development can be considered as being in receipt of a subsidy.

may be seeking to enter the development business. Others are long-established builders, property investors and managers, property developers, traders and speculators. And within any of these groups, significant variation is likely. Thus the capacity of a developer to bear the costs of development obligations and the time period within which such obligations can be fulfilled is highly variable.

3.4.3 Standardized or negotiated requirements

Faced with this variation, administrative simplicity and legal equity suggests that a system of standardized charges and fees would be a sensible way forward. The desirability of such an approach has been strongly argued by US writers, notably Nicholas *et al.* (1991). There are considerable pressures to introduce a similar approach in the UK as noted above. Precursors are already available in the system of standard water charges for developments introduced under the Water Act 1989, now contained in the Water Industry Act 1991. The Department of Transport is also interested in introducing standard payments for hook-ups to the national highway network (DTp, 1992) and DoE interest in impact fees has already been referred to (Goodchild and Henneberry, 1994). This apparently efficient and equitable solution is not necessarily fair as between developers or effective in meeting developers' requirements or in mitigating adverse impacts. As noted earlier, schemes of equal scale and value may have different requirements and impacts. Standardized charges may neither ensure the provision of the infrastructure investment needed for a developers' project nor mitigate the specific adverse impacts of a project. This point has been made in comment on the Berkshire Infrastructure Charges (Barton Willmore Planning Partnership, 1991).

This is one reason why the negotiation of obligations is still favoured by many developers. However, without a clear planning policy framework, permissions will be obtained in return for benefits by the larger, knowledgeable and well-connected developers at the expense of the less powerful firms and those who only occasionally engage in the development process. This puts the onus on the regulatory system to provide clear general principles with respect to the negotiation of obligations, which recognize explicitly the variability in development projects, development conditions and developers. This is a tough challenge for the regulators. It also requires some re-thinking of long established planning and legal principles, such as the principle that planning regulation should focus on land *use* and not consider the *users* of a site (Healey *et al.*, 1993a), and the meaning of equitable treatment as between different developers.

3.5 IMPLICATIONS

The **market** that the planning system is expected to regulate, that is, the processes of land and property development, is thus highly diverse and segmented. The traditional approach was to ignore this diversity and focus on fair treatment of all **applicants** for planning permission. The current reliance on market processes and private-sector investors and developers to produce development has encouraged the system to become more **market aware**. With this has come increasing realization of the diversity and complexity of the development process and the development industry. The challenge for the planning system is to find ways of treating development industry interests fairly, while working sensitively with this diversity.

The diversity makes it difficult to generalize about the ability of projects and developers to cover the social costs of agreements and other measures to deal with the adverse impacts of projects. Also factors influencing the ability to pay may work in contradictory ways. Nevertheless, projects which are likely to be able to cover such costs typically have the following characteristics:

- buildings involving standardized products (e.g. a number of similar houses);
- on large sites, with few development problems;

- schemes which substantially upgrade the land market status of the site;
- projects within a buoyant market sector and segment;
- in a healthy local economy;
- the developer involved has project management capability and adequate financial backing.

Projects which may have difficulty covering their costs, in contrast, are likely to have the following characteristics:

- an unusual or complex project;
- relatively high and unpredictable costs;
- sites with difficult topography or pollution and ground clearance problems;
- small sites;
- projects within a difficult market sector or segment;
- in a relatively weak local economy;
- inexperienced developers, with limited financial backing.

One clear consequence of this conclusion is that larger projects on green-field sites will be more likely to cover their social costs than complex redevelopment projects and infill projects within the urban area. A planning regime which relies too much on the negotiation of development obligations without any ability to subsidize redevelopment will therefore tend to encourage urban extension rather than urban regeneration. This has significant implications for contemporary environmental debate. One approach to addressing the new environmental agenda is to require all projects to cover the costs of their adverse impacts by compensation measures of some kind. But if only those projects on easy-to-develop greenfield sites can cover such costs, such a strategy will encourage urban extension. In contrast, a policy which seeks to contain urban extension by forcing development to seek out difficult urban redevelopment sites may find that projects are unable to cover the costs of any adverse impacts, or even of site clearance and de-contamination. A planning regime which emphasizes the negotiation of obligations to deal with environmental impacts and infrastructure requirements will also tend to favour larger, well-financed developer firms, based on the site-by-site negotiation of impacts, and thus continue the long-standing tendencies in the British development industry, as described at the start of this chapter. Such a regime is thus not particularly fair as between developers (Rodriguez-Bachiller et al., 1992). As we have noted several times, moves towards greater clarity and predictability as to infrastructure needs and social costs requirements nevertheless have the capacity to improve the opportunities for the smaller development interest, the occasional developer, and the less locally knowledgeable development firm.

This suggests that a market-aware planning regime which also strives for fairness should provide clear policy guidance on its approach to development obligations. Such advice should focus first on what is required from projects in terms of obligations relating to payment for the infrastructure needs of projects. This should be followed by an indication of the particular areas where social costs will be assessed (the fields of impact), with an indication how this will be done. A planning authority could also indicate what factors will be borne in mind when considering the circumstances of individual projects and specific developers. This would set clearly the *baseline for negotiation* over individual projects. If a project could not cover its social costs, yet was desirable for a particular planning objective (economic development for example), at least it would be clear that a *de facto* subsidy from the community was involved and why this was justifiable.

Improving clarity and predictability could help many developers, as the scale of costs arising from the planning regime would tend to be known early on in the development process. It should therefore be more efficient overall, help to build costs into the land price, reduce time spent in negotiating planning permission and help to provide fair demands as between developers. It would, however, reduce the opportunities for development entrepreneurs and traders by stabilizing market conditions, although planning authorities with a sophisticated understanding of local markets could still provide opportunities for such firms by careful phrasing of planning policy. However, the diversity of developers and of projects argues against over-standardization of the demands on developers. Caution therefore needs to be exercised with respect to the introduction of standard impact fees and utility service charges.

In Part Two, we examine in more detail evolving practice with respect to the types of obligations being negotiated. We return in Part Three to discussion of the dimensions of a more systematic approach to the negotiation of development impacts as outlined above. What this chapter has sought to stress, however, is that the form of the relation between development activity and the planning system is not just a question of the detailed operation of a regulatory regime. How it works has consequences for the organization and structure of the development industry and of land and property markets. It also has consequences for society as a whole, in terms of both the efficiency of the provision of land and buildings for society's activities and the environmental and social consequences of the particular way the built environment is produced.

NOTES

1. In some places, buildings are moved from place to place. This is unusual in Britain.

2. Derived from Lichfield and Darin-Drabkin (1980) and Healey *et al.* (1988).
3. It is often suggested that all developers are risk-seeking entrepreneurs. They are more appropriately seen as risk-minimizers.
4. This produces the separation between land submission evident in Australia, the US, Canada and France.

4

THE LAW AND THE LEGAL DEBATE

4.1 THE ROLE OF LAW IN ENABLING DEVELOPMENT OBLIGATIONS TO BE CREATED

In English law, the most usual way a private individual can create a legally binding obligation with respect to another private individual is through the common law mechanism of a contract. As local planning authorities are the creatures of statute, they need statutory authority to enter into contracts. Section 111 of the Local Government Act 1972 provides a general power to enter into contracts which are calculated to facilitate or are conducive to the discharge of any of their functions. Moreover there are several specific statutory powers which enable local authorities to enter into agreements relating to the use and development of land. While a contract is primarily a private law mechanism, when used by public authorities, it is subject to the rules of public law as well as private law; at least where there is a recognizable public law element and the authority is not acting in a purely commercial or private context.

Public law consists mainly of the statutes which set up public authorities and vest in them various duties and powers. The courts play a vital role in interpreting these statutory duties and powers. This is normally done by the High Court by way of an application for judicial review, or through a specific statutory right of challenge, or appeal set out in the statute which confers the function on the public authority.[1] In exercising this jurisdiction it is generally accepted that the courts are doing more than simply interpreting the will of Parliament and that they draw on what are in substance free-standing principles. These principles reflect judicial values as to fairness, human rights and what is in the public interest. So judicial decisions on the scope and materiality of development obligations are not sealed off from the wider debate about their efficacy and morality. Indeed the judgements often reflect and are influenced by this wider discourse; albeit that the judgements transform these arguments into more stylized legal language.

This chapter reviews the legislation authorizing agreements and undertakings and the legal arguments that have taken place over the scope and content of obligations and the extent to which they can be taken into account in granting planning permission. However, it is important to realize that even where there may be doubts over the legal validity of an agreement or a grant of permission, there is normally no incentive for the immediate parties to test the matter in the courts. Most challenges in the courts have been mounted by aggrieved third parties such as rival developers. The parameters of the discourse are therefore dictated by the fairly arbitrary process of litigation and there are, as yet, still only a handful of cases which have been decided by the courts. Nevertheless, the principles to be deduced from these judgements set the framework for future negotiations and are extremely influential on the practice of negotiation. Unfortunately, the jurispudence which has so far evolved has been confused and inconsistent.

4.2 THE LEGAL MECHANISMS AVAILABLE TO DEAL WITH THE IMPACTS OF DEVELOPMENT

4.2.1 The application for planning permission

The developer can use the planning application itself as the means of incorporating into the development proposal features, such as roads, sewers and public space, which may make it both acceptable to the planning authority and workable in its own terms. Any significant departure from the terms of any subsequent grant of permission will normally mean that the development is totally unauthorized. Therefore enforcement action could be taken against the developer for failing to implement the development as set out in the application. By its nature, this form of development obligation is restricted to on-site matters and will often be supplemented by conditions or separate planning agreements to make enforcement easier. Because developers are usually aware of what local planning authorities require or expect with regard to a development, it is a frequent but often unnoticed form of development obligation. In this regard the research commissioned by the Department of the Environment found

> that community facilities were often included in the applications themselves, perhaps after negotiations between applicant and authority, without the need for this subsequently to be secured by an agreement (Grimley J. R. Eve *et al.*, 1992, para. 7.10).

4.2.2 Planning conditions

This is the traditional method in the British planning system of minimizing impacts and making an otherwise unacceptable development acceptable. The power to impose conditions is contained in section 70(1) of the Town and Country Planning Act 1990 and gives the determining authority an apparently unrestricted discretion to impose 'such conditions as they think fit'. Faced with such absolute statutory powers, the courts have nevertheless held that such powers cannot be used arbitrarily or oppressively or for what are seen as improper purposes. In the case of planning conditions, the House of Lords held in **Newbury [1980],**[2] that a condition must comply with three basic principles. First, the condition must be imposed for a planning purpose and not for some ulterior purpose. Second, the condition must fairly and reasonably relate to the development being permitted. Third, the terms of the condition must not be so unreasonable that no reasonable planning authority could have imposed such a condition.

In the past, these principles have been applied strictly. Conditions have been quashed by the courts where they have been seen not to be sufficiently related to the permitted development or to be too unreasonable. Thus, in **Royco Homes [1974],** the Divisional Court held that conditions were invalid which in substance required a private developer to provide social housing by restricting the type of houses to be developed and the persons to whom the houses would be let and on what terms. Then, in **Hall & Co. [1964],** the Court of Appeal quashed a condition requiring a developer to build a service road and dedicate it to the public. The basic rationale of such decisions is that the planning powers should not be used for a taking of property rights especially where there exist alternative statutory powers whose use would involve the payment of compensation. This approach was more recently upheld by the Court of Appeal in **Bradford [1986]** where the Court further held that a condition requiring a road to be widened was still invalid, even if the applicant agreed. Lord Justice Lloyd stated:[3]

> If the condition is manifestly unreasonable, the willingness of the developer is irrelevant. *Vires* cannot be conferred by consent (p. 64).

However, conditions will be valid if they are worded in such a way that they do not positively require the developer to give away their land or to do something which as yet they have no power to do. Thus in **Britannia [1978]** the court upheld a condition, attached to a grant of permission for a housing estate, which required provision of children's play areas, public open space and a social/shopping centre. The Deputy Judge[4] distinguished this from the the **Hall & Co**. case on the grounds that the condition did not positively require any land to be dedicated to the public. It therefore followed that the spaces would not become dedicated and adopted, except under some other agreement or by the operation of other statutory powers. In fact, in that case, there existed a planning agreement under which the public were to be given rights to the land. This makes clear that a condition can require what may be termed planning gain if the condition itself stops short of requiring a transfer of property rights.

Grampian Regional Council v City of Aberdeen District Council

Grampian Regional Council applied for planning permission to carry out industrial development. As the City of Aberdeen failed to determine the application within the required period, the application was deemed to be refused. On appeal the reporter, who held a public inquiry into the deemed refusal, said that he would have granted permission, if it not been that the development would have caused unacceptable traffic danger at a road junction some yards from the site of the proposed development. He had considered imposing a condition requiring the closure of part of the road between the site and the junction but had concluded that such a condition would have been invalid as the applicants could not ensure that the closure order would be confirmed. The reporter's decision upholding the refusal of permission was challenged in the courts on the ground that, while a condition *requiring* the road to be closed would have been invalid for unreasonableness, the reporter had misdirected himself in failing to consider whether to impose a condition to the effect that development was *not* to commence until the road in question had been closed. The House of Lords held that the reporter's decision should be overturned. There was in this context a crucial difference between a positive and a negative condition. Compliance with a negative condition is within the control of the applicant and is therefore readily enforceable by the planning authority. While a condition positively requiring the road to be closed was unreasonable as the applicant might not be able to comply with the requirement. The reporter should have considered imposing a negatively worded condition. Such a condition, which makes the commencement of the development or part of the development conditional on certain circumstances being satisfied, has become known as a **Grampian** condition.

Figure 4.1 The Grampian condition (Grampian [1984] case)

A similar device is the negatively worded or **Grampian** condition, as it has become known since it was given the approval of the House of Lords in the case of **Grampian [1984].** (The facts of this case are set out in Figure 4.1.) Here the condition does not positively require land to be dedicated or works to be carried out. Instead, it requires that the development should not be carried out or completed until the land has been dedicated or works carried out. However, until recently, the effectiveness of this form of condition was restricted as the courts had held that such a condition is only valid where there is a *reasonable prospect* of the condition precedent being satisfied (see **Jones [1991]**). Thus, in the case of **Eagle Star [1992]**, the only planning objections to a proposed extension of a shopping centre were the traffic problems which would be created by the development. These traffic problems could be solved by off-site highway works but these works would require the compulsory purchase of land. As there were likely to be objections to any compulsory purchase orders and the public body which would have to make the orders (the Highway Authority) was unwilling to use their compulsory purchase powers, the Secretary of State, on appeal, not surprisingly found that there was no reasonable prospect of the improvements being completed. The justification for holding a condition invalid in such a case was that it is totally unreasonable for a planning authority to impose such a condition as it shuts out any reasonable prospect of the permission being implemented and so undermines the grant of permission. It did not matter if the applicant consented or even positively asked for such a condition. This very paternalistic approach has been overruled by the recent decision of the House of Lords in **British Railways Board [1994]**. In this decision, Lord Keith of Kinkel said that:

> the mere fact that a desirable condition appears to have no reasonable prospects of fulfilment does not mean that planning permission must necessarily be refused.

He nevertheless accepted that there could be circumstances where permission might be refused on the grounds that there would be difficulties in complying with the pre-conditions.

The development of such devices as the **Grampian** condition, along with signs of a more liberal judicial approach to planning conditions, mean that conditions are a much more viable alternative to planning agreements than is often realized. However, even where local planning authorities are aware that the planning objective could validly be achieved through a condition, they may often prefer to negotiate an agreement or undertaking either as an alternative to, or in addition to, a condition. One reason often cited in our interviews with planning officers was that, because agreements are agreed by the parties and not imposed by the local planning authority as with conditions, it is perceived that there is less likelihood of the obligation being broken. Agreements are also seen as more easily enforceable, should there be default, as the authority can go direct to the courts for an injunction without having to go through the complicated and time-consuming process of serving an enforcement notice. However, the reforms introduced by the Planning and Compensation Act 1991, which provide for breach of condition notices and the use of injunctions to enforce planning control, have increased the effectiveness of the enforcement of planning conditions. More significant in tipping the balance of local authority preference for the use of agreements, rather than conditions, is the fact that, once planning permission has been granted subject to conditions, it is always possible for the developer to seek permission to implement the permission shorn of its condition. If this is refused, there is an immediate right of appeal to the Secretary of State. In the case of agreements or undertakings, there now exists a right to ask for the obligation to be varied or discharged but this has the important restriction that five years must elapse before an application can be lodged.

The government's policy has always been that, where there is a choice between imposing a condition and entering into a planning obligation, the imposition of a condition is preferable because it enables a developer to appeal. This position has been re-iterated in circular 16/91 (DoE, 1991b). The research conducted for the Department of the Environment (Grimley J. R. Eve *et al.*, 1992) found that there was widespread disregard of this policy and that there was frequent replication of conditions by agreements. This is often known, colloquially, as the **belt and braces** approach. There is, how-ever, nothing unlawful in a local planning authority doing this even if the objective is to preclude an appeal to the minister. In the case of **Good [1994],** the Court of Appeal, in upholding the decision of the High Court, agreed with the Vice-Chancellor, Sir Donald Nichol's[5] view, that, while there was a certain lack of attractiveness about a local planning authority deliber-ately seeking to bypass the minister, this action was not unlawful. The Court of Appeal added that as long as the local planning authority used its power to enter into agreements in good faith and took into account all material considerations, it did not matter that the council was aware that they were exercising their powers in a way which was disapproved of by the Secretary of State. It was pointed out that the developer did not have to go along with the local planning authority and can always refuse to enter into an agree-ment. Certainly it would be invalid for a local planning authority to refuse a planning application on the grounds that the applicant had refused to sign an agreement when the same objective could be achieved by a condition.

4.2.3 Collateral agreements and undertakings

The Town and Country Planning legislation has, from its inception, pro-vided a power for local planning authorities to enter into agreements with developers. However, it is important to realize that such 'planning agree-ments' are only one form by which development obligations can be created. Indeed one of the problems is that there is considerable overlap and confu-sion between the various mechanisms, and the practice of local authorities varies with respect to the legal instrument they use when concluding devel-opment obligations, as we show in Part Two. We now examine the legal scope and consequences of these mechanisms.

4.3 AGREEMENTS AND UNDERTAKINGS UNDER THE PLANNING ACTS

Tucked away in paragraph 13 of the fourth schedule to the first Act to contain the word 'planning' in its title, the Housing, Planning etc. Act 1909, was a power for planning authorities to make agreements with owners. This power is to be found in all the Town and Country Planning Acts that followed. Section 34 of the Town and Country Planning Act 1932 provided that planning agreements were enforceable against successors in title. The provision contained in the Town and Country Planning Act 1947 (section 25) set out in more detail the purpose of such agreements and introduced the requirement of ministerial consent. (This requirement was to be removed in 1968.) This was repeated in the wording of section 52 of the 1971 Town and Country Planning Act. During the 1970s and 1980s, planning agreements were commonly referred to as 'section 52' agreements. The wording of the provision in these Acts was taken by many lawyers to mean that only negative obligations could be the subject of planning obligations and that in any case only restrictive obligations were enforceable against successors in title to land which is the subject of the agreement. Fortunately many of these arguments have been resolved by the Planning and Compensation Act 1991. This substituted a new wording for section 106 of the Town and Country Planning Act 1990. This in turn replaced section 52 of the 1970 Act.

4.3.1 The scope and content of planning obligations

Before the statutory changes which were made by the Planning and Compensation Act, section 106 provided that the purpose of a planning agreement was 'restricting or regulating the development or use of the land' which was the subject of the agreement. This led to doubts as to whether covenants to carry out positive acts, such as landscaping, could be correctly termed as 'restricting or regulating'. The new wording resolves such doubts by setting out a detailed list of the matters that can be included in an obligation whether by agreement or by a unilateral undertaking. These are now set out in section 106(2) and are obligations:

- restricting the development or use of land in any specified way;
- requiring specified operations or activities to be carried out in, on, under or over land;
- requiring the land to be used in any specified way; or
- requiring a sum or sums to be paid to the authority on a specified date or dates or periodically.

The last three categories are all new and allow for all manner of positive obligations. In the **Plymouth [1993]** case (the facts of which are set out in Figure 4.2). Lord Justice Evans said that the statutory provisions now reflect the political objective of permitting the greater use of private capital for what are described as 'off-site infrastructure costs', which formerly were borne by the public sector alone. Hence the increasing incidence of community benefits and planning gain (p. B86).

This case rapidly became notorious. Many thought it had overstepped the boundaries of what could legitimately be required in obligations.

By the late 1980s, no conference on planning gain was complete without a story being recounted, usually without any names or details, about solicitors on behalf of developers handing over large cheques to local planning authorities in order to get planning permission. The express reference in the Planning and Compensation Act 1991 to 'sum or sums to be

---

R v Plymouth Council ex parte Plymouth and South Devon Co-operative Society

This major case involved three applications to develop major food stores in Plymouth. The draft alteration to the local plan had selected three out-of-town areas for stores and stated that stores were expected to provide community benefits. Both Tesco and Sainsbury were in competition to develop stores on different sites at one of these areas, Marsh Mills. Sainsbury suggested that permission be given for both stores and Plymouth Council invited both organizations to make submissions setting out the community benefits that would be offered. Both Tesco and Sainsbury offered substantial packages of facilities both on and off the superstore sites; Sainsbury's amounted to £3 662 000. These benefits included crèches, park and ride schemes, a wildlife habitat, a birdwatching hide, an art display, a tourist information centre and infrastructure for an alternative industrial site. Tesco's offered a similar amount. Both applications were approved but on the same day, an application, by the South Devon Co-operative Society, for a store on one of the other areas identified in the draft plan, was deferred as it was considered that, in the light of permissions granted to Tesco and Sainsbury, the capacity was now too large. Although the Society was subsequently granted permission, they applied to the High Court for the grants of permission to Tesco and Sainbury to be quashed on the grounds that Plymouth Council had erred in law by taking the packages of community benefits into consideration. Both the High Court and the Court of Appeal held that all the community benefits were material considerations even though many were not necessary to overcome any planning problems. The decision therefore means that a developer can attempt to get an advantage over a rival developer by offering benefits which are contrary to the policy in circular 16/91 (DoE, 1991b).

Figure 4.2   The Plymouth [1993] case

paid' now means that an undertaking to pay over large sums is presumably perfectly legal as long as the monies are to be used for a planning purpose. Thus, in the **Crest Homes plc [1994]** case, the Court of Appeal upheld the validity of a series of agreements under which the landowners agreed to pay to the local planning authority between 17% and 20% of the increase in the value of the land caused by the granting of permission for industrial/commercial use. (The facts of this case are set out in Figure 4.4.)

The obvious omission is that, although a planning obligation under section 106 can only be entered into by a person who is 'interested in land in the area of a local planning authority', there is no express provision for the owners of land to undertake to transfer or sell that land. This apparent omission has already caused problems. In the **Wimpey Homes [1993]** case, it was held that an undertaking to transfer land to another person was not an obligation restricting the development or use of land and so did not come within section 106(1). However, it would seem that this difficulty could be got around by the equivalent of a **Grampian** condition, in that the development of the site could be made conditional on land being transferred. This would be an obligation restricting the development or use of land.

Support for this approach is to be found in the case of **Springimage Ltd [1994]** , where it was similarly argued that a planning obligation under section 106 could not be used to restrict a developer's rights to requisition a sewer. The Deputy Judge accepted that where there was concern about the capacity of sewers, an agreement could validly restrict the development of the site until some proper sewerage arrangement had been made. The point also arose in the case of **Crest Homes plc [1994],** where agreements contained an obligation to convey land free of charge to a local planning authority. In the High Court, Mr Justice Brooke[6] commented that it would be very odd if an owner was allowed to create a planning obligation to pay the council the money required to buy, say, neighbouring land for a car-park, but was not allowed to bind him/herself to transfer part of his/her own land free of charge for this purpose. On appeal, the Court of Appeal said that this could be lawfully done under section 106, if the transfer of the land was done in order to restrict the use of the land or to ensure that it was used in some specific way.

There also used to be doubts as to whether a positive obligation could be enforced against successors in title to the land which was burdened by the obligation. This was based on an analogy with the general law on positive covenants. The wording of section 106 puts beyond doubt that all obligations are enforceable both against the person entering into the obligation and any person deriving title from that person, though complications could still arise where the obligation concerns both on-site and off-site land and there is later fragmentation of ownership.

The legislation has never made clear *why* persons interested in land should wish to enter into burdensome obligations. In practice, it is obvious that, in most cases, the reason will be to enable a valuable planning permission to be granted. In this respect, a specific undertaking by a local planning authority to grant permission might be held by the courts to be invalid and unenforceable, as an improper fetter on the statutory discretion given to local planning authorities to determine whether or not to grant planning applications. Whether or not this is so, in practice, it presents no problem as obligations can be made conditional on planning permission being granted and implemented. Thus, the standard procedure is for the agreement or undertaking to be executed first. The local planning authority then goes on to resolve to grant permission. It may be noted that in such a case the obligation would become binding, even if in fact the authority granting permission had not had regard to the obligation in granting permission. Of course the law still requires that the creation of the agreement should not prevent the authority from considering fairly the merits of any opposition to the planning applications. However, as Mr Justice Brooke admitted in the **Crest Homes plc [1994]** case:

> It is, of course, a truism that Parliament's willingness to allow councils to enter into planning agreements with developers in order to attract private capital into infrastructure and related works may make it more difficult for councils to avoid giving the impression that they are favouring one developer over others; but so long as they comply with the law and take into account only material considerations when judging the appropriateness of granting a particular application, the courts won't intervene (p. 952).

There similarly used to be debate over whether an agreement would be invalid because the local planning authority was apparently giving no reciprocal undertakings in return for the developer's undertakings. This is termed lack of consideration in contract law. However there would seem to be no reason why common law rules of contract should invalidate an obligation which has complied with the formalities laid down by the section itself. In any case obligations made by way of deeds are enforceable without consideration.

4.3.2 The validity of planning obligations and their relationship to the grant of planning permission

Although section 106 is silent as to why an owner of land should enter into a planning obligation, the fact that most obligations are entered into in the context of the grant planning permission, or the prospect of one, means that it has been argued that planning obligations are not valid unless the obligation fairly or reasonably relates to the permitted development. This assumes that the tests as to whether a planning condition is valid apply equally to planning obligations. This approach was first indicated in the Court of Appeal decision in the **Bradford [1988]** case where Lord Justice Lloyd thought that, if an obligation could not be imposed as a condition (because it was manifestly unreasonable), it could not be imposed as part of a planning agreement. Then, in **Monahan [1990]**, known as the **Royal Opera House** case, Lord Justice Kerr approved Lord Justice Lloyd's view and went further by stating that:

> But if a particular condition would be illegal – on the grounds of manifest unreasonableness or *otherwise* then it cannot acquire validity if it is embodied in a section 52 agreement whether at the insistence of the applicant himself or not [our emphasis] (p. 117).

The 'otherwise' would include a condition which was illegal because it did not fairly or reasonably relate to the permitted development. The obvious objection to such a rule is that planning obligations are not imposed on the grant of permission but are created under a free-standing legal document made under a separate statutory provision. There would seem little point in establishing a distinct statutory mechanism for creating planning obligations, if this mechanism was to be confined to those matters which could be dealt with by way of conditions. Moreover it would appear that Lord Justice Kerr had not been referred to two previous decisions of the High Court which had expressly held that undertakings made under section 52 do not have to fairly or reasonably relate to any connected permission; see **Parham [1989]** and **Charles Church [1990].**

The Court of Appeal in the **Good [1994]** case, held that the scope of planning obligations is not limited in the same way as planning conditions. This decision concerned a grant of planning permission for a dwelling-house. The grant was subject to an agricultural occupancy condition, but in addition, the applicant entered into a covenant under a planning agreement that the house should not be sold away from the land comprising the farm on which the house was to be erected. It was argued that, as the condition was invalid, the covenant was equally invalid. Lord Justice Gibson, who gave the main judgement, rejected this argument on the grounds that the statutory power to enter into a planning agreement is not controlled by the nature or extent of the powers to grant planning permission. He stated:

> The two statutory powers are distinct and the exercise of either of these distinct powers has separate consequences and is subject to different procedures (**Good [1994]**, p. 167).

He therefore ruled that the scope of the power to enter into planning obligations is only limited by the actual words of the authorizing section. The decision concerned an agreement based on the old wording of section 52 which authorized agreements for 'the purposes of restricting or regulating the development or other use of land'. Lord Justice Gibson therefore argued:

> If such an agreement was required by a planning authority, and the requirement was made for such purposes, with true regard to relevant considerations, and is not unreasonable (see the first and third requirements stated in the **Newbury** case), such a requirement is not ultra vires merely because the purpose could not be validly achieved by the imposition of a condition under section 29 (**Good [1994],** p. 166).

It has already been pointed out that the statutory change in wording far extends the purposes for which planning obligations can be entered into under section 106 of the 1990 Act. This means that it will be very difficult to argue that a planning obligation is invalid.

Unfortunately for the clarity and certainty of the law, in the decision of **Crest Homes plc [1994]** (a decision which was made before the **Good** case, but not referred to the Court of Appeal), Mr Justice Brooke took the authorities to hold that:

> The legal validity of a planning agreement depends on whether it is material to the proposed development and fulfils Viscount Dilhorne's three tests in the **Newbury** case (**Crest Homes plc [1994],** p. 946).

This is of course completely contrary to the Court of Appeal's ruling in the **Good** case. Mr Justice Brooke relied upon a statement of Lord Justice Russell in the **Plymouth [1993]** case where, as an aside, Lord Justice Russell stated that the tests of the validity of a condition must also be true of a section 106 obligation.

However, the whole focus of the **Plymouth** case was not on whether the agreements were valid or not, but on whether the obligations contained in them were material to the grant of permission. We would therefore argue that the approach in the **Good** case is legally the correct approach. In practical terms the issue probably does not matter that much, as the grant of permission can be held by the courts to be invalid if it is based on immaterial but nevertheless valid planning obligations. As previously stated, most obligations will be drafted so that they are only enforceable if permission is subsequently granted and implemented (see the examples in Chapters 5 and 7). Also, even if the same abstract tests apply to planning obligations as to conditions, the different wording is likely to mean that the application of the tests to specific circumstances will give different answers. Thus, in the **Crest Homes plc [1994]** case, it was accepted that the new form of section 106 considerably widened the express ambit of planning agreements. The decision concerned a series of agreements under which the local planning authority received 20% of the increase in the value of the land caused by the grant of permission. The monies were to be used towards the creation of infrastructure which would be made necessary by the proposed development. Both the High Court and the Court of Appeal rejected the argument that this was the equivalent of a development land tax. A condition requiring 20% of the *development value* however, would have almost certainly be held to be invalid. As a planning obligation under section 106, it only became valid when used as a proxy for calculating development costs, rather than a tax on development profits. The need for, and the difficulties of, making these distinctions have already been discussed in previous chapters. This sequence of cases shows that the courts accept that the 1991 changes to the wording of section 106 have extended the scope and content of planning obligations.

It is finally worth noting that in the **Tesco (Witney) [1994]** case, to be discussed later in this chapter, Lord Justice Beldam took the view that section 106(3)(d) should be interpreted so that a planning obligation, requiring a sum or sums to be paid to the planning authority, should be for a planning purpose or objective which should, in some way, be connected, or relate to the land in which the person entering into the obligation had an interest. (The facts of this case are set out in Figure 4.3.) So it may be that, although the test will not be applied so strictly as with a planning condition, there does have to be some sort of relationship between the obligation and the development of the land that is the subject of the agreement or undertaking.[7]

Overall, despite the recent statutory changes, and the judgements arising from litigation, there still remains confusion over the legal limits to the scope and contents of planning obligations which can be entered into under section 106.

4.4 OTHER TYPES OF AGREEMENTS AND RELATED STATUTORY PROVISIONS

4.4.1 Section 111 of the Local Government Act 1972

As indicated earlier, this is a general enabling power. Most agreements entered into by local authorities will recite[8] this as well as another, more specific, statutory powers. The provision authorizes local authorities to enter into contracts so long as the contract is calculated to facilitate, or be conducive or incidental to, the discharge of any of their statutory functions. The House of Lords has held in the **McCarthy & Stone [1991]** case that this power does not authorize a local planning authority to charge for pre-application advice, as the giving of such advice is not a function of the authority (though it was incidental to the function of determining planning applications). The courts have as yet not had to adjudicate on the extent to which section 111 can be used to create development obligations, but the **McCarthy & Stone [1991]** decision emphasizes that there will have to be a close connection between the undertaking and an independent function of the local authority which is benefiting from the undertaking. If undertakings are made under seal they are enforceable against the person who made the undertaking but they will not be enforceable against successors in title.

4.4.2 Section 33 of the Local Government (Miscellaneous Provisions) Act 1982

This power expressly provides for positive undertakings to carry out works. It therefore often used to be recited alongside the appropriate provision in the Town and Country Planning Act because of doubts over the scope of that provision. The amendments to section 106 of the Town and Country Planning Act 1990 made by the Planning and Compensation Act 1991 have largely removed those doubts. The 1991 Act also provided that section 33 cannot be used for the purpose of facilitating the development of land or in connection with the development of land. This effectively means that section 33 cannot now be used where undertakings are being given in connection with the granting of planning permission.

4.4.3 Local Acts

During the 1960s many local authorities used private Acts of Parliament to obtain wide powers to enter into planning agreements with developers (Henry, 1983). Most of these private Acts ceased to have effect by the end of 1984 by virtue of section 262 of the Local Government Act 1972. Nevertheless some local authorities took the opportunity to promote local consolidation Acts which retained special powers to enter into agreements. Such powers can therefore be used as alternatives to section 106 agreements or in conjunction with such agreements. It is difficult these days to see the justification for some authorities having more extensive local powers than those provided for all local authorities in general Acts.

4.4.4 Agreements under the Highways Act 1980

While the power to enter into agreements under the planning legislation is often used to get developers to build or to contribute to the cost of highway improvements, there exist specific provisions under which both on-site and off-site roads are provided by developers. In the case of on-site roads the normal procedure is for the developer to construct the highway and for the highway authority to agree to adopt the highway once it has been constructed. This is done under section 38 of the Highways Act 1980 (as modified by the New Roads and Street Works Act 1991). The main concerns of the highway authority are to ensure that the road is constructed to an appropriate standard and that it is not left with any costs should the developer default.

More significantly, under section 278 of the Highways Act 1980, any highway authority (including the Department of Transport) can enter into agreements under which they undertake the execution of works on the terms that the developer pays the cost. These works will normally be off-site, such as road widening, access to existing roads, roundabouts or entirely new roads. Under the old wording, the agreement could only be entered into with someone who would derive a special benefit from the timing or the manner in which the works were constructed. This requirement has been omitted in the new version of the provision provided by the New Roads and Street Works Act 1991. Now the only pre-condition is that the authority must be satisfied that the works will be of benefit to the public. This change must mean that the need for the works does not have to flow from any development being carried out by the person entering into the agreement. An important feature is that the agreement can require that the developer pays not only for the direct cost of the works but also for the later maintenance costs.

4.4.5 Charges and new connections to water mains and sewers

Section 146 of the Water Industry Act 1991[9] creates what are in effect impact charges or fees. This is because section 146(2) authorizes the imposition of charges for the connection of premises to a water supply or a public sewer as long as the premises have never at any previous time been connected to either a supply of water for a domestic purpose or to a sewer used for drainage for domestic sewerage purposes. Such charges are over and above the payments which have to be made towards the directs costs that flow from the requisition of water mains and public sewers and the actual costs of connection. These water charges are in effect a form of impact fee. Section 146 is concerned with the costs that will arise from the extra load on water and sewerage services and relates to the capital costs of providing new capacity. It only applies where the connection is 'for domestic purposes' and so charges cannot be levied for commercial or industrial developments. As these fees will have to be paid if the development is to go ahead, it is hard for a water undertaker to justify extra payments towards water and sewerage infrastructure as a price of granting planning permission. When the original provision was being introduced in the House of Lords, the minister in charge of the Bill stated explicitly that

> the need for individual agreements to pay for infrastructure associated with the granting of permission will be unnecessary.[10]

The scheme will only work effectively if the charges are sufficient to ensure that there is enough income overall to pay for all the improvements needed because of the increased demand caused by new connections. In this regard the instrument creating the new water companies, who receive the charges, requires an infrastructure charging scheme to be in place and a ceiling has been placed on all charges; which are subsequently geared to the Retail Price Index. The development industry has contested the charges arguing that they are poorly related to the real infrastructure costs; see Goodchild and Henneberry (1994). The Director of OFWAT is at present reviewing the use of charges; see OFWAT (1992).

4.5 DEVELOPMENT OBLIGATIONS AS MATERIAL CONSIDERATIONS

The most important characteristic of the British statutory system of development control is the amount of discretion which is given to local planning authorities in determining a planning application. Section 70 of the Town and Country Planning Act 1990, which sets out the power of determining planning applications, only requires the determining authority to:

> have regard to the provisions of the development plan, so far as material to the application and to any other material considerations.

The status of the development plan has recently been strengthened by the insertion of section 54A by the Planning and Compensation Act 1991. This imposes an additional requirement that, where the provisions of the development plan *are* material:

> the determination shall be made in accordance with the plan unless material considerations indicate otherwise.

In the case of **St Albans [1993]**, it was held by the High Court that this creates a presumption in favour of the plan unless material considerations indicates otherwise. Nevertheless the overriding principle, always stressed by the courts, is that as long as the decision-maker does not misdirect him or herself or make a totally perverse decision, the actual weight or balance that is given to conflicting considerations is entirely a matter for the body in which the statutory authority has been vested.

4.5.1 The scope of material considerations

Even where there is no express statutory instruction, the courts have required bodies exercising statutory powers to keep to what can be termed the *relevancy* principle. This legal principle requires that all relevant considerations must be taken into account in making a decision and no irrelevant considerations brought into the judgement. Section 70 is therefore an express statutory formulation of this principle and the courts will overturn grants of permission, where material considerations have not been regarded or immaterial considerations have been regarded in coming to the decision. The courts exercise this power flexibly however, and will not strike down grants where the error has not affected the outcome. The consequence is that the scope of the power to determine planning applications is effectively determined by the definition of what are and what are not material considerations.

The courts are the final arbiters of the meaning of words used in statutes, though they may decline to define terms and leave their application to the public body which is administering the scheme. In the case of **material considerations**, the courts have come forward with the open-ended definition that:

> any consideration which relates to the use and development of land is capable of being a planning consideration (Mr Justice Cooke in **Stringer [1971]**, p. 1294).

The courts have then held that this definition includes financial and social factors as long as they can be seen to affect the use and development of land. Most recently in the case of **Mitchell [1994]**, the Court of Appeal held that an application for a change of use from multiple occupation (some 20 bedsitting rooms) to seven self-contained flats could be refused on the grounds that it would lead to a loss of affordable housing. Lord Justice Saville stated that

> It is undoubtedly the law that material considerations are not confined to strict questions of amenity or environmental impact, and that the need for housing in a particular area is a material consideration within the meaning of what is now Section 70(2) of the 1990 Act.

The broad scope of 'material considerations' is crucial to the evolution of development obligations, as the justification for such obligations often turns on the need to offset the impacts of development proposals. The more the social and economic impacts of development can be classified as being 'material considerations', the wider the scope for negotiating development obligations.

While it is clear that the courts have the ultimate jurisdiction as to what considerations are *capable in law* of amounting to material considerations, there is some confusion over whether it is equally for the courts to determine whether, on the *particular facts* an issue is material or whether it is a matter of fact and degree for the decision-maker. In the case of **Bolton**

[1991], Lord Justice Glidewell stated that it was for the judge to decide whether a matter was one which the decision-maker should have taken into account. The courts have since held that the question, of whether the statutory duty (set out in section 70) has been discharged, was one of law to be decided by the courts (see **Fairclough Homes Ltd [1991]** and **Wansdyke District [1992]).** However as the Deputy Judge recognized in the **Fairclough Homes Ltd** decision, whether something is material in a particular case may turn on questions of fact. The relevance and significance of such questions of fact would be for the decision-maker to determine and the courts should not overturn that determination unless it was unreasonable.

4.5.2 The Newbury tests of relevancy

Loughlin (1980) has pointed out that, while the courts are prepared to countenance a broad interpretation of the goals or objectives of the planning system, they are more ready to strike down conditions and other mechanisms for achieving planning objectives, if they consider that they are unfair or unreasonable. Loughlin points out that:

> the concept of 'material considerations' has a dual aspect. The first aspect relates to the potential goals of planning policy (the considerations the LPA may have regard to in controlling development or refusing permission). The second aspect ... focuses on the means by which these policies can be achieved (the proper function of this power to control development or refuse permission within the entire armoury of powers available to achieve planning policies) (Loughlin, 1980, p. 177).

So, even if it is accepted that a development obligation is fulfilling a proper planning purpose, this does not mean that the obligation or the lack of such an obligation, is automatically a material consideration. In particular the courts have held that the same tests as apply to planning conditions (known as the Newbury tests), also apply to the issue of whether a consideration is in fact material in the particular circumstances. This was first indicated in the **Royal Opera House** decision **(Monahan ([1990])** and has now been firmly laid down by the Court of Appeal in the **Plymouth [1993]** case. So, to be a material consideration, a development obligation must therefore not only have a planning purpose but must also fairly and reasonably relate to the permitted development. Further, the taking into account of the obligation or its absence must not be totally unreasonable.

4.5.3 Unreasonableness and the necessity for development obligations

As Lord Justice Hoffman pointed out in the **Plymouth [1993]** case, only the first two tests are strictly tests of 'materiality', that is, whether the obligation is a relevant consideration. If an obligation achieved a planning purpose and fairly and reasonably related to the proposed development, it would be material. But the courts also make a judgement on whether a requirement is 'reasonable'. This raises the difficult question of when it would be unreasonable to take into account an obligation which would otherwise be material to the planning application. It is important to emphasize that here the courts are using the term 'unreasonable' to mean 'totally unreasonable' and they disclaim any power to judge the merits of the application. Basically it means that the decision must be found to be irrational or to have contravened some fundamental legal principle such as fairness or human rights.

In this respect, the courts have repeatedly stated that it is a fundamental principle that planning permissions cannot be bought and sold. On this basis, it could be argued that it is totally unreasonable for a local planning authority to take into account either the existence or the absence of obligations, which are material to the application, if the application is otherwise acceptable. Certainly, it is at present government policy that it is unreasonable for local planning authorities to seek benefits when a development proposal is acceptable. The policy is that planning obligations should only be sought .

> where the benefit sought is related to the development and necessary to the grant of permission [and that] Local planning authorities should ensure that the presence or absence of extraneous inducements or benefits does not influence their decision on the planning application (DoE, 1991b).

However, it is unfortunately far from clear whether in law a local planning authority is acting unlawfully if it takes into account the existence or absence of planning obligations, which, although not strictly necessary to make the proposed development acceptable, serve a planning function and fairly and reasonably relate to the development.

The problem presents itself in two distinct categories. The first is where permission is *refused* because of a failure to provide development obligations. The second is where the local planning authority, in *granting* permission, takes into account development obligations. The courts are far more likely to hold the first category of decisions to be invalid, as it can be seen as an unfair imposition on developers. In this regard in the **Plymouth [1993]** case Lord Justice Hoffman said that the government policy statements:

> embodied a general principle that planning control should restrict the rights of landowners only so far as might be necessary to prevent harm to community interests (p. B90).

The Judge recognized this as the continental law principle of **proportionality** but was uncertain as to the extent to which that principle was a

part of English law. In any case, he considered that in the particular circumstances of the Plymouth case, this principle could not be invoked by a rival
developer to challenge the validity of a planning permission when the
developer was not arguing that his liberty to deal with his land had been
disproportionately restricted.

The situation is very different when the applicant is refusing to enter into
the development obligations. In the **Westminster Renslade [1993]** case, it
was held to be invalid to refuse permission on the grounds that the developer
had failed to provide public car-parking. In this case, Mr Justice Forbes
accepted that:

> while if the developer freely chose to give away his rights, because it
> was more likely he would get planning permission if he did, then it
> might be legitimate to take into account what he was providing as
> planning gain (p. 457).

But he went on to state:

> You would not in his view, get round that the fact that a condition
> would be ultra vires by making clear that you were going to go on
> refusing planning permission until a developer made provision for
> that which a condition could secure, but which to secure by condi-
> tion, it was accepted would be ultra vires! (p. 457).

However, we would argue that the **Westminster Renslade** case was
wrongly decided, as in that case the development remained unacceptable
because of the lack of parking. It is a very different matter where the development is acceptable even without the extra benefit. We would argue that
normally it would be totally unreasonable, and therefore unlawful for a local
planning authority to refuse permission for development which was acceptable in planning terms, because the developer had failed to come up with
additional benefits, even if those benefits did have a planning purpose and
related to the development.

The difficult issue is whether the absence of planning benefits can make a
development unacceptable. Mr Justice Glidewell rejected this approach in
the **Richmond-upon-Thames [1984]** case. In this case, the policies in
the development plan said that office developments would normally be
required to show planning advantages. However, he accepted that:

> if no legitimate planning objection could be raised apart from lack of
> planning gain, if there were lack of planning advantage under policy
> 29, nevertheless there is still no good ground for refusing permission
> (p. 26).

This argument, however, has not been maintained in the case of affordable
housing. Here, the courts have accepted that failure to provide an element of

affordable housing can be a reason for refusing permission. The Court of Appeal first established in the **Mitchell [1994]** case that affordable housing is a material consideration. In that case, permission was refused because the development would result in the loss of affordable housing. The judgement of Lord Justice Balcombe in this case in particular accepts that it is valid for planning authorities to encourage developers to provide affordable housing by requiring specific densities. The Department of the Environment's Planning Policy Guidance on housing accepts that Development Plans can include 'an overall target for the provision of affordable housing throughout the plan area based on evidence of need' (DoE, 1993). The Guidance suggests that one method of achieving this target is to lay down quotas for specific sites.

This can be perceived as requiring private housebuilders to subsidize affordable housing. However the latest High Court decision indicates that the courts will uphold refusals of permission based on such policies. In the **ECC Construction [1994]** case, the court rejected a challenge to a decision of an inspector refusing permission for residential development for an area of 8.4 hectares because of a failure to secure an element of affordable housing. In furtherance of the Department's policy guidance, the council had adopted a policy of seeking affordable housing. The court held that the refusal was justified on the grounds there was a recognized need for affordable housing in the area and that the failure to satisfy this need would cause demonstrable harm.

This decision can be criticized in that neither the inspector nor the Judge explained in what way the proposed development would cause harm, if it went ahead without an element of affordable housing. The clear inference must be that where there is a recognized need, a development proposal can be refused, if it could but does not help to satisfy that need. In this way the failure to provide planning obligations can be seen as 'unacceptable' if it is based on clear planning policies. This shows that the line between what is acceptable and what is not can rapidly be changed.

In the second category, where permission is granted, it is obviously more difficult to argue that it is unreasonable for the local planning authority to take offers into consideration just because they are strictly unnecessary, if it is otherwise material to the proposed development. Accordingly, in the **Plymouth** case, the Court of Appeal had no hesitation in holding that, where the obligation is *offered*, it can be taken into account even if it is strictly unnecessary. However, this can be seen as an encouragement to local planning authorities to seek such benefits and for them to be offered by developers. Of course, in theory, local planning authorities cannot *require* extra benefits in such circumstances but developers may be prepared to offer them to get a quick permission or where it is not clear-cut as to whether the development is acceptable or not as it stands. In this sense, it is possible to 'buy' permissions.

Also, where rival developers are competing to obtain planning permission where only *one* permission can be granted, the **Plymouth** decision would suggest that, where there are two proposals, both acceptable in planning terms, one application can be refused because another application is being granted which includes a package of community benefits. So this amounts to a refusal because of a failure to provide sufficient community benefits.

This scenario arose in the important Court of Appeal decision in the **Tesco (Witney) [1994]** case (see Figure 4.3). All three Judges in this case in the Court of Appeal considered that the Secretary of State's decision was valid because he had gone on to state that, even if he had taken into account a partial contribution towards the road, he would have still come to the same decision on planning grounds. However, they also considered that the Secretary of State was entitled not to take account of the offer to build the road. Unfortunately, as is often the case when all three Judges give separate judgements, no clear principle can be derived from the case, as they all gave different reasons why the offer could be disregarded. Sir Thomas Bingham, the Master of the Rolls,[11] concluded that even if the offer was material, it was open to the Secretary of State to give it no weight as a matter of policy, on the grounds that the offer was not necessary to make the development acceptable. Lord Justice Steyn in contrast took the view that:

> In my view he [the Secretary of State] was entitled to take the view that Tesco's offer of funding, having plainly failed the test of necessity in Annex B of Circular 16/91, is not a material consideration within the meaning of section 70(2). And I would reject the contention that because Tesco's offered the funding, that the Secretary of State was not entitled to apply the policy set out in Annex B of Circular 16/91 (p. 934).

Neither Judge's reasoning is very satisfactory. Sir Thomas Bingham's argument seems to confuse the question of whether the offer had any planning advantages (which is clearly a matter for the decision-maker) with the question of whether to ignore those planning advantages as a matter of policy (which contravenes the statutory instruction to have regard to those planning advantages if they are material). The approach of Lord Justice Steyn goes against the principle that it is for the courts, and not the Secretary of State, to determine whether a particular benefit is or is not material.

We would argue that, on the facts of the case, there was ample evidence for holding that the offer of the road was not a material consideration, not because it was unnecessary in order to make the development acceptable, but because the offer did not fairly and reasonably relate to the proposed development. This would seem to be the approach favoured by the third Judge, Lord Justice Beldam, who considered that:

> In a case in which the person interested in the land offers to enter into an obligation to pay a sum of money to provide planning benefits off-site, the nature and extent of the relationship and the degree of

connection with the land in which he is interested must be factors which in any particular case determine whether the obligation is a material consideration (p. 931).

The case can therefore be explained on the basis that the Secretary of State determined that the offer to fund the roadways not a material consideration because the new superstore would not cause the need for the road and the small amount of extra traffic that it would generate would equally be created by permissions already granted for that site.

So it is still not clear what is the legal position where one developer outbids another by offering benefits which, while not strictly necessary to make the development acceptable, serve a planning function and relate to the proposed development. The judgement in the **Plymouth [1993]** case holds that a local planning authority can take the offer into consideration, while the majority view in the **Tesco** case holds that, if the decision goes to the

---

Tesco Stores Ltd v Secretary of State for the Environment (1994) JPL 919

Both Tesco and Tarmac wanted planning permission to build a superstore on the outskirts of Witney in Oxfordshire. Tesco offered to pay for a much needed new road through the town but Tarmac considered that it was inappropriate for any of the superstore developers to contribute to the funding of this road. The inspector appointed to hold a public inquiry into applications to develop three rival sites concluded that there was little to chose between them but thought that permission should be granted for only one. She concluded that although there was a relationship between the development of the superstore sites and the new road, it was very tenuous as the development would not generate a great deal more traffic than the other permitted uses of the sites. She however thought it would be perverse to turn away the offer of the road and took it into consideration in her decision which was to recommend that Tesco's application be granted and Tarmac's appeal be dismissed.

The Secretary of State in contrast, applying the policy in circular 16/91, concluded that it would be unreasonable to seek even a partial contribution towards the funding of the road and that 'it cannot be treated either as a reason for granting planning permission to Tesco or for dismissing either of the two ... appeals'.

This decision was challenged in the High Court. Deputy Judge Nigel MacLeod quashed the Secretary of State's decision on the grounds that he had been wrong in law to ignore the offer of funding as it was a material consideration. The Court of Appeal, in its turn, reversed the decision of the High Court.

Figure 4.3 The Tesco (Witney) [1994] case

Secretary of State, he can use the necessity principle as the basis for ignoring the offer. This is totally unsatisfactory, as it means that decisions will be decided differently depending on the level of decision-making. Therefore local planning benefits and developers will still consider it worth while to provide such benefits. Lord Justice Steyn was very aware of this danger and was particularly concerned that the philosophy of the bazaar should be rejected.

We understand this concern. The present position means that, where there is competition to win planning permissions, the developer with the largest purse will be at an advantage. On balance, however, we consider that this has to be accepted as long as the benefits actually make the development superior in planning terms and they are not extraneous to the project. We would argue that the main safeguard, therefore, against the development system being distorted, lies not in the necessity principle, but in the need for the development obligations to fairly and reasonable relate to the permission being granted. In the **Plymouth** case, Lord Justice Hoffman argued that:

> materiality was an entirely different matter, because there was a public interest in not allowing planning permissions to be sold in exchange for benefits which were not planning considerations or did not relate to the proposed development (p. B90).

In the same case, Lord Justice Evans stated that:

> The test of materiality, strictly applied, in his judgement was a sufficient safeguard against its abuse (p. B86).

The problem is that the courts have not yet provided clear guidance as to what constitutes a fair and reasonable relationship. Confusion thus remains over what can and what cannot be properly taken into account. We now address that issue.

4.5.4 The relationship between the obligation and the grant of permission

The tests developed by the courts

First of all there is the problem of terminology. While the standard test used is whether there is a **fair and reasonable relationship**, it has also been suggested that there should be **a direct relationship** between the planning benefit and the development; (see **Barber [1991]** and **Safeways Property Limited [1991]**). Other terms that have been used include **recognized and real relationship (British Airports Authority [1979]**) and **clear and direct nexus (Wansdyke DC [1992]**).

The importance of physical proximity

It is perhaps more useful to examine the kind of situations where the courts have held or indicated that obligations and benefits would or would not be material. First, it is clear that **physical proximity** is important. If an obligation relates to the site of the proposed development, then it will be very hard to argue that it is not a material consideration. Where the benefit flows directly from the nature of the development, it is self-evident that it must be material. Most development projects have both desirable and undesirable consequences in planning terms and the job of the decision-maker is to weigh up all these consequences. It is more problematic when the advantages are specially built into the development proposal or arise by way of an agreement with, or an undertaking by, the developer. In the **Plymouth [1993]** case (see Figure 4.2), at the invitation of the local planning authority, both Sainsbury and Tesco offered to provide on-site special features such as a tourist information centre, a bird watching hide, a static art feature and a moving water sculpture. These features were not required to make the development acceptable and were neither inherent to, nor even the normal attributes of, out of town superstores. Nevertheless, Lord Justice Russell stated:

> So far as benefits which were to be provided on site, there does not appear to me to be the slightest difficulty or room for argument. They made the development more attractive and that must be surely in the public interest (p. B84).

Similarly Lord Justice Hoffman said of the benefits which were constructed on or adjacent to the site that:

> They were matters of benefits to the developer as well as to the community. I do not see how it can possibly be said that such embellishments did not fairly and reasonably relate to the development (p. B90).

As has been pointed out (Ashworth, 1993), this approach would seem to establish that any benefit which is in the 'public interest' is material but it was undoubtedly the close physical relationship between the benefits and the development site which was conclusive in arriving at a judgement. In the **Monahan [1990]** case, Lord Justice Staughton gave the example of a developer applying to build an office block who also offered to build a swimming pool at the other end of town. Now it may be in the public interest to have an extra swimming pool, but Lord Justice Staughton said that:

> It would be wrong for the planning authority to regard the swimming pool as a material consideration, or to impose a condition that it should be built. That case seemed very little different from the developer who

offered the planning authority a cheque so that it could build the swimming pool for itself (p. 121).

In contrast he found that the benefit of restoring the Opera House was
relevant to the application to build offices because it was all part of one
composite development. The other two judges also placed importance on
the physical congruity of the sites.

The necessity for the obligation

Where there is not a physical relationship, a benefit will nevertheless be a
material consideration if it solves a planning problem which would otherwise be created by the development. This is of course an aspect of the
necessity principle referred to in the **Plymouth** case, as the obligation is
necessary to alleviate or solve the planning problems. However while that
decision established that a benefit does not have to be necessary if it has
another basis for being a material consideration, it was accepted that necessity could itself be a basis for materiality. The obvious example is where the
development will cause highway problems because of the increase in traffic
which it will create. In the **Plymouth** case itself one of the obligations was
to provide £800 000 as a contribution to park-and-ride facilities which were
needed to reduce the traffic problem which would be caused by the proposed superstore. All their Lordships therefore felt that although the facilities were provided off-site, they were sufficiently related to be a material
consideration. Again, in the **Safeway Properties [1990]** case, Safeway
made an offer of £1 000 000 for a traffic management scheme. The case
turned on whether the need for the works arose wholly or substantially
from the proposed supermarket. It was evidently accepted by the Court of
Appeal that provided they did, the offer was a material consideration.
Finally the Court of Appeal in the **Crest Homes plc [1994]** case (see
Figure 4.4) accepted that where residential development made additional
infrastructure necessary or desirable, it was lawful for planning authorities
to seek contributions to that infrastructure from major developers and to
take such contributions into account in deciding the grant of permission.

The scale of the obligation

Difficult problems arise when the offer goes substantially further than is
necessary to cure the need created by the development. The government's
policy is that local planning authorities should only seek contributions
which are 'directly related in scale to the benefit which the proposed development will derive from the facilities to be provided'. An extreme example

is the **Tesco (Witney) [1994]** case (see Figure 4.3), where there was only a tenuous relationship between the offer to fund the new road and the development of the superstore by Tesco. Deputy Judge Nigel Macleod concluded that the Secretary of State should have taken into account the whole offer of funding on the grounds that there was a fair and reasonable relationship, because the roadworks would solve the existing severe traffic problems which the proposed store would make worse. In reversing the deputy judge's decision, the Court of Appeal was mainly concerned about whether the Secretary of State was right to exclude the whole offer (see above). The court however seems to have accepted that, if the offer had to be considered at all, only a partial amount (proportionate to the need created by the superstore) could be taken into account.

The point directly arose in the **Crest Homes plc [1994]** case (see Figure 4.4) where the main challenge was to the formula by which the amount of the contribution was calculated. In the High Court, Mr Justice Brooke understood the legal decisions to show that:

> There is an important public interest in not permitting planning permissions to be bought and sold in exchange for benefits which are not legitimate considerations or do not relate to a proposed development: Even if the proposed benefit is of a type which can properly be regarded as material, it must not be so disproportionately large as to include a 'significant additional benefit' over and above that which could properly be considered to be material (p. 947).

In upholding his decision, the Court of Appeal accepted that a benefit disproportionate to the adverse planning impact of the development would not fairly and reasonably relate to that development. Lord Justice Henry, who gave the only judgement, admitted that the formula used (a percentage of the increase in land values caused by the grant of permission) might well be unlawful as an unauthorized development land tax, if the local planning authority had sought to recover more than the cost of the related infrastructure or merely imposed an arbitrary standard contribution without any attempt to calculate the cost of future infrastructure needs. However, he went on to hold that the formula was lawful in the present case because there was no evidence of the council recovering more than the cost of the infrastructure properly related to the expansion of the town. Further, the contribution made by each development was not disproportionate to the impact of that development. The judge went out of his way to underline the particular facts which made the formula lawful in this case. He stated:

> I would re-emphasise the crucial importance in this case of the facts; the genuineness and lawfulness of the policy, the legitimate treatment of Towcester as a unity, the identification of the infrastructure required and the attempts to distribute that cost (or some of it) equitably among

the developers. Those facts are crucial because they legitimise a formula which, used in other factual contexts, could be struck down as constituting an unauthorised local development tax (ibid.).

The decision is nevertheless of general importance as it means that, in law, the local planning authority does not have to attempt to work out exactly the proportion of infrastructure the need for which will be created by a particular development. Mr Justice Brooke proposed that the test was:

> whether it is certain that all contributions will be paid for purposes which are material in the sense that they are for a planning purpose, that they reasonably and fairly relate to the proposed development, and that they are not disproportionately large (ibid.).

Lord Justice Henry, in the Court of Appeal, generally agreed but thought that it was too strict to require 'certainty'. He considered that:

> the question should be whether the contribution agreed or assumed by the developer is one which can property be regarded by the planning

---

R v South Northamptonshire District Council ex *parte* Crest Homes plc

Crest Homes plc challenged in the High Court the validity of decisions made by South Northamptonshire District Council relating to an elaborate scheme worked out by the Council and a consortium of developers. The objective of this scheme was to ensure that the residential expansion of the area around Towcester was accompanied by the necessary improvements to the infrastructure and other services required to support such an expansion of the town. The developers were to enter into planning agreements under which land was to be freely transferred and funds provided for the improvements. The amount to be contributed by each developer was 20% of the enhanced land value derived from the grant of permission for residential proposals and 17% for industrial/commercial proposals. The facilities to be provided included roads, schools, playing fields, footpaths and cycle ways. These agreements were conditional on both a local plan in a particular form being adopted and planning permission for development being granted. One developer fell out with the local planning authority over the phasing of the expansion and applied to the High Court to have the agreements which were entered into by the other developers, the grants of permission and other resolutions of the Council, held to be invalid. The application was rejected on the grounds that it was made too late but Judge Brooke made it clear that he considered that the scheme was valid. On appeal, the Court of Appeal held all the actions of the Council to be completely lawful.

Figure 4.4   The Crest Homes plc [1994] case

authority as a genuine pre-estimate of that developer's proper contribution to the related infrastructure (ibid.).

This could create problems where it turns out that all or particular contributions are too high. In the particular circumstances of the **Crest Homes plc** case, the drop in land values meant that, by the time the agreements were signed, the amounts produced by the formula were only sufficient to carry out a limited amount of works. In one of the agreements, there was a clause which provided that, if there was a surplus, the monies would be spent on 'further community benefits in Towcester and its environs'. Mr Justice Brooke was doubtful as to whether, if monies had been available for this purpose, it would have fairly and reasonably related to the development. Lord Justice Henry did not allude to this particular agreement but he did accept that if later the monies were not applied to the infrastructure or proved to be more than was required, then the developer might have other remedies.

We would argue that such problems are inherent in a formula based on development land values, as the amount of the contributions must inevitably vary according to the arbitrary factor of the increase or decrease in land values. A more credible formula would be to require each developer to pay a proportion of the total estimated costs based on a rough estimate of the impact of what will be caused by that development. This would clearly differentiate such a development obligation from impact fees or development land taxes.

In certain circumstances, developers may have no option but to offer a disproportionate amount, if they are to obtain planning permission. Where existing infrastructure is already desperately overloaded, the local planning authority may be justified in refusing permission for a development which increases that overloading, even by a small amount. In practical terms it may not be sufficient for the developer to contribute only a proportionate amount towards improving the facilities. If a totally new road or school is needed, a contribution of say 5% of the cost will not solve the problem. In this regard it has been held by the courts to be irrelevant that the works will benefit other users who are not contributing to the improvements. In the **Pickavance [1994]** case, permission was refused for development which the inspector concluded would cause traffic problems. The local planning authority had proposed that the applicant should enter into a section 106 agreement under which he would pay for the necessary road-widening. Other existing users would benefit from these improvements but there was no way in which they could be forced to contribute to the cost. The applicant therefore refused to enter into the proposed agreement. The court upheld the inspector's decision to reject the appeal as the improvements were necessary to make the development acceptable.

So if the developer does decide to pick up the whole cost by agreeing to pay for the total cost of the new facilities, this will of course ensure that permission cannot be refused on that basis. However, if there are other reasons for refusing permission, it would seem that the developer's generosity in solving the existing traffic problems should not be taken into consideration.

Enabling development and the compensatory principle

The courts have countenanced what has become known as **enabling development** whereby the profits from one development will be used to enable another desirable development to take place. In this way an obligation resulting from the grant of permission for one development can be given weight as counterbalancing other planning disbenefits which will be caused by that development, as long as it enables other desirable and related development to take place. This happened in the case of **Wandsyke [1992]**. There, it was argued that the granting of permission for the development of a sports facility would enable redevelopment of another site which would have benefits for the Bath conservation area. It was accepted that the development of the sports facility would cause harm to another conservation area, the Bathampton Conservation Area about a mile away. The court held that the inspector had acted legally in holding that the benefits to the Bath Conservation Area outweighed the harm to the Bathampton Conservation Area. There was no agreement that if permission was granted the other site would be developed. The inspector however held that there was a reasonable prospect that this consequence would follow and the Judge held that there was no need for a copper-bottomed guarantee underwritten by an agreement or an undertaking.

Similarly, in the much earlier case of **Brighton [1979]**, the court held that the possibility that the profits from a residential development would be used to maintain and refurbish an important listed building was a material consideration in determining whether to grant permission for that residential development. The residential development was to take place on land near to the listed building and on a site which was all in one ownership, though it does not seem to have been regarded as composite development as in the **Royal Opera House** case (**Monahan [1980]**). In the **Wandsdyke** case, there was a relationship between the benefits and disbenefits in that they all related to conservation areas, albeit different conservation areas. In the **Brighton** case the functional relationship was not so strong, as the benefits to the listed building had to be balanced against the arguments that the residential development was contrary to the development plan and would detract from the amenities and the character of the area. The case can therefore be used to establish a general principle that *any* planning advantage that will result from the grant of permission can be used to justify that grant. In the **Northumberland CC [1990]** case, Deputy Judge Spence took this approach to extreme lengths by holding that, as long as financial benefits flowing from a development were connected with the use or development of other land, this was a material consideration to be taken into account in determining whether to grant permission for the enabling development. In this case the Judge held that, in an application to carry out opencast coalmining, the fact that the profits could be used to invest in new deep mines was a material consideration which could be weighed against the damage to the environment. He stated:

> What he had said was subject always to the proposition that the consideration to be sought to be brought into play in assisting upon the judgement as to whether permission should be granted, be it financial or otherwise, must relate to the use and development of land. I repeat that the land does not as a matter of law have to be identified. Nor in my judgement does it have to be land that is in close proximity to the land which is the subject of the application (**Northumberland CC [1990]**, p. 705).

This in effect means that as long as it can be shown that the granting of permission is likely to result in planning advantages relating to the development of land somewhere, those planning advantages are material considerations. It will not matter if the land which will receive the benefits is remote from the development application which is being determined or has not even been identified. Nor will it matter that the planning advantages have no relationship to the harm that the development may cause. This would allow for developers to buy permission for profitable development, by undertaking to use part of the profits for the use and development of land, perhaps even the hypothetical swimming pool. The **Northumberland CC** case could be distinguished on the grounds that in the particular circumstances, the profitability of the proposed development was material as the public interest in cheap supplies of energy is a material consideration in itself. Nevertheless, until the scope of the principle as stated by the Judge is restricted by the higher courts, it undermines the repeated assertions by the courts that planning permissions cannot be bought and sold. We would argue that, unless the 'enabling development' is an intrinsic consequence of granting the proposed development, it should only be a material consideration if it is necessary to make the development acceptable. This would apply if the enabling development alleviates planning problems to be caused by the development as in the case of road works or, as in the **Wansdyke [1992]** case, balances out disadvantages in the same policy area.

4.6 THE ROLE OF THE DEVELOPMENT PLAN

It is only recently that most local planning authorities have made it a practice to include in the their local plans detailed policies on development
obligations. As these plans have to be publicized and there is a right for objectors to appear at a local inquiry, the inclusion of policies in the statutory plan
gives them a higher political legitimacy. The increased status given to
approved development plans by section 54A of the Town and Country
Planning Act 1990 (as amended by the Planning and Compensation Act 1991)
means that there is an added incentive for local planning authorities to put
their policies on development obligations into the these plans.

This does not mean that a local planning authority can only rely on policies
which are set out in the plan. The courts have in the past held that decisions
based on policies in emerging statutory plans or in statements which are
never intended to become statutory plans, are nevertheless valid. On the
other hand, the House of Lords in **Westminster CC [1985]** held that part of
a local plan was invalid because it stated that the exceptional circumstances in
which office development might be permitted outside a certain zone should
be dealt with by non-statutory guidance. Lord Scarman pointed out that there
was a statutory requirement to include in the plan 'the authority's proposals
for the development and use of land' and the planning authority were failing
in that duty, if they had policy proposals but did not include them in their
plan. The court, however, appeared to accept that there was a distinction
between policy matters which must go into the plan and matters of detail
which could be left out. The Department of the Environment's current
Planning Policy Guidance on development plans (DoE, 1992b) makes a similar distinction between non-statutory planning guidance which supplements
the policies and proposals of the plan itself, which are said to be useful, and
informal or **bottom drawer** plans and policies. It is these latter which are
said to be incompatible with the requirements of the 1991 Act. So, a local
planning authority might be in breach of its statutory duties, if the policies as
to when community benefits and facilities were to be expected or required
were to be found in non-statutory plans or documents. However this is
unlikely, as long as the basic policy is set out in the plan and the non-statutory
document is supplementary to that policy. Certainly the courts have, since
the **Westminster CC [1985]** case, shown a reluctance to apply widely the
principle laid down in that case (see for example **Simplex [1988]** and
Morris [1992]).

More importantly, both the courts and government policy stress that policies which are to be found in up-to-date plans can be given more weight than
policies in non-statutory plans. In the context of planning obligations, there is
also the important and difficult issue of whether the inclusion of a policy in
the statutory plan precludes any challenge to the validity of that policy.
Section 287 of the Town and Country Planning Act 1990 provides a right to

apply to the High Court within six weeks to question the validity of all or part of a plan. Section 284 provides that the validity of a plan shall, otherwise, not be questioned in any legal proceedings whatsoever. The courts have construed such exclusion clauses strictly and have refused to entertain challenges out of time. Further in the **Westminster CC [1985]** it was held that the provision prevented the courts not only from considering a direct challenge to the validity of a development plan out of time, but also an indirect challenge in the course of challenging the validity of a determination of a planning application. Strictly applied this would mean that if the development plan required that permission should be refused unless the developer undertook to contribute large sums to the authority, it would be impossible to challenge in the courts a refusal based on such a policy. The only remedy would be for the Secretary of State to make a direction that the plan should be altered. However in the **Richmond-upon-Thames [1984]** case, Judge Glidewell refused to accept that the inclusion of a policy in the development plan expecting planning gain contributions meant that permission could be refused simply because of a lack of planning gain. Finally in the **Northumberland [1990]** case, the Deputy Judge appeared to take the view that even if the support for deep coalmining was not normally a material consideration, the inspector and the Secretary of State had to have regard to this policy as it was an approved structure plan policy. However it was not argued in that case that the policy itself was invalid; it was only its application to the particular appeal that was under challenge.

The views of academic commentators reflect this judicial confusion. Alder (1990) considers that, while the validity of the development plan cannot be challenged out of time, the application of the policies in the determination of planning applications could be challenged on the grounds of relevancy. In contrast, Jeremy Rowan-Robinson (1994) argues that, if an applicant failed to provide benefits which the plan expects to be provided, the application could be refused even though the benefits would not otherwise satisfy the test of a fair and reasonable relationship.

The inclusion of a policy of expecting community benefits in the development plan must strengthen the argument that such benefits are material considerations. We would nevertheless agree with Alder's view that this should not automatically determine whether the existence or absence of benefits is a material consideration in a particular case. We would therefore expect the courts in an extreme case to outlaw what was seen to be a sale of planning permissions even if this sale was underwritten by the development plan.

4.7 CONCLUSIONS

The courts, when required to adjudicate on the legality of development obligations and their role on the development control system, have come up against the same issues that we set out in Chapters 1–3. The jurisprudence has traversed the same territory as the policy and practice discussion of the rationales for obligations. However, instead of giving authoritative guidance, the courts have provided conflicting signals to both planning authorities and developers. The courts have still not made exactly clear the scope of section 106 planning obligations. There remains confusion as to how far the application for planning permission can be used as an occasion for the local planning authority to negotiate specific benefits which are not strictly necessary on planning grounds. The only real safeguard against abuse by either local authorities or developers, i.e. blackmail or bribery, is the need for the obligation to relate to the proposed development. This is still loosely defined and applied by the courts. The courts have also, by upholding development obligations where the scale of the contribution is based on the increase in land values, got near to legitimizing a form of impact fee. While repeatedly affirming that permission cannot be bought and sold, the concept of enabling development has been expanded to allow developers to obtain permission by funding other unrelated desirable developments.

At the time of writing, it is understood that the **Tesco (Witney)** decision is to be appealed in the House of Lords. Hopefully this opportunity will be used by the House of Lords to provide planning authorities and developers with authoritative and workable guidance as to the kind of development obligations that can be legitimately negotiated. The next chapter analyses the actual practice of negotiating obligations within the present rather slack and confused legal framework. Part Three considers law and policy changes that would help to clarify the legitimacy of the demands for obligations being made by planning authorities.

NOTES

1. The courts disclaim any power to impose their views as to the merits of a decision and only decree whether the public body has exercised its powers lawfully.
2. All legal cases are highlighted in bold text. Full citations in Appendix 2.
3. Lord Justice is the title given to male Lord Justices of appeal who sit in the Court of Appeal.
4. A Deputy Judge is an experienced Barrister who is appointed to decide cases from time to time in the High Court.
5. The Vice Chancellor presides over the Chancery Division of the High Court.
6. Mr Justice is the title given to male judges appointed to the High Court.
7. The House of Lords has now settled the issue by holding that a planning obligation to be valid does not have to relate to any development (see **Tesco (Witney)** case and the Supplement on p. xix).
8. By recite we mean that the preamble to the agreement would set out the statutory provisions authorizing the agreement.
9. First contained in section 79 of the Water Act 1989.
10. House of Lords Debates, Vol. 508, vol. 55, 22 May 1989.
11. The Master of the Rolls is the President of the Civil Division of the Court of Appeal.
12. Judgement has now been given and is discussed in the Supplement.

PART TWO

THE PRACTICE

5

DEVELOPMENT OBLIGATIONS IN CONTEMPORARY PLANNING PRACTICE

5.1 INTRODUCTION

In Part One, we argued that the practice of negotiating development obligations through the planning system is increasing in scale and significance. We have also identified considerable controversy and confusion over what is the proper scope and content of obligations and other forms of development impact mitigation. This chapter examines evidence from practical examples. Chapter 4 provided one 'window' on practice through the cases which have come to the attention of the courts. Most cases, of course, do not. This chapter looks at the available empirical evidence on practice in England to address the following questions:

1. What is the *scale* of the negotiation of obligations, particularly through planning agreements, in relation to applications for planning permission generally, and how has this changed?
2. What is the is *scope and content* of such obligations and how has this changed?
3. What *form* did obligations take, and how has this changed?
4. What *types* of development, developer and development conditions give rise to agreements?
5. What are the advantages and disadvantages of *negotiating* obligations, from the point of view of local authorities, other agencies seeking obligations, and developers.

A major problem with research on development obligations in Britain is the lack of systematic records. Since 1968, when it no longer became necessary for central government approval of agreements under planning legislation, there has been no means of assessing the scale and scope of the negotiation of obligations, apart from special surveys or case studies conducted from time to time. Until the 1980s, there was very little research on either development control practices in general, or the negotiation of agreements in particular. More recently, the increasing salience of the negotiation of agreements has lead to many more surveys and qualitative case-based assessments. Nevertheless, these have not necessarily focused directly on the above questions. This chapter therefore draws together the available data from a number of sources, including our own research, to address these questions. It is organized into two parts. In the first, we review evidence from national surveys and reviews and set the practice in historical perspective. In the second, we examine the evidence from detailed case studies of five local authorities from 1986–91.

5.2 FROM INNOVATION TO NORMAL PRACTICE

5.2.1 Early innovation

The demand for legislation reviewed in Chapter 2 shows that local authorities have been negotiating agreements with developers from time to time for many years. As far back as the 1930s, there are examples of land being dedicated for community development purposes and infrastructure needs. These mechanisms worked well where the development involved was primarily urban extension, adding new residential neighbourhoods on the expanding periphery, and where the public sector was responsible for building the community facilities and infrastructures needed to service the development. But by the 1960s, local authorities were facing more complex circumstances. Many office and retail projects involved the redevelopment of the urban fabric, creating multiple local impacts. Authorities, notably in London, began to engage in complex negotiations with developers, to help shape projects with local objectives in mind (Marriott, 1967). Authorities on the urban periphery and beyond were preoccupied with problems of infrastructure provision, and sought a framework for negotiating with developers over infrastructure contributions. Legislative authority for the agreements used to finalize negotiations was found in the various laws outlined in the previous chapter.

Some evidence on the numbers of agreements negotiated can be found in Jowell's summary of agreements negotiated under section 37 of the 1962 Town and Country Planning Act, the precursor to section 52 (see Table 5.1).

This omits all agreements under local legislation as well as highway construction agreements. Section 37 only enabled agreements relating to 'regulating or restricting' the use of land. The numbers recorded are very small indeed, compared to the overall numbers of planning applications at this time and to the levels of agreements found in surveys in the 1990s.

Table 5.1   Number of agreements approved by national government: 1964–68 (under section 37, TCPA, 1962)

	Received	Approved	Not approved	Withdrawn
1964	55	55	–	–
1965	90	83	4	3
1966	141	139	1	1
1967	159	157	2	–
1968	97	95	1	1

Source: Jowell, 1977, p. 416.

Other research suggests that in greenfield residential development, in the buoyant markets of the outer South East, the negotiation of agreements on infrastructure questions had become fairly routine (Henry, 1983, 1984; Davis and Healey, 1983).

This practice was given positive encouragement by central government in the early 1970s. By the late 1960s, there was considerable concern that insufficient land was being made available for housing. A key issue here was the cost of providing infrastructure services in the expanding areas on conurbation peripheries and beyond. Bringing serviced land forward for development and negotiating contributions from developers for infrastructure provision become a major preoccupation of the short-lived Land Commission. As discussed in Chapter 2, when this was abolished, the *Sheaf Report* on servicing development promoted such negotiation (DoE, 1972). This encouraged the use of agreements for infrastructure purposes and accepted the need to expand the then section 52 provisions to enable positive covenants to be entered into through agreements (see Chapter 2). The report notes as examples of matters covered by agreements:

> the carrying out of specified site works as a prelude to development, contributions to the cost of sewerage works, and the conveyance of land to local authorities for public purposes (DoE, 1972, Annex D, para. 3).

From case studies of city centre redevelopment projects, there is also evidence of agreements negotiated over office and retail schemes although in these cases, a local authority usually had a landownership role through which to negotiate (Marriott, 1967; Morley, 1980) (see Figure 5.1) More use began to be made of agreements within urban cores, in relation to major office schemes in London. This was pioneered by the Greater London Council.

The London Borough of Harrow negotiated an office redevelopment scheme in 1972–3 which included the following benefits:

- a community centre built by the developers, which was leased back to the local authority at a peppercorn rent;
- 18 residential units (to diversify the mix of uses, as sought by planning policy);
- financial reimbursement for the construction of a roundabout and pedestrian underpass to the site;
- provision of car-parking spaces accessible to the adjacent railway station.

Although in line with Greater London Development Plan principles on community benefits, this scheme did not proceed as it fell foul of other strategic planning policy objectives.

Source: Loughlin, 1978.

Figure 5.1   An office development agreement in London: 1972–73

In the early 1970s in London, these practices were consolidated into policies encouraging contributions to community benefits on major office schemes (Jowell, 1977; Loughlin, 1978).

In 1975, Jowell (1977) undertook the first recorded survey of the negotiation of agreements. He sampled 28% of English local authorities with a questionnaire survey, and undertook in-depth interviews with 20 authorities. Of the 87 authorities in the sample, 44 (51%) admitted to achieving 'planning gain'. In London the proportion was higher. Jowell found that the negotiations for planning gain focused on particular types of projects, primarily large-scale commercial developments in buoyant property markets. He found considerable problems in classifying the gains achieved, as what was considered a gain depended on the particular planning policy context. In some cases, Jowell notes, what was sought as a 'gain' was intended to offset a loss to the local authority. (Jowell's example is the provision of community benefits 'in exchange' for permission to build at a higher density.) Jowell identified the following 'gains' achieved:

- specification of use (restricting use; requiring additional uses);

- public rights of way on developers land;
- dedication of land for public use;
- extinguishing existing user rights;
- provision of community buildings;
- rehabilitation of property;
- provision of infrastructure;
- gift of site or buildings for residential use;
- commuted payments for car-parking.

Of these, the most commonly cited were the first four categories. These were justified in terms of the **regulatory and restrictive** purposes of planning legislation. In the light of practice and debates in the early 1990s, it is of interest to note that agreements relating to community facilities and contributions of land for social housing purposes were already being nego-tiated in the 1970s. Jowell's evidence suggests that the relative incidence of such agreements was not dissimilar to that in the early 1990s.

Infrastructure issues were of great significance in some areas. In Wokingham in Berkshire, one of the most pressured areas in the outer South East from the 1960s to the 1980s, planning agreements were negoti-ated for the three main land allocations of Lower Earley (5000 dwellings), Woosehill (2300 dwellings) and Woodley Airfield (1500 dwellings). These related to the construction of local distributor roads, provision of water mains and satisfactory land drainage arrangements, provision of open space within the development and the reinstatement and preservation of wood-lands (Davis and Healey, 1983). Henry (1983) suggests that the negotiation of such infrastructure contributions and other matters relating to the impact of both large and small developments had become normal practice in the District by the mid-1970s. Research on large-scale residential and commercial projects on peripheral sites in the West Midlands and Greater Manchester indicates that such negotiations were normal here too by the early 1980s (Healey *et al.*, 1988).

The general pattern up to the 1980s thus seems to be a sophisticated use of agreements to deal with questions of infrastructure provision and amenity on major greenfield development sites around the large conurba-tions, and particularly in outer south-east England, complemented by an evolving practice in inner London, focused on community gains from office development. Otherwise, agreements were primarily used to restrict the mixture of uses on a site or to enable public rights of way through sites.

5.2.2 The routinization of negotiative practice

In contrast to earlier periods, a flood of studies of the negotiation of develop-ment obligations became available by the early 1990s. These were generated by increased awareness of the phenomenon in practice, as well as by the debate on the evolving nature of the planning system as discussed in Part One. The most authoritative study is that undertaken for the Department of the Environment by Grimley J. R. Eve *et al.* (1992). This aimed to provide a detailed quantitative assessment of the use of planning agreements in England in a sample of local authorities from April 1987 to March 1990. Research was undertaken in 23 Districts (including Metropolitan Districts and London Boroughs) and five counties.

This complements a study by Durman and Rowan-Robinson (1991) undertaken for the Scottish Office. This was based on a survey of all local authorities conducted in 1991, followed up with detailed studies in 14 local authorities and interviews with developers. Other studies attempting a general picture of the practice of negotiating development obligations are Elson (1990a, b), KPMG Peat Marwick Management Consultants (1990) and MacDonald (1991). There have also been a few studies focused on particular kinds of benefit. Whatmore and Boucher (1992) examined the use of agreements to negotiate environmental benefits. Elson and Payne (1993) looked in particular at obligations relating to sports and recreation. Barlow and Chambers (1992), Williams *et al.* (1991) and, to an extent, Bramley (1993) examined obligations linked to the provision of affordable housing.[1] The findings of these studies are reviewed under the headings of the questions listed at the start of this chapter. We supplement them with comments from our own interviews with developers, planning authorities and others involved in the negotiative process.

Scale

The main findings from all the large-scale systematic surveys show that numbers of agreements are a very small proportion of total numbers of planning decisions, but that their use has been increasing. Grimley J. R. Eve *et al.* (1992) estimate that agreements are associated with only 0.5% of all decisions in England. In Scotland, Durman and Rowan Robinson (1991) found less than 1% of planning applications were linked to an agreement. Whatmore and Boucher (1992), Barlow and Chambers (1992) and MacDonald (1991) broadly confirm these small numbers.

Our research suggests that these studies may underestimate the scale of use of agreements in development projects.[2] Durman and Rowan-Robinson (1991) note that there is little statistical relationship in any case between the numbers of planning decisions an authority makes and numbers of applications. Other factors were more important in shaping the incidence of the use of agreements,

> such as the attitude of planning officers and elected members and the particular circumstances of the planning applications (Durman and Rowan-Robinson, 1991, p. 5).

The various studies nevertheless stress two trends in the 1980s. Firstly, more local authorities began to make use of planning agreements. Secondly, most authorities negotiated more agreements towards the end of the decade. Grimley J. R. Eve *et al.* (1992) also note that developers offered contributions more readily by the early 1990s in the expectation that obligations would be required of them. Even in local authorities with difficult urban problems, more agreements were being negotiated by the end of the 1980s (Pears, 1989).

Interestingly, both Durman and Rowan-Robinson (1991), and KPMG (1990) suggest that, after a period where the practice increased, there was by 1990 some stabilization. This could be due to the penetration of the practice across most local authorities. It could also be due to the collapse in confidence in the development market in the early 1990s. However, as both the legal cases reported in Chapter 4 and our own case studies show (see section 5.3 of this chapter), local authorities continued to negotiate development obligations into the 1990s.

The relatively small numbers of agreements negotiated in relation to the flow of planning decisions appears to belie the degree of interest in the practice discussed in Part One. This paradox may be explained by the spread of the practice across all local authorities, as noted in the surveys; by the likelihood that any large or complex project will lead to some kind of agreement; by the symbolism of agreements as an expression of the negotiative practice around planning regulation which was well-established by the 1980s (Healey *et al.*, 1988; Brindley *et al.*, 1989), and by the impact of these trends on developers who have reacted by offering obligations.

There has been no comprehensive study of the scale of the negotiation of agreements since 1991. DoE Circular 16/91 (DoE, 1991b) is likely to have promoted the practice. On the other hand, property market conditions were stagnant until at least 1994. It is probably only by the late 1990s that it will be possible to tell whether shifts in government policy have produced a quantum change in the use of agreements, or whether the policy has merely consolidated existing practice.

Scope and content

There are no simple ways of classifying development obligations. One approach is to distinguish between obligations which merely restrict the rights of use a landowner has and those which require a positive action by a developer, through transferring land, undertaking works or making a financial payment. Another approach is to classify obligations according to the relation to the development site, distinguishing between on-site and off-site obligations. This classification is attractive to those who prefer to concentrate on the role of obligations in enabling development to go ahead, rather than their role in addressing adverse impacts, which could as easily be off-site as on-site. A further possibility is to classify agreements by planning purpose in some general way, or by specific policy objective or by the form of the obligation. The problem here is that such purposes are likely to vary from authority to authority, depending on local policies and local conditions.

Most studies use a mixture of these classificatory principles, as can be seen from Tables 5.2 and 5.3. For example, the Grimley J. R. Eve classification merges the substantive purpose of an obligation (e.g. **environmental/ecological measures**) with the form of an obligation (e.g. **financial contributions and payments**). The Whatmore and Boucher classification puts more emphasis on purposes, but mixes up ends (e.g. **public open space**) and means (e.g. **phasing**).

Both the English and Scottish surveys conclude that agreements have primarily been used to enable development to proceed. By implication, most have dealt with on-site issues, though the survey material does not discuss this distinction. Drawing on the various surveys, it may be concluded that agreements have been primarily used for the following purposes:

- to control development and restrict the use of development;
- to deal with highway and other infrastructure matters;
- to control and/or promote provision for car-parking;
- to provide landscape and public open space.

Table 5.2 Matters for agreement in planning agreements (as classified by Grimley J. R. Eve *et al.*, 1992, p.21)

Category*	Frequency
1. Control of development	754
2. Limitations on use	615
3. Financial contributions and payments	461
4. Highway improvements	290
5. Legal costs	276
6. Environmental/ecological measures	153
7. Infrastructure provision	112
8. Avoidance of nuisance	91
9. Conservation and built environment measures	54
10. Full provision of community facilities and services	44
11. Part contribution towards community facilities and services	35

* It should be noted that many agreements deal with more than one category at one time.

Table 5.3   The content of agreements
(as classified by Whatmore and Boucher, 1992, para. 8.6)

	Wansdyke DC	South Cambs DC	Hart DC	Yorkshire Dales NP
		(% of agreements falling into each category)		
Access	1.75	6.19	4.84	3.41
Agricultural development	11.70	0.00	0.54	0.00
Car-parking	2.92	0.52	6.45	1.41
Community facilities	1.75	1.56	4.84	2.27
Elderly users	7.60	3.61	11.38	0.00
Environment and amenity	4.08	10.31	7.07	25.01
Existing S52/Plan. P	1.75	4.64	3.23	1.14
Future development	5.26	7.73	5.91	5.68
Highways	8.94	3.09	2.15	0.00
Infrastructure	4.68	5.67	4.30	0.00
Land transfer	0.59	1.56	3.60	0.00
Local/employed user	1.17	4.12	1.61	26.14
Phasing	7.77	7.73	5.91	5.68
Public open space	0.59	1.56	18.36	0.00
Size restrictions	0.00	5.16	0.00	0.00
Social housing	0.00	0.52	0.00	0.00
Temporary development	1.17	3.61	0.54	1.14
Use restrictions	35.67	33.00	17.28	27.41
Unknown	0.59	1.03	1.61	0.00

Note: the category 'environment and amenity' has been quite broadly defined, and includes for example, landscaping, advertisement and noise control. For the purposes of this table, public open space forms a separate category.

Although there is some evidence of an increase in the use of agreements to secure social and community benefits, and to enhance or protect the biospheric environment, these remain relatively small in number compared to the other purposes for which agreements are used.

Yet Durman and Rowan Robinson (1991) note little evidence of the dramatic gains reported anecdotally from England. The legal cases discussed in Chapter 4 include several increasingly complex arguments about the relationship between projects and their impacts. Barlow and Chambers (1992) illustrate the potential for a 'stretched' relationship between a development project and obligations negotiated with respect to social housing. These begin to take on the quality of the kind of 'linkage' agreements negotiated in the United States. The Grimley J. R. Eve *et al.* (1992) study reports that most agreements in their study are likely to be 'inoffensive' in relation to current law and policy (p. 29).

The conclusion from these studies thus suggests that the scope and content of agreements has changed little since the 1970s. However, several of the studies draw on interview evidence with planning officers and developers to suggest some significant shifts. The recent legal cases reported in Chapter 4 seem to support this conclusion, as do the comments from planning officers and developers in our own research. This suggests two trends. Firstly, while most obligations relate to the development site, there has been an increasing tendency to negotiate off-site obligations. Secondly, the content of agreements is being extended to encompass social, cultural and environmental benefits.

Thus the rhetoric of 'community benefits' and 'planning gain' which dominated the literature and public debate in the early 1980s receives only limited support from practice until the early 1990s. Nevertheless, the discussion, and the encouragement given by government policy in the 1990s, seems to have lead to significant shifts in scope and content by the mid-1990s.

The form of obligations

Many obligations take the form of a restriction on future rights to use and develop sites. They are embodied in the agreement and are 'tied' to the site by the terms of section 106 (and the preceding section 52). Where the developer is required to take some specific action, this may take one of the following forms:

1. conveyancing of land to a public authority (as in the dedication of school sites, or areas of communal open space);[3]
2. carrying out of physical works, for example building an access roundabout, providing for internal site services, building a proportion of low-cost housing units; the works built may then be conveyed to a public agency or other appropriate body;
3. making a financial payment to a public agency, to enable it to undertake works, or to cover ongoing maintenance costs.

The various studies give little attention to this question, although Tables 5.2 and 5.3 show that financial contributions and land transfers were involved in a number of agreements. Financial transfers would also have occurred under highway agreements, but these have been omitted in most studies.

Yet from the various case studies, the interviews and lists of types of agreement, it is clear that all the above forms of obligation are used regularly. Both the Grimley J. R. Eve *et al.* (1992) and the KPMG (1990) studies note an increased tendency towards making financial payments. The Grimley J.R. Eve study even attempts a calculation of the scale of financial payments and other cost implications involved in agreements. Our own research, discussed in section 5.3, casts more light on the form of obligations, and concludes that they vary according to the particular circumstances of the parties more than the type of project. However, because the circumstances in which both developers and local planning authorities find themselves these days are different from those in the 1970s, the patterns of preference for forms of obligations are changing.

Variation by development conditions

The discussion in Chapter 3 suggests that there could be considerable variation in the way agreements are used, depending on the development sector involved (industrial, retail, residential etc.), the size of project, the type of developer and the nature of local development conditions. In part because of data problems, the various studies provide little information on these questions.

There is most evidence on the type of development. Grimley J. R. Eve *et al.* (1992) found that 61% of the agreements in their study related to residential development (see Table 5.4).

A similar dominance of residential applications was found by Durman and Rowan-Robinson (1991) in Scotland, though agreements on minerals applications were of greater significance.

Table 5.4   Numbers of agreements by type of development (Grimley J. R. Eve *et al.* study: 1987–90)

Residential	522	61%
Industrial/commercial/storage	53	9%
Offices	67	9%
Retail	65	8%
Leisure/tourism	70	8%
Minerals	16	2%
Agriculture	18	2%
Other	41	5%
	852	104*

* Error due to rounding up.
Source: derived from Appendix F. in Grimley J. R. Eve *et al.* (1992), p. 67.

The studies are agreed that development obligations are linked to both large and small projects. (Durman and Rowan-Robinson, 1991; MacDonald, 1991; Elson and Payne, 1993). It is possible that off-site community benefits and substantial infrastructure contributions are predominantly linked to larger projects, but the evidence on this is uncertain. The KPMG (1990) study claimed that 'planning gain' was always expected for large commercial and retail parks, at least in the view of developers. This study also suggested that there were most opportunities for negotiating obligations on larger residential and office schemes.

Little attention is given in the research studies to the relation between agreements negotiated and the nature of the developer, apart from what may be inferred from the spread of agreements across large and small projects.

Theoretical analysis discussed in Chapter 3 and the findings from earlier periods suggest that local market conditions are a major factor in the opportunity for negotiating obligations. Attractive sites in strong markets create the opportunity to negotiate obligations. Poorer sites in weaker markets do not. But this easy link no longer seems as clear cut as the literature suggests. Pears (1989) notes the extension of the use of agreements in local authorities deliberately selected for their problematic local economies. Social housing obligations are being achieved in areas with a wide range of local market conditions (Barlow and Chambers, 1992; Williams *et al.*, 1991). This suggests that the practice of negotiating obligations has shifted from a reliance on the increment of 'development gain' or 'economic rent' associated with the limitation on land supply due to planning restrictions, to a widespread practice needed because the public sector can no longer afford to facilitate development by the advance provision of infrastructure, or to provide community benefits and deal with adverse environmental impacts. Thus the increase in the use and scope of agreements may relate as much to the changing roles of the public and private sectors in the development process as to local market conditions.

The advantages of obligations

Most of the studies comment on the mutual benefits the negotiation of obligations brings. For planning authorities, the main benefits noted by Durman and Rowan-Robinson (1991) were:

1. to remove an obstacle preventing planning permission being granted, for example to ensure infrastructure was provided;
2. to provide a more robust control over development, for example to provide greater strength than was possible through a condition, or enable more rapid enforcement.

They were also valuable, according to the Grimley J. R. Eve *et al.* (1992) study, in dealing with the issues raised by large and complex development applications and in particular to sort out who should pay for what in relation to infrastructure development.

For developers, advantages of agreements noted in the studies included:

1. removing an obstacle to planning permission;
2. bringing forward public infrastructure programmes;
3. avoiding delay through an appeal;
4. enabling a trade-off between advantages and disadvantages of a project, so allowing it to proceed;
5. producing a public relations benefit and influencing public opinion;
6. enhancing the development itself;
7. providing added support to a case if an appeal becomes necessary (Durman and Rowan-Robinson, 1991; Elson, 1990a; KPMG, 1990; Grimley J. R. Eve *et al.*, 1992).

Developers nevertheless were reported in the studies to have some concerns over the practice. Grimley J. R. Eve *et al.* (1992) note that some developers found obligations negotiated at the height of the property boom were no longer possible to deliver by the early 1990s. Durman and Rowan-Robinson (1991) comment on the transaction costs of negotiation leading to delay, and the impact of obligations on overall project finance and restrictions on future value. Despite these reservations and despite the rhetoric of anxiety over the practice put forward by some commentators on the negotiation of obligations in the 1980s, these studies generally show a reasonable acceptance by developers of the practical case for the negotiation of obligations.

5.2.3 Conclusions

Even though agreements affect relatively few applications, the research discussed above describes a practice which seems to have become routine among most local authorities during the 1990s. The practices identified in the 1960s and 1970s in only some authorities, in some parts of the country, have now extended across the system. Despite the rhetoric of local planning authorities making extortionate demands from developers for 'planning gain', the reality seems to be that such negotiations have a useful role for most parties in managing the development and regulatory relationship in contemporary conditions.

If there are concerns emerging from the research studies reported here, these relate in part to the tendency for an **upward ratchet** in the expectations of planning authorities and others involved in negotiating contributions. This is seen in the tendencies to expand the range of obligations negotiated, and a greater interest in the negotiation of off-site contributions. But the studies also report concerns about the management of the negotiation process, and the legal issues which are raised.

The research reviewed above does not go into detail on these management and legal issues. Nor does it provide much insight into how the practice varies as between local authorities and types of project; the differential impacts it may have on developers; or the overall costs of the obligations incurred and the process. Our own research adopted an intensive approach in order to fill out our understanding of the practice of negotiating environmental and community impacts. It centred on detailed case studies of practice in five local authority areas. These were selected to cover a range of different development situations. In the remainder of this chapter, we describe the agreements negotiated, using the same headings as in the previous section. In Chapters 6 and 7, we examine the arguments being made to justify the obligations negotiated, and the practices which have evolved for negotiating and managing agreements.

5.3 DEVELOPMENT OBLIGATIONS IN FIVE LOCAL AUTHORITIES

5.3.1 The case study areas

The five areas for our research were chosen to represent diverse development and planning situations (see Table 5.5). In each, the local planning authorities had made some use of planning agreements, and had included planning policies with respect to development obligations in recent local plans (Healey, 1991b).

Table 5.5   Population trends in the case study districts

	Population 1991	% pa change 1971–81	% pa change 1981–91
Solihull MBC	195 586	+0.32	–0.14
Wandsworth LB	239 161	–1.67	–0.66
Newcastle City CC	264 069	–1.05	–0.50
Tewkesbury BC	69 523	+1.15	+0.60
Harlow DC	73 524	+0.15	–0.73

Source: 1991 Census.

Three of the five case study areas are unitary authorities.

Solihull is a metropolitan district in the West Midlands conurbation. It lies to the east of Birmingham, and contains both residential suburbs and villages within the Birmingham/Coventry green belt and substantial business locations, particularly around Birmingham Airport and the National Exhibition Centre, and adjacent to the M42. Solihull has seen a substantial amount of development in the post-war period, with major allocations for housing development in structure plans since the 1970s.[4] The Council was in Conservative control until 1991 when it became a hung council.

Wandsworth is an inner London Borough. The population level has been steadily falling since the 1960s, though at a slower rate in the 1980s. It is a largely residential area, including a number of large parks and open spaces. Development in the 1980s concentrated on riverside sites, where there were redundant warehouse premises, and in the various centres in the Borough. There are significant levels of commuting into the Borough. Residential development is primarily small scale; the larger development projects are for business, retail and leisure. Most of these involve the redevelopment of redundant industrial and commercial sites. The council changed from Labour to Conservative control in 1978.

Newcastle is a metropolitan district in the Tyne and Wear conurbation. It covers the conurbation core, Newcastle City Centre, substantial areas of active and redundant industrial land primarily on the riverside, residential districts, and green belt land to the west, part with coal reserves. The riverside areas include part of the Tyneside Enterprise Zone and were included within the territory of the Tyne and Wear Development Corporation.[5] There has been a substantial decline in the area's traditional industrial base with high levels of unemployment in manufacturing. This has been balanced by the expansion of the service sector. Major development opportunities are limited by the long-standing weakness of the local economy and are clustered around the riverside as a result of urban policy incentives, and around the recently opened A1 western by-pass, which runs through the green belt. The council has been in Labour control for many years.

Tewkesbury is a county district within Gloucestershire. The Structure Plan: First Alteration (1992) targets the district for major growth in housing and employment. The district's main preoccupation is with providing the infrastructure for this growth. The primary problems were: accommodating new housing and resolving drainage issues; the pressure on Tewkesbury's community facilities and town centre as a result of an expected 50% expansion; and accommodating the needs of rural villages while limiting their growth. Tewkesbury council is in independent control and rural parish councils are an important element of local politics.

Harlow is a small county district within Essex. It is a former London New Town, and its area is largely built up. There has been some decline in the town's industrial base, leading both to rising unemployment and redundant sites. These sites, along with Brenthall Park (now known as Church Langley), a greenfield site, formerly in neighbouring Epping Forest district, were the focus of considerable development interest in the 1980s. The council has been in Labour control for a long time.

Our research involved interviews with planning officers, officers in other departments, local councillors, developers and some interest groups. Using planning case files and other records, we constructed as comprehensive a list as possible of all agreements made between 1984 and 1991 in each authority. We examined case files and conducted interviews to provide more detailed information on a selection of case studies in each authority area. We prepared a report on each case study authority and discussed this with the local planning officers (see Appendix 1 for further details). It should be noted that our study period largely preceded the government's own re-statement of policy in circular 16/91 (DoE, 1991b) and should be treated as a record of practice up to the early 1990s. We discuss the findings of our resarch using the same headings as the previous section.

5.3.2 Scale

The total number of agreements identified in the period 1984–91 in the five authorities was 206 (see Table 5.6). This data is incomplete as systematic records were rarely kept. It should therefore be treated with caution.[6] Nearly all of these agreements involved the use of Section 52 of the Town and Country Planning Act 1971 (Section 106 of the 1990 Act). Many used more than one legal source (see Appendix 1).

Table 5.6 Numbers of agreements in case study districts

	1984–91*
Solihull	52
Wandsworth	58
Newcastle	21
Tewkesbury	63
Harlow	12
Total	206

* The date used is the date the agreement was signed.

Solihull, Wandsworth and Tewkesbury had the largest numbers of agreements. In Newcastle and Harlow, few agreements were signed, in total, although the numbers increased significantly in the late 1980s. The reasons for these low numbers are not the same. In Newcastle, economic conditions suppressed development interest until late in the decade. The trend in Harlow was affected by the winding down of the New Town Development Corporation, which had powers to enter into agreements through land deals.

The numbers of agreements in each area were very small compared to the overall number of planning decisions, confirming the findings of the studies cited in the previous section. Taking the period 1986–91, for which planning permission data is readily available, agreements in our case study authorities represented only 0.3 % of all *decisions*. A more significant statistic is the proportion of agreements to major, minor and minerals *permissions* granted, given that total planning decisions include householder applications, advertisement and listed building consents (see Table 5.7). Even so, the numbers of agreements were very low (1.07% overall).

Table 5.7   Agreements in relation to applications in case study districts

	Nos of agreements *1986–91*	*Nos of significant permissions granted (major, minor minerals 1986–91) +, **	*Overall nos of decisions (all decisions, including refusals and all householder decisions)*
Solihull	31	2766	10 240
Wandsworth	49	5118	12 667
Newcastle	18	3159	10 815
Tewkesbury	43	2565	9608
Harlow	12	649	2470
TOTAL	153	14 257	45 800
Agreements as a % of significant permissions		1.07%	
Agreements as a % of all decisions			0.3%

+ Figures for 1988 for Wandsworth and Harlow are derived from data for six months.
* Major developments are those of ten dwellings (or 0.5 ha) or more, or 1000 m² (or 1 ha) or more. Minor developments are projects less than this in scale, which constitute development rather than change of use.
Source: DoE Planning Application Statistics.

The numbers of agreements in the five authorities fluctuated between 24 and 30 per year, but the pattern of agreements over time was affected by very particular local circumstances, such as the signing of major agreements in Solihull related to a major housing allocation at Cranmore-Widney, and the inclusion of agricultural occupancy agreements in Tewkesbury until 1986, when the authority switched to the use of conditions. Nevertheless, except in Solihull and Wandsworth, where planning officers were operating practices established since the 1970s, the other three authorities commented on the increasing significance of agreements as the 1980s progressed. However, it is only in Newcastle that the data clearly supports this.

Although it is not possible from the data to distinguish large from small schemes, an impressionistic picture emerges from our fieldwork. Agreements for small schemes were quite usual, for example with respect to agricultural or age occupancy restrictions (Tewkesbury, Newcastle). Many agreements, however, related to large and complex schemes.

In Solihull and Tewkesbury, most of the developments which were the subject of agreements went ahead to completion. In the other three authorities, a significant number of cases were affected by the difficult development conditions which emerged in the later 1980s and early 1990s, with developers not proceeding with projects, or seeking variations or discharge of obligation requirements. Some developers went into liquidation. There is no clear data on whether obligations were implemented, as much depended on the terms of an agreement and on the monitoring processes in place (see Chapter 7).

5.3.3 The contents of agreements

Classifying obligations

We have noted in the previous section the problem of classifying development obligations. Our approach has been to divide obligations into *negative* obligations, which are a restriction on the rights of landowners, such as occupancy obligations and in the way in which particular facilities in a development are provided (such as car-parking, crèches and public facilities), and those which in require some specific further action to be undertaken. We refer to these as *positive* obligations. This classification superficially resembles the legal distinction between negative and positive covenants in land law. In law, it is much more difficult to enforce a positive covenant against successors in title. Positive planning *conditions* are more likely to be held to be invalid. In this way, the legal distinction confirms the idea that positive covenants are more radical and more far reaching. However, whether in law an obligation is construed as a negative or positive obligation often turns on the formal wording rather than the substance of the covenant. A good example is the

Grampian condition, discussed in Chapter 4, where in substance the developer is required to carry out the specific actions but the condition is drafted so that the development should not be commenced until these actions have been completed. Much of the controversy surrounding the negotiation of obligations has focused on positive obligations as discussed in Chapter 4. These are often difficult to achieve through the mechanism of a planning condition (for example, making a financial contribution). We therefore believe this distinction is a useful one in the light of current debates, although it creates difficulties. Both negative and positive obligations may be controversial. An obligation related to affordable housing may take the form of a negative obligation, limiting the occupancy of housing to those in particular income categories. Or it may require that a developer builds a specified number of units and makes these available to a housing association. Both cases are directed at a social policy objective.

In this section, we provide considerable detail on the agreements involved and what the various parties thought about them. This provides empirical material which we draw upon in later chapters. An agreement may relate to one or several obligations. In the 206 agreements in our five local authorities, we identified 524 obligations (see Table 5.8). Of these obligations, around one-third related to negative restrictions and two-thirds to positive requirements. In interviews, our respondents emphasized that, in the 1980s, there had been a significant increase in the numbers of positive agreements.

Negative obligations

Sixty-five per cent of the agreements identified in our five local authorities between 1984 and 1991 contained negative obligations. These were most commonly associated with residential projects (48% of agreements and 42% of negative obligations). However, retail, hotel/catering/leisure and mixed development schemes generated around 10% each of all negative obligations.

Table 5.8 Obligations in agreements in case study districts

| | Nos of obligations | | |
	Negative	Positive	Total
Solihull	46	109	155
Wandsworth	59	85	144
Newcastle	16	15	31
Tewkesbury	66	85	151
Harlow	7	36	43
TOTAL	194	330	524

Our categorization omits obligations restricting the use of the development until positive obligations have been fulfilled, that is the **Grampian** type obligations (see Figure 4.1). These were very common with respect to infrastructure works and in this discussion are subsumed within the relevant positive obligations. We grouped the remaining negative obligations into four main categories:

1. *Development control administration*

   Obligations in this category are adjustments to existing permissions (e.g. extinguishment of prior permission) or the limitation of a prior permission (e.g. temporary permission). We include here two cases relating to agricultural dwellings in Tewkesbury. In one case a mobile home had to be removed once a dwelling was completed. In another, the applicant was required to increase the acreage devoted to horticulture, to make his holding viable.

2. *Controlling development*

   Negative obligations in this category are concerned with the control of the development phase of a project and may focus on the control of construction traffic noise, levels or hours of operation. They may also focus on development phasing or timing. Case 4 from Newcastle provides an example of restrictions designed to control traffic movements around mineral workings. Case 5 from Tewkesbury is a good example of phasing permissions.

Case 4: Dewley Mill, Newcastle

Development type: Mineral

Developer: H. J. Banks & Co

Proposal: extension to existing quarry for the excavation of clays, shales and restoration of final void by infilling with waste materials

The main aim of the agreement was to bring a 1972 consent under the control of current planning legislation with a view to preventing further applications for extraction.

The agreement also contained negative obligations to control the flow of traffic to and from the site. Permissible routes for vehicles removing extracted minerals or depositing waste materials are specified. These restrictions applied to the developers' vehicles. The developer was only liable to make 'best endeavours' to ensure that lorries driven by other operators followed permissible routes.

Case 5: Gloucester Trading Estate, Tewkesbury

Development: mixed

Developers: Arlington Securities, Arlington Business Parks Ltd, Bovis Homes Ltd, Gloucester Business Park Ltd

Proposal: B1, B2, B8 development and residential development

In the highway agreement concluded with Gloucestershire County Council, the development is phased to permit the highway authority to control the development.

The development cannot be commenced until adequate bonds to cover the highway works have been secured and the developers have submitted a satisfactory programme of works to the authority. The developers may commence on-site highway works, landscaping, drainage and public utilities works prior to commencement of the development.

They are allowed to construct 50 dwellings but these are not to be occupied until one of the road junctions forming part of the highways works is completed and the Department of Transport has commenced construction of the by-pass.

The agreement contains phasing provisions linking the completion of works to stages of residential and office development.

---

3.   *Control after development*

This is by far the largest category of negative obligations. The primary purpose of obligations in this section is to control the use of land or the development after completion. This category includes restrictions on site use, conditions of use (limitations on hours, restrictions on sales etc.) and occupancy restrictions.

Two sub-groups of obligations in this category are of particular interest. They are management and maintenance obligations, and affordable housing obligations. Management and maintenance obligations were used by local authorities to regulate the future use and operation of facilities provided by developers. In some instances such facilities are provided as part of the application (e.g. car-parking). In other cases the facilities are a positive obligation provided under a legal agreement. Thus in Solihull and Tewkesbury these obligations were required in conjunction with positive obligations to provide landscaping. In Newcastle, an exceptional case required a minerals operator to maintain woodland and wetland areas provided as part of land restoration. In Wandsworth, the most extensive user of such obligations, developers were required to maintain and manage car-parking (provided as part of the application), public toilets and crèches (generally provided as part of an agreement) to local authority standards (Case 6).

Case 6: Putney Exchange, Wandsworth

Development type: Mixed

Developer: Guardian Royal Exchange

Proposal: 45 shopping units ranging from 13 sq. m to 1520 sq. m and ten flats on a 1.26 ha site

GRE agreed to provide sewerage, public toilets, car-parking and a crèche. Wandsworth council's concern was to ensure the long-term management of these facilities for the benefit of the public.

The agreement contains detailed specifications covering these facilities:

(a) car-park – details of charging and opening, i.e. availability to the public;
(b) public toilets (including disabled toilets and baby care unit) – must be available to the public free of charge when the shopping centre is open;
(c) crèche – to be run by GRE initially though later it could be run by a licensee with Wandsworth's consent.

Negative affordable housing obligations fall into two categories. In the first, small sites developed by a housing association in Tewkesbury were covered by obligations which aimed to ensure that the housing will remain available as low-cost housing in the future.[7] In the second category, negative housing obligations are normally linked to positive housing obligations (see Case 17 under positive obligations). A distinctive form of negative obligations were those negotiated by developers directed at exhorting employers to use their 'best endeavours' to employ specific groups in the area, thereby restricting their freedom to employ whom they chose (Case 7).

4.   *Modification*

These obligations related to changes to previous agreements. We discuss these in more detail in Chapter 7.

Most negative obligations related to control after the development process (see Table 5.9).

The reasons for such control varied significantly from authority to authority.

Case 7: Battersea Power Station, Wandsworth

Development type: Leisure

Developer: Battersea Leisure Ltd

Proposal: leisure and entertainment complex

Battersea Leisure's proposal to establish a theme park on a redundant power station site was seen by Wandsworth as an opportunity for new employment. The developer estimated that there would be 4500 jobs created by the scheme. A primary concern for the Council was to ensure that disadvantaged groups had the opportunity to secure employment.

To this end the agreement contained schedules which included:

(a) an Employment and Positive Action Policy;
(b) a list of target groups (school-leavers, long-term unemployed, black people, women, people with disabilities);
(c) a positive action programme;
(d) an employment profile for the scheme.

The operation of the Positive Action Policy was to be monitored by an Advisory Panel (whose membership included community groups).

The extent of the obligation was limited by the agreement. Battersea Leisure agreed to 'endeavour' to implement the Positive Action Policy while the Council acknowledged that the company's operations might preclude total fulfilment.

Table 5.9 Negative obligations in case study districts

	S	W	N	T	H	Total
Numbers of agreements	32	34	12	49	5	132
Development control administration	3	1	1	2	–	7
Controlling development	4	7	7	13	4	35
Control after development	39	49	5	50	3	146
Agreement modification	–	2	3	1	–	6
Total number of obligations	46	59	16	66	7	194

In Tewkesbury, a number of obligations related to occupancy restrictions on agricultural dwellings, as well as affordable housing purposes. In Wandsworth, we found 15 obligations relating to the management and maintenance of facilities after development.

Negative obligations in our case study areas were primarily concerned with on-site matters. A few were concerned with off-site matters but directly related to the project in question (for example, the regulation of construction traffic). Local authorities used negative obligations to obviate problems caused by a development, with the aim of ensuring that the development was acceptable in planning terms. The main exceptions were affordable housing obligations, management and maintenance obligations and Wandsworth's employment and training obligations. Here, a connection was made between a project and its social and economic consequences elsewhere in an area. Several of the obligations related to social rather than physical considerations (e.g. occupancy restrictions).

Positive obligations

The extent of positive obligations varied from agreement to agreement. An obligation might entail provision of pedestrian or vehicular access for minor residential development or a single substantial obligation such as car-parking, or more comprehensive provision for a major residential development. Once again, we faced classification problems in describing these obligations. Table 5.10 summarizes our categories. This focuses on the purpose of an obligation. The table shows the dominance of infrastructure obligations, as found in the other research studies, and the importance of landscaping and open space obligations, again in line with other research. However, our research found proportionately more obligations for community facilities than in the Grimley J. R. Eve *et al.* (1992) survey.

Table 5.10   Positive obligations in case study districts

	S	W	N	T	H	Total
Numbers of agreements	31	42	13	23	12	121
Highways	51	25	9	27	15	127
Sewerage and drainage	20	6	–	16	6	48
Landscaping and open space	29	34	–	17	3	83
Parking	6	4	4	1	3	18
Community facilities	–	6	2	11	1	20
Conservation and restoration	–	3	–	3	–	6
Social policy	–	6	–	1	4	11
Other	3	1	–	9	4	17
Total no. of obligations	109	85	15	85	36	330

We now discuss each of these groups of obligations in turn.

1.   *Highways obligations*

For minor residential developments (less than ten dwellings), obligations related to vehicular and pedestrian access to the site. For large developments, obligations may require major on-site highway works, access and off-site works. Case 1 from Tewkesbury quoted in Chapter 1 illustrates a package of infrastructure and related requirements for a large residential project. Case 8 illustrates the highway requirements in the West Midlands Renaissance Area around the National Exhibition Centre and Birmingham International Airport. This is a major business location involving a range of different land parcels, serviced originally by a local country road network.

Case 8: West Midlands Renaissance Area, Solihull

Development type: Mixed

Developers: various

According to Solihull estimates, £20 m was required to provide an adequate highway network. Solihull expected 60% of this to come from developers. The remainder was to be provided by the European Community and the local authority.

In this development Solihull was not able to set the agenda. The planning authority acted as 'honest broker' to ensure that developers paid pro rata contributions based on the impacts of their development to finance the highway network.

Highway obligations are generally seen to be uncontroversial. However, there was debate about the scale of contribution in relation to a development's impacts. The Clapham Junction developer (see Case 22 in Chapter 7) argued that:

One of the problems that you have with local authority Highway Departments is that [when an agreement is negotiated] the Highway Department goes and looks through its files and sees all the problems within half a mile of the site and hopes we'll pay for it.

The Solihull Highway Engineer, on the other hand, argued that it was important to consider the impacts of a project on the wider network over a long-term period:

> We go slightly beyond certain advice which essentially says that if it works on day one, that's the end of the developer's interest. We say, as far as we're concerned and as far as the developer's concerned, we may need a road and we think it's a waste of resources to carry out improvements to the highway if it's only going to have a life of one or two years. So we say to the developer, we're looking at these improvements that are only necessary because of your development. We want it to work in 15 years' time. We don't want to come back in five years time and do further works ... it will disrupt your business activities.

Highway works in the West Midlands Renaissance Area are devised with this 15-year time scale in mind. Another approach adopted by Solihull was to require contributions in order to pay for possible future improvements to the general upgrading of the highway network in addition to making provision for the immediate impacts of the development (see Case 8).

A similar situation occurred in relation to the Church Langley development in Harlow with respect to highway infrastructure provision. In addition to constructing access works to link the development to the A414, the developer was required to make a contribution of £3 300 000 to cover the cost of any highway improvements deemed necessary by Essex Highway Authority within a radius of four miles from the site 'so as to assist the accommodation of such extra traffic as may be generated by the development'. The developer was to receive a refund of any amounts of the contribution unspent by the completion of the development (see Case 11 below).

There was evidence from our case study authorities that the scale of highway obligations was increasing, encouraged by the Department of Transport[8] and by the increasing size of development projects in the late 1980s. Typically highway obligations were required to deal with the impacts of the development. In Wandsworth, all agreements related to applications for redevelopment of redundant sites. Off-site highway obligations were for improvements to existing highways. Such obligations were often substantial (see Case 20 in Chapter 6). In Newcastle, the City Treasurer stated that a developer must pay for highway works as the local authority was unable to finance the necessary infrastructure (see Case 21 in Chapter 6). This echoed the view of the Solihull Highway Engineer:

> You've got to get the money from somewhere, [to enable the development to go ahead]. If you can't get it from the rate-payer or the government, where else can you get it from?

2. *Sewerage and drainage*

Sewerage obligations, prior to the Water Act 1989, were the outcome of negotiations between the developer and the water authority. (Negotiations are now with the water company.) A local authority may have acted as agent for the water authority or as 'management contractor' for a water company. Sewerage obligations may be negotiated directly with the sewerage undertaker without the local authority being a party to the resulting agreement. Consequently it is possible that the number of sewerage obligations is under-recorded in this study.

Though local planning authorities generally incorporate sewerage phasing obligations in a section 106 agreement which is attached to the planning application, this does not always happen. Tewkesbury's engineer explained:

> Part of the development control process is that developers shall ensure that the site is sewered to the satisfaction of the Local Planning Authority (standard practice). The agreement that follows is a section 18 [Public Health Act 1936] agreement. That in itself ties in the developer on performance.

Generally a planning agreement is negotiated where a local authority acts as agent (management contractor) for the water authority (water company) and where the local authority is to undertake construction of off-site sewerage. A residential project in Tewkesbury provides an example (see Case 9).

Thames Water Utilities argued that the sewerage obligations required for the Church Langley project (see Case 11 below) did not constitute 'planning gain':

> The purpose of the agreement was to ensure that Church Langley wasn't built or occupied until sewerage and drainage arrangements were in place. It wasn't a case of asking the developer to pay for something that Thames Water would normally pay for.

On redevelopment sites, in Wandsworth for example, the need for sewerage provision occurs because the development may overload the existing system. This can lead to the developer providing a new sewer, as in the Putney Exchange mixed retail and residential development described in Case 6 above.

In our data, sewerage obligations were most frequently related to the development of greenfield residential sites (see Case 9). While the range of sewerage requirements varies from site to site, this example typifies agreements covering sewerage obligations. Drainage obligations in our case study areas were primarily concerned with the

Case 9: Manor Farm, Up Hatherlery, Tewkesbury

Development type: Residential

Developer: McAlpine Homes West

Proposal: outline application for residential development on 11.3 ha of land including the construction of a new estate road and method of disposal of foul and surface water

Under the agreement, the developer was to submit a general scheme for the disposal of on-site surface water and foul drainage to ensure adequate provision at each stage of the development. A temporary surface water balancing system was to be provided by the developer whose design was to be approved by the Council.

The sum of £203.00 (index-linked) per dwelling was paid quarterly until completion of the development to Severn Trent Water Authority. These were contributions towards the provision of a new public sewer which connected with the existing sewer system. The developer was allowed to build 55 dwellings connected to the existing system prior to the completion of the sewer. If the new sewer was not completed by a specified date, he could not build further houses connected to the existing sewer system.

Upon completion of each dwelling, the developer was to contribute £350.00 (index-linked) to Tewkesbury Council towards the cost of an off-site land drainage system to be constructed by the Council.

The developer was to provide a surface water drainage system which was to drain into a nearby brook via the off-site land drainage system.

drainage of land not attached to buildings, i.e. land drainage on green-field sites both large and small (as the Tewkesbury data shows). Developers are usually responsible for the provision of land drainage facilities, though the local authority has discretionary powers to secure adequate provision. The water authority (now company) is responsible for catering for the run-off from land drainage. Typically drainage oblig-ations require a developer to provide the local authority with a land drainage scheme prior to the commencement of development and to provide adequate land drainage facilities. This provision can be seen in Case 9 above.

3. *Landscaping, open space, footpaths*
    Another major group of obligations related to footpaths, cycleways, play areas, riverside walks and other areas of recreational and

environmental amenities. The Grimley J. R. Eve *et al.* (1992) study found a similarly large number of obligations of this kind, which they classified as 'environmental and ecology' obligations. However, we have made a separate category for conservation benefits, as those with a direct nature conservation purpose were relatively few in number, as Whatmore and Boucher (1992) discovered. The local authority concern was firstly with the standard of provision and secondly with the responsibility for long-term maintenance. Typically, where the maintenance was to be undertaken by the owner, the standards and future management are dealt with by a condition.

Local authorities have no specific statutory powers to secure what they consider to be satisfactory landscape provision. They may have a local policy which can be embodied in standard conditions. For residential development, Solihull had a requirement that at least 2.4 ha of open space be provided for every 1000 population (see Case 10).

Case 10: Hillfield West, Area D, Solihull

Development type: Residential

Developer: Bryant Homes Ltd

Proposal: outline application for residential development

This site was part of the Cranmore–Widney development. All developers made contributions to open space provision. This included:

(a) footpaths, contributions towards the cost of laying out playing fields and public authority open space at the rate of £200 per acre;
(b) open space laid out to Solihull standards;
(c) commuted sums for open space maintenance at the rate of £50 per sq. m.

Agreements are used where the facility is to be transferred to the local authority. Exceptionally an agreement may be used to require the developer to manage and maintain landscape.

The majority of landscaping and open space obligations in our case study areas related to residential development. Developers generally preferred the local authority to assume responsibility for long-term maintenance. Agreements provided a much more powerful tool for this purpose than conditions (see Chapter 4). This arrangement enabled the local authorities to secure some control over landscape and open space design. All agreements of this type contained obligations requiring the developer to submit landscape schemes to the local authority for approval.

On the Church Langley project in Harlow, the Parks Manager was able to convince the developer that provision of landscaping, open space and play facilities was mutually beneficial (see Case 11 below).

> The playground provision in Church Langley is a classic example. I had no real power to require it. It was a question of 'I think it would be mutually beneficial' because (a) the council would like to see its policy maintained across the town and (b) in terms of you selling your houses, if you've got a playground sited sensibly from the minute you are selling your houses, that then becomes an additional saleable item in terms of that house. They jumped at it and wanted to know how to tackle it ... We got it agreed. It was more a question of drawing out the idea and showing them the benefit of having that incorporated and them realising that the cost of that provision would be more beneficial than not.

The aim was to ensure that the provision for Church Langley matched the standards of Harlow New Town. As he explained, he was able to do this because

> The impression that I got speaking to their landscaping people and the people involved in the negotiations on their side was this – Anything you want – say so – as long as it's within the context of the developer's brief.

On large-scale residential projects, developers were more willing to negotiate with the local authority over provision. With smaller schemes, there were fewer options. The issue, according to Solihull's landscape architect, was which land would be given up. Frequently the land that developers want to give up is undevelopable. The options for open space and landscaping were further restricted by requirements to set land aside for sewerage and highways. Once these areas are decided, the area available for open space became limited. On large housing developments the issue was less problematic. On smaller developments, the open space provision often ended up as an 'arbitrary pocket', as Solihull's landscape architect explained:

> It is the bit after they work out the back gardens, the house layout and the highway layout. Something gets left over ... They always want to give us the bits of ground they can't deal with.

On completion of the development, the land was usually transferred to the local authority either free-of-charge or for a nominal sum.

Case 11: Church Langley, Harlow

Development type: Residential

Developer: Brenthall Park Ltd

Proposal: 3500 dwellings

In total four agreements have been concluded with respect to the Church Langley development. The developer and landowners were party to all agreements.

(a) Highway agreement (with Essex County Council). This covered provision for estate roads, access between Church Langley and the A414 and included £3.3 m to cover highway improvements within four miles of the site which were deemed necessary over a ten-year period.

(b) Sewerage and Drainage agreement (with Thames Water Utilities). This included provision of on-site sewers, link sewer to main network and land drainage facilities.

(c) Landscaping agreement (with Harlow District Council and Epping Forest District Council).

- Brenthall Park Ltd agreed to provide structural landscaping, (including woodland conservation) noise attenuation features, play areas, play equipment, a water feature and woodlands.
- Developers were also required to provide sums for the maintenance of these features. The agreement contains two schedules which provide a method of calculation for maintenance contributions for each of these provisions and base units for calculating the commuted sums.
- Harlow Council also binds itself to ensure the maintenance of each area of landscaping and play equipment and the water feature in perpetuity.
- Harlow's Parks manager had to ensure that the new development's landscaping would be consistent with that existing in Harlow. The Leisure Department wanted to ensure that there was adequate play provision and that commuted sums were available for maintenance.

(d) Social Housing and Community Facilities (with Harlow). Not less than 20% and not more than 25% (at least 800) of dwellings were to be provided as social housing. The developer was also required to provide sites for community buildings at nominal cost and to provide 25% of construction costs either by way of financial contribution or by provision of labour or materials.

Further negative obligations were then used to limit future uses for landscaping and open space.

Increasingly, local authorities were only willing to accept the transfer of land if the developer made a commuted lump sum payment to cover the cost of maintenance. Agreements might contain formulae for calculating the amount to be paid (see Case 10 above). These formulae were notionally derived from the level of maintenance required, though the Solihull landscape architect stated that the figures used were arbitrary. Whatever the basis for calculation, the process of securing payments stemmed from a pragmatic rather than a policy-based approach. An exception was Tewkesbury, where a policy for landscape and open space maintenance had been in operation since the early 1980s, though, according to one officer, it has not been uniformly implemented throughout the period.

In contrast, play areas, cycleways and other such provision were typically required for major residential developments such as Church Langley (see Case 11 above), but were secured through negotiation rather than being demanded as a matter of express policy.

The provision of a riverside walk negotiated by Wandsworth did represent the application of an expressed policy. A long-term aim of London riverside authorities was to secure provision of a continuous walkway alongside the River Thames. During the period covered by this study (1984–91), Wandsworth negotiated 14 agreements which provided for riverside walkways (see Case 12) and three others which secured access to the riverside.

4. *Parking*

Parking obligations were a well-established part of both applications and planning agreements. There was considerable variety among local authorities in the way adequate parking for a development was secured. A negative obligation may be utilized requiring that part of a site be used for parking. Alternatively, parking obligations could require a developer to provide adequate on-site and/or off-site spaces or commuted car-parking payments.

All the case study authorities had standards for car-parking requirements. These varied according to development type. Ideally car-parking was to be provided on-site. The local authority sought to ensure that developers made provision for the parking impacts of their development. Where provision could not be secured, developers were required to make commuted car-parking payments to the local authority. In Harlow, the developer of a mixed retail and office development paid the local authority for provision of off-site car-parking spaces. In Solihull, the developer of a mixed office–retail development made an obligation to provide commuted car-parking payments (see Case 13).

Case 12: Albert Wharf, Wandsworth

Development type: mixed

Developer: Petmoor Developments

Proposal: Eight/nine storey block: retail; two-storey office workshops

The agreement included a specification for the laying out and construction of the riverside walk (a general specification was adopted in 1986) which covered materials to be used, paving and street lighting. The agreement also contained a schedule of landscaping requirements to which the developer must conform.

The riverside walk was to be laid out and constructed by Petmoor under the supervision of the Borough Engineer. The work was bonded with a sum of £105 000.

This figure also covered provision of riverside walk extensions and a lifting bridge. Both were to be constructed according to Wandsworth's specifications.

When the riverside walk and riverside walk extensions were completed to the satisfaction of the Borough Engineer, they were to be adopted by Wandsworth who would take responsibility for the maintenance of the surface, landscaping and the lifting bridge. The developer remained responsible for maintenance of the parapet wall, the river wall and the dock wall.

Case 13: Solihull Cinema Site, High Street, Solihull

Development type: Mixed

Developer: Solihull Picture House Company

Proposal: demolition of cinema and erection of banking hall with two floors of offices above

As this was a town centre site the developer had to provide adequate car-parking spaces, i.e. 32 on-site spaces (one for every 28 sq. m office space).

The developer could only provide ten on-site spaces without impairing the building's design which was itself acceptable to Solihull.

The issue was resolved by the developer agreeing to pay a commuted sum of £40 000 for public car-parking spaces.

The precise figure was the result of negotiation. The figure used as Solihull's starting point for negotiations was an average based on the cost of provision of a parking space in the authority's multi-storey car-park and the cost of a parking space in a low-level car-park.

Commuted car-parking payments were also found in Harlow and Tewkesbury.

Generally, the formula for calculating the commuted sum depended on the number of car-parking spaces and the cost per space negotiated between the developer and the local authority. Commuted car-parking payments often create disquiet among developers. As one developer stated, local authorities often consider commuted payments as a financial contribution which may not necessarily be used for the purpose for which it was intended.

In Newcastle, a unique variant of car-parking obligations was found (see Case 3 in Chapter 3) which involved the purchase of contract car-parking tickets. This method resulted in no extra car-parking spaces but placed pressure on existing provision. It must therefore be seen as a relaxation of policy to enable a development to proceed rather than a measure to deal with the adverse impacts of a project.

The Wandsworth practice was different again. According to officers the local authority did not seek commuted car-parking payments, as it wished to avoid taking on the long-term management of facilities. Instead Wandsworth aimed to ensure that provision was made by, and managed by, developers. However, the authority could not require, by using a condition, that on-site car-parks provided by developers were made available for use by the general public at charges set by the local authority, as this would have been an unacceptable infringement of property rights. As in Case 6 above, agreements negotiated with developers allowed use by the general public. Charging mechanisms were defined in schedules attached to the agreement. Similar provisions were contained in agreements covering the Clapham Junction development (see Case 22 in Chapter 7).

5. *Community facilities*

This category covers community services, sport and recreational facilities. Our study found a greater number of such obligations than the Grimley J. R. Eve *et al.* (1992) study. They were secured in Wandsworth, Harlow and Tewkesbury in particular. In Tewkesbury and Harlow, the obligations were associated with large residential schemes. On the Bishop's Cleeve development in Tewkesbury (see Case 1 in Chapter 1), provision was made for a primary school site and a playing field site. In addition, the sum of £500 000 was made available to the Parish Council for recreational and community uses.

In the Church Langley agreement in Harlow, the developer agreed to provide sites for the construction of community facilities (see Case 11 above). Tewkesbury and Harlow justified these obligations as being both needed for the development and to cope with the impact of the development on the wider community. In Wandsworth, the emphasis was on the preservation of existing facilities after site redevelopment (see Case 14). Wandsworth was also concerned with the provision of public toilets in superstore projects.

Case 14: Convent of Notre Dame, Wandsworth

Development type: mixed

Developer: William Sapcote and Co.

Proposal: alterations to provide light industrial, residential units, office, community hall, shop, restaurant/bar

Wandsworth's view was that the development of redundant hospital sites and school sites (this example) can lead to the loss of community facilities. Wandsworth aimed to ensure that part of the building be retained for community use.

In the agreement Sapcote's were required to refurbish part of the building as a community hall as specified in a schedule of works contained in the agreement. The refurbishment consisted of a hall with capacity for 200, disabled access, toilets, office, kitchen, electricity supply, heating, water and sewerage.

Occupation of the hall was restricted to a community group approved by the council. The hall was to be for rent or purchase, between Sapcote and the tenant or purchaser at a price agreed. In default of agreement between the two, the Council's Valuer was to arbitrate.

Sapcote observed that they were not happy with the obligation to provide a community facility. It was the boom conditions of the 1980s which provided the impetus in order that a permission would be granted.

In both Wandsworth and Tewkesbury, there was evidence of strong local demand for the facilities concerned. Wandsworth maintains a list of groups who seek premises. In Tewkesbury, the parish council sometimes got involved in negotiations. Case 15 illustrates such a case, though in this case an agreement did not result for legal reasons.

6. *Conservation*

Very few obligations related to either building or nature conservation, or to archaeological matters. The small numbers of building conservation obligations may reflect the nature of our case study areas. Only one obligation was found relating to nature conservation specifically (in Tewkesbury), though nature conservation provisions were also found

---

Case 15: Butts Lane, Woodmancote, Tewkesbury

Development type: residential

Developer: Skymarch Developments Ltd

Proposal: two detached dwellings

The site itself was near an Area of Outstanding Natural Beauty on the edge of an area of open countryside. The planning department wanted to prevent encroachment into the area of open countryside. In the opinion of the borough planning department, to allow the proposal would establish a precedent for further development.

The developer secured the support of the parish council by offering them part of the site so that a scout headquarters could be built upon it. One Woodmancote parish councillor stated that there was a need for a scout headquarters in the village.

Two applications were submitted – the first for the scout headquarters and the second for the dwellings. Both sites were inspected and approval given.

From the planner's point of view, the offer was a clear inducement which could be seen as bribery. From the parish council's point of view it 'was a straight bargain to get planning permission' which was acceptable.

---

as part of landscaping provision (see Case 11 above). This confirms the findings of both the Grimley J. R. Eve *et al.* study (1992), and Whatmore and Boucher (1992) specifically on environmental agreements. However, four cases were being negotiated, two in Solihull, and one each in Harlow and Newcastle. These seem to have arisen opportunistically, rather than in response to well-established local policy (see Case 16).

Historic building obligations were for on-site matters, directly related to a project. The few nature conservation obligations related to both on-site and off-site works, and the relationship with the development was less direct.

7. *Social policy*

These included child care, employment training and housing obligations with a social policy intention. Both Wandsworth and Harlow had negotiated a few such obligations, while Tewkesbury had negotiated an agreement involving affordable housing obligations. Wandsworth and Harlow had secured obligations relating to public transport. It is striking that our study found four child-care obligations as well as a single positive employment and training obligation, while the Grimley J. R. Eve study for the DoE found none. Harlow had attempted to secure

---

Case 16: National Exhibition Centre, Solihull

Development type: Leisure

Developer: NEC Ltd

Proposal: relocation of existing personnel building, construction of new tractor bays and general store/workshop to form estates management complex

Both the Warwickshire Nature Conservation Trust and the Nature Conservancy Council expressed concern regarding the impact of the development on local wildlife. The NCC proposed that a section 106 agreement be used to ensure that a management scheme for the plantations was secured. The developer was willing to take responsibility for the upkeep and maintenance of Bickenhill Plantations under a woodland management scheme to be drawn up with the NCC and to construct the management complex so that impact on the plantation was reduced.

Solihull has approved the scheme as an exception to green belt policy subject to a section 106 agreement which would include: (a) a full definition of the extent of Bickenhill Plantations to be protected; (b) an agreed management scheme; (c) re-creation of a wetland area being discussed in relation to another NEC proposal.

---

child-care provision on a retail development scheme, but had been informed by the superstore operators that this was not possible as it would create a precedent. The district was also unsuccessful in securing contributions to a child-care trust.

Fundamental to Harlow's assessment of needs was the type of development proposed. Office development would attract female workers, many of them returning to work after starting a family. The developer was expected to cater for their needs. The justification for seeking child-care obligations was that women with children should, under equal opportunities policies, be afforded the opportunity to take up local employment. The Equal Opportunities Officer explained Harlow's reasoning behind the negotiations over the Harlow Business Park (see Case 17):

> We indicated to them that because the business park was on the periphery of the town removed from other services, there was a need in that concentrated business area for provision of what we saw as a certain number of basic facilities to serve the people who were working there. It wouldn't be feasible in their lunch-hour to get out into the town centre to do the sort of things people need to

Case 17: Harlow Business Park

Development type: Office

Developer: ARC Properties

Proposal: 71 322.5 sq. m B1 offices

ARC properties were to provide a temporary nursery building once 19 509 sq. m of office space was occupied.

The temporary facility was to have 30 child spaces (2.3 sq. m per child). Ancillary accommodation (e.g. toilet and kitchen area) was also to be provided.

Permanent facilities were to be provided by the time 53 082 sq. m of office space was occupied.

Permanent facilities included a nursery of 37 sq. m plus ancillary facilities, a small shop, a management-training centre and, if possible, a cash point.

The agreement also contained a clause which released ARC from liability for provisions if these facilities did not generate a commercially viable level of demand within five years.

do. We envisaged that there would probably be quite a substantial number of people working up on the site – hence the crèche and all day nursery, the small mini-shop and banking facilities. We developed that. We saw that they would be recruiting a lot of untrained labour into there. We suggested there should be a business management centre which could be used for training purposes etc. These were essentially going to be little, small units – not able to accommodate within themselves anything meaningful but if we had one centre various businesses could make the use of it.

Harlow secured contributions for on-site child-care facilities through a section 106 agreement on this scheme and the provision of a management/training centre.

Harlow was also able to secure a number of social policy contributions without using agreements. IDC (UK) contributed £15 000 to fund research into out-of-school child care. An application made by Countryside Properties and SIDA Properties for office development included provision of a single-storey crèche. In addition, Countryside Properties made voluntary commitments by letter to use local sub-contractors, to take on two YTS trainees and to hire 20 labourers from the Harlow Job Centre during the course of construction and to extend their catchment area for management trainees to cover Harlow.

While crèche and public toilet facilities have been secured in

Wandsworth on schemes negotiated in the mid- and late-1980s, the employers' crèche, community facilities and public transport obligations associated with the Battersea Power Station project have not yet been provided as the development has not commenced. The recession also hit the Harlow Business Park project. Less than 20% of the development had been completed by 1994. However, in this case, the developer provided a permanent nursery ahead of time as required in the agreement. Apparently, the public relations benefit of provision was valuable for this scheme.

Confirming the findings of recent studies by Barlow and Chambers (1992), we found few obligations relating to social housing. Tewkesbury and Harlow each had secured one agreement including affordable housing obligations. Both related to major residential developments. In both cases the local authority view was that the development should cater for housing needs in the area.

Tewkesbury has operated an Affordable Rural Housing Policy since 1988. The Stonehill/Wheatpieces scheme provided the first opportunity to secure affordable housing plots on a major residential scheme (Case 18).

Harlow secured obligations which would provide for at least 800 affordable dwellings (out of a total of 3500) on the Church Langley project (see Case 11 above). This agreement, negotiated in the mid-1980s, was in part secured because the developers required Harlow's support at an appeal inquiry against non-determination by Epping Forest DC (the site was at that time in that local authority area). Countryside Properties, one of the developers, argued that the final development should be considered as a neighbourhood with a mix of housing tenures available to the residents. Local authority officers and the developers interviewed reported that the negotiation of further affordable housing obligations was limited due to the economic recession and the difficult housing market conditions.

The examples of obligations reported here provide an idea of the complexity and diversity of many agreements. They also show how practice has evolved. As suggested in the previous section, some authorities had a well-developed approach to the negotiation of obligations. Others were turning their approach into a more developed and strategic one. Wandsworth, a London Borough, negotiated positive obligations as a matter of routine, building on practices evolved since the 1970s. So too did Solihull, which had negotiated more obligations than the other authorities, but over a narrower range than the others. Both Tewkesbury and Harlow were in the process of transforming their practice from an occasional *ad hoc* approach to a more routine one, and were beginning to articulate clearer policies. Newcastle, with a few obligations, was nevertheless changing to a more

Case 18: Stonehill and Wheatpieces, Tewkesbury

Development type: Residential

Developers: J.S. Bloor (Newbury) Ltd and Bovis Homes Ltd*

Proposal: 1054 dwellings

These sites were allocated for residential development under the Tewkesbury–Ashchurch Local Plan (Case 23 in Chapter 7). Under the section 106 agreement, developers were to provide 10% affordable housing as part of the development. That provision was to take the form of the transfer of plots to a specified housing association.

The development as a whole was to consist of five stages. Each stage was determined by the number of dwellings completed or a specified date (whichever was later). Twenty plots per stage were to be transferred. If further planning permission was granted for residential development, one plot was to be provided for each multiple of ten dwellings in excess of 1050 dwellings.

Tewkesbury was to make no payment towards the transfer of plots other than a fixed payment of £10 000 (index-linked) which was a contribution towards the cost of highways, drainage and landscaping works and community and/or social facilities. The plots transferred were to be provided with all necessary services (e.g. drainage, sewers, access roads up to a convenient point agreed between the developers and the borough).

All affordable housing plots were to be the subject of covenants intended to ensure that they remained as affordable housing.

The developers had the option of transferring completed buildings which would reduce the number of plots to be transferred.

* Only J.S. Bloor signed the agreement. Contributions from Bovis were secured through a collaboration agreement between the two developers.

systematic approach. All authorities expected to continue to negotiate obligations at least on the same scale and with the scope achieved in recent years. Further, authorities were persistently extending the scope of the practice, to negotiate more substantial obligations covering a wider range of matters.

5.3.4 The form of obligations

As noted earlier, obligations could take several forms. They could involve a land conveyance to a public agency; or a developer could undertake to carry out works; or a financial payment could be made to a public agency by a developer. Increasingly, obligations involved some kind of financial burden to the developer. However, the scale of this burden cannot always be identified from records of agreements, as it may be more convenient for the developer to undertake the works directly. If so, a local authority will seek some form of assurance that the works will take place to an appropriate standard. Local authorities may prefer this arrangement for ideological or financial management purposes. Developers may prefer it because the work is then undertaken by their own labour force to their own timescale.

Where the developer undertakes highways, sewerage and drainage works in this way, it is usual for the local authority to require a performance bond to be provided as a safeguard with respect to timing and quality of works. It also acts as a security in case a developer goes into liquidation. Case 19 illustrates such bond arrangements.

Case 19: Marshall Lake Road and Oakenshaw Road, Solihull

Development type: B1 offices

Developer: Sears Men's and Children's Wear plc

Proposal: outline application for development of B1 business units with associated car-parking, service area, landscaping and road improvements

Sears were required to construct road improvement works and a new traffic roundabout for their development. The cost of the roundabout was estimated at £350 000.

They were required prior to the commencement of works, to procure a bond as a guarantee of good performance of the works. The value of the bond was to be £150 000 for which Sears paid £3000.

The bond value was to be adjusted according to changes in the Retail Price Index if the works were not started by the second anniversary of the agreement.

Upon completion of the works, Solihull as Highway Authority, were to issue a Completion Certificate. For a period of 12 months after the date of the Completion Certificate, Sears were liable for making good any defects in materials or workmanship. From that date also, the value of the bond was to be reduced to 10%, remaining in force for the period of maintenance.

Local authorities saw the bond as a means of ensuring that the works were completed to their satisfaction. The Wandsworth engineer expressed the matter succinctly. The borough council are able to guarantee completion of works:

in the end because we've got the bond. Because they want it [the highway] accepted. ... We've got something over them. ... Otherwise, you haven't got anything, you've got no control over them.

In the case of major highways works such as those required at Bishop's Cleeve (Case 1 in Chapter 1), each phase of the highways scheme was bonded separately in order to reduce the overall burden on the developer. Where the developer contracted the work out, a tender list of contractors might be agreed with the local authority. Developers were also required to provide bonds to cover sewerage works, as in the Church Langley development (see Case 11 above).

Where the local authority undertook highways works, as was the preferred option in Newcastle and Harlow, then financial payments to the local authority were made. With local authorities who had Direct Labour Organizations, the work may be given directly to them. In Wandsworth's case, the Annual Contractor selected by the Competitive Contract Tendering process undertook such work. Where local authorities put the work out to tender, a list of suitable contractors will be agreed with the developer.

Local authorities vary in their approach to collecting payment. In Harlow, the payment for highway works is made prior to the commencement of works. Solihull and Newcastle adopt the same procedure. In Wandsworth, though agreements contain provisions to invoice a developer monthly, these provisions are rarely used when the amount is £100 000 or less. The management of these payments and the monitoring of physical works is discussed further in Chapter 7.

Land conveyancing either involved outright transfer to the local authority, typically at minimal or reduced land values, or a dedication of the land surface for use for public access. In this latter case, the original owner retained the land interest. Land transfer was common for the provision of open space, community facilities and affordable housing.

Our case study authorities also illustrate different ways of dividing responsibility between developers and local authorities over who should undertake works. This division operated both between local authorities and between different development projects. Solihull preferred developers to carry out highway works in established urban areas as this often involved negotiations with statutory undertakers which could prove to be expensive and time-consuming. All agreements requiring developers to undertake highway works placed the responsibility for dealing with statutory undertakers with the developer. Though willing to undertake highway works, one developer stated that local authorities did not provide adequate support in dealing with statutory undertakers (now the utility companies).

On the other hand, Solihull's engineer argued that, where there were a number of interested parties, the local authority should co-ordinate the works:

The Renaissance Area – partly it's improvements of existing works and partly it's new road. And it goes through some different landownerships and a similar number of developers ... or a very busy BR line. All sorts of complications like that which in practice would be impossible ... for a single developer to do. ... I mean you need to widen a road on both sides and you need land off this person and land off that person. Now if this person wants to develop a year before that person does, when do you actually get the works done? And what happens if the other changes their mind? Because there is substantial public benefit we think that in this case where there are such problems we'd be able legitimately to use highway CPO powers. Not to help the development but to get the bits of highways through which we think are necessary as Highway Authority to get through.

A primary concern for local authorities is that the highway works are completed to a satisfactory standard. Hence local authorities always supervise the design and construction of highways works and are paid for this by the developer. The major concern for developers is to ensure that the highways are completed before the development is ready. Some developers expressed a preference for carrying out highways works themselves as they would have greater control over the timing of works.

On-site sewerage works are typically undertaken by the developer. Off-site link sewers may be constructed by the developer or the water company and its agent. The same considerations regarding satisfactory completion that apply to highways works also apply to sewerage.

Landscaping and open space provision are typically the province of the developer. The provision of other facilities varies with the nature of the development obligation and the extent of the developer's contribution. Thus crèches, public toilets, and the Notre Dame Convent community facility in Wandsworth (see Case 14 above) were all on-site and hence constructed by the developer. Developers only made a 25% contribution to community facilities on the Church Langley development, Harlow (see Case 11), and responsibility for construction lay with Harlow Council.

We found that developers commonly undertook works themselves, even where off-site works were involved. This affects the calculation of the financial costs of obligations. The Grimley J. R. Eve *et al.* (1992) study found relatively small sums involved in actual financial payments, as noted in the previous section, though these were increasing. However, local authorities were increasingly prepared for the developers to undertake the works themselves. The local authorities could avoid constraints on public capital projects, and for developers, the work was often a valuable addition to their portfolios. Clearly, however, the cost of obligations to developers includes these direct works, as well as direct financial payments.

Variation by development conditions

In Chapter 3, it was argued that type, scale and form of obligations were likely to vary with various attributes of a development, for example, the nature of a project, the type of developer and local market conditions. The difficulty in examining this aspect resulted in only limited evidence on patterns of variation in the studies reviewed in section 5.2. We encountered similar data problems, particularly with respect to the type of developer. In contrast, it is relatively simple to classify agreements by land use involved.

Table 5.11   Negative obligations by development type

	Rs	Of	Rt	HC	Ag	Mx	In	Mn	O	Total
Number of agreements	61	9	7	7	5	13	5	3	22	132
Development control administration	4	–	–	–	1	1	–	–	1	7
Controlling development	10	4	5	2	1	8	–	2	3	35
Control after development	62	8	17	13	8	14	4	1	19	146
Agreement modification	1	–	1	1	–	–	2	–	1	6
Total no. of obligations	77	12	23	16	10	23	6	3	24	194

Key: Rs = Residential; Of = Offices; Rt = Retail; HC = Hotel, catering, leisure; Ag = Agricultural activity; Mx = Mixed use; In = Industry; Mn = Minerals; O = Other.

This shows that obligations were most commonly associated with residential projects, but their incidence was considerably lower than in the other studies discussed.

Forty-six per cent of all agreements associated with negative obligations were for residential projects. The majority of these obligations related to occupancy restrictions. Retail, hotel, catering and leisure projects generated considerably more obligations than agreements, indicating the complexity of some of these projects. Our data did not classify development projects by scale of project or by type of developer. Nevertheless, our impression was that negative obligations could be negotiated with large or small projects and many types of developers, in line with the findings of other studies.

Residential projects are less dominant when it comes to positive obligations. Agreements with such obligations constituted only 36% of the total of agreements with positive obligations. However, 47% of all obligations were linked to residential projects, indicating the range of obligations negotiated in individual residential agreements (see Table 5.12).

Table 5.12 Positive obligations by development type

	Rs	Of	Rt	HC	Mx	Ag	In	Mn	O	Total
Total no. of agreements	41	13	22	7	19	2	2	2	13	121
Highways	59	19	17	7	15	–	2	1	7	127
Sewerage and drainage	32	8	–	3	5	–	–	–	–	48
Landscaping and open space	40	4	14	2	16	2	2	–	3	83
Parking	4	1	4	3	3	–	–	–	3	18
Community facilities	8	–	3	1	7	–	–	1	–	20
Conservation and restoration	3	2	–	1	–	–	–	–	–	6
Social policy	2	2	2	4	1	–	–	–	–	11
Other	7	3	–	1	4	–	–	–	2	17
Total no. of obligations	155	39	40	22	51	2	4	2	15	330

Key: Rs = Residential; Of = Offices; Rt = Retail; HC = Hotel, catering, leisure; Ag = Agricultural activity; Mx = Mixed use; In = Industry; Mn = Minerals; O = Other.

Retail schemes, mixed development projects and office projects also generated a considerable number of obligations. This data is significantly affected by the large proportion of such projects in Wandsworth. These were typically associated with a range of obligations. Most of the social policy obligations negotiated related to such non-residential projects, as did the parking obligations. Sewerage and drainage obligations, in contrast, were primarily associated with residential projects

Behind these figures, and drawing on the evidence of the cases reported here, it is possible to suggest that the negotiation of positive obligations continues the pattern initiated in the 1970s. Positive obligations are most likely to be negotiated on larger greenfield residential projects, and linked to substantial commercial schemes, whether in redevelopment or greenfield locations. Given that the majority of such schemes are developed by relatively sophisticated developers, investors and retail companies, it is a likely hypothesis that most agreements containing positive obligations are negotiated with developers who are knowledgeable about, and skilled in, negotiative practice.

5.4 CONCLUSIONS

The evidence from our research thus confirms many of the tendencies found in the research reported in section 5.2. Two authorities, both in metropolitan areas, had been negotiating agreements in a systematic way since the 1970s. A third metropolitan district, with a much weaker local economy, was beginning to use agreements for a wider range of issues. Both county districts, one a former new town, were developing coherent strategies towards negotiating obligations. In all of them, there was a tendency to negotiate an increasing range of obligations, to expand the number and range of positive obligations sought and to introduce more complex packages of negotiations.

Two pressures were particularly evident in the trends identified; the difficulty of funding public facilities and services, from roads to sports fields, without private contributions; and the widening scope of the fields of impacts which a project was seen to generate. As a consequence of both, obligations addressed a range of off-site as well as on-site issues. Most obligations related to highway and landscape/open space matters, but community and social considerations were successfully secured, against both on-site and off-site. Further, the relationship between a development scheme and the obligations secured often rested on an argument about wider impacts rather than the immediately evident impacts of a project.

The value of agreements in securing development obligations was seen by those involved in our case study authorities to be as follows:

1. they were clearly seen to attach to the site which was the subject of the agreement;
2. they committed all those with an interest in the site over time;
3. they provided a contractual basis for the transfer of land, the payment of money, or the undertaking of works (this applied to positive obligations only);
4. they were seen by both *developers* and *authorities* to be more effectively enforceable than a condition;
5. positive obligations helped *developers* co-ordinate with other developers and landowners; a contractual basis was helpful in sharing obligations;
6. they also helped *planning authorities* co-ordinate action among several developers and landowners;

7. agreements were more effective in securing long-term control over the management and maintenance of public facilities in private buildings; and over the subsequent occupation of affordable housing;
8. they indicated an additional commitment from developers;
9. they reduced the likelihood of an appeal.

So, while the disadvantages of conditions are sometimes exagerated, it is clear that both planning authorities and developers value the contractual format with its emphasis on negotiation. The detailed views of developers are discussed further in Chapter 6.

Combining all the evidence from recent research, it seems fair to conclude that, by the early 1990s, the negotiation of development obligations had become routine, especially for larger projects. Because of the lack of any systematic recording of agreements and obligations, and the difficulty of attempting this, trends in the use of agreements, in their range, scope and form, and their variability between development types and developers, can still only sketchily be perceived. What seems clear, however, is that the negotiation of positive obligations is not merely related to the buoyancy of market conditions. The practice helps to sort out some of the problems associated with complex redevelopment projects or projects with adverse local impacts. It also becomes increasingly necessary as the burden of dealing with the impacts of development on physical and social services is increasingly pushed onto developers and as there is greater consciousness of a wider range of environmental impacts.

The local authorities in our case studies were not merely developing a negotiative routine. They were actively considering how best to provide explicit policies to guide the practice. This meant that they had to clarify their rationales for the practice and consider how to express these in policy statements in development plans. Chapter 6 reviews the rationales for negotiating obligations generally, and in relation to government policy and legal judgement, before discussing how our five case study authorities developed rationales and policy guidance for their practices. Chapter 7 then explores the problems local authorities faced in the management of the negotiative process.

NOTES

1. In addition, there have been some studies undertaken by postgraduate students which expand our knowledge of practice, for example, Pears (1989), as well as a number of case studies of development control practice which make reference to agreements (for example Glasson and Booth, 1992).

2. Firstly, the total number of planning decisions includes advertisement provisions and householder applications where agreements are unlikely to be involved. These represent around a half of all planning decisions. Secondly, records of agreements reached are often incomplete and some are never concluded. Thirdly, agreements concluded under related legislation were left out of the studies. As our research shows, agreements under section 278 of the Highway Act 1980 were particularly significant.

3. Such an obligation is, however, not specified in section 106 (i); see Chapter 4.

4. See the West Midlands Structure Plan 1982 and the West Midlands Strategic Guidance (DoE, 1988a).

5. Our data excludes the Development Corporation's area.

6. This number represents the number of agreements for which contents were identified. There were at least another 40 for which contents were not traced, and others whose existence we suspected but no details could be discovered. Our figure may thus be only four-fifths or less of the total number of agreements signed in these authorities in these years, although the discrepancies were evenly distributed between authorities.

7. Tewkesbury consolidated its approach in its Rural Housing Policy statement.

8. See DTp, 1989, 1991, 1992.

6

THE PURPOSES AND RATIONALES FOR AGREEMENTS

6.1 INTRODUCTION

Chapter 5 has described the increasingly sophisticated scope, content and form of development obligations. In this chapter, we explore the purposes behind this negotiation of obligations. As we argued in Part One, the practice of negotiation attracts continued controversy because of conflicting views and confusing interpretations as to the purposes for which it is legitimate to pursue such practices.

In Chapter 1, we argued that the purposes for which development obligations are used can be reduced to three broad rationales:

- rationale 1 which is concerned with the implementation of planned development;
- rationale 2 which focuses on the impact of development;
- rationale 3 where the developer is seen as having a duty to return some of the profit from the development to the community.

These rationales refer to the arguments made to justify a planning obligation, not to the content of the gain or advantage itself. Obligations such as improvements to a highway, a community hall in a development scheme, a wildlife reserve, a public sculpture or other work of art, commuted car-parking payments, contributions for child-care provision, and the inclusion of social housing in a development project, may be justified by more than one rationale. This is one reason why classifying obligations is so difficult.

It is also important to emphasize that the crucial difference between rationale 1 and 2 is not whether the obligation is related to the site of the proposed development, or is off-site, or whether it is positive or negative in form, but whether the need for, and the precise nature of, the obligation required is inherent in the nature of the development itself. Both developer and planning authority will expect specific attributes to be provided, such as access roads or landscaping. In designating a site for a large housing estate, a local planning authority is likely to set out in the development plan the infrastructure and facilities needed to service the development. If there are insufficient public funds available to build the infrastructure and facilities, developers may have to contribute to the provision of these planned projects before they will be granted planning permission to develop the site. We would place this in rationale 1. On the other hand we would place in rationale 2 the situation where the development plan did not attempt to predict in advance all the specific social costs of future development projects and left this to be negotiated project by project. In both cases the essential justification is the social costs which would otherwise be imposed on the community in the form of poor quality development, congested roads and overcrowded schools.

Rationale 1 therefore focuses more on the development itself rather than on the impact of the development. The emphasis is on the site and the physical form that the development is to take. In this respect, rationale 1 can be linked to what Loughlin (1980) has termed the architectural/engineering model of the planning system, where the goal of planning is the orderly arrangement of physical resources. In contrast, rationale 2, by focusing on the impact of the development, inevitably moves away from the site itself. It also tends to encompass the social, environmental and economic consequences of the development. It involves a shift in perspective from how to make a development work in its own terms to how to accommodate a development within a wider area. While the rationale requires there to be a well-reasoned connection between a project and its impact, this rationale has far more potential for justifying development obligations, depending on how far the formula can be stretched to include what some might see as very tenuous and vague impacts.

Loughlin (1980) saw this kind of purpose as reflecting a social cost model of planning, as it required the developer to internalize social costs by paying to alleviate those which otherwise would be borne by neighbours or the community at large. Here an important distinction must be made between the alleviation of those costs and compensating the community by providing other planning advantages. The alleviation of the impact is a much more attractive and legitimate approach as the planning problem or objection is removed. In the case of compensation, the adverse impact will still take place but will be seen to be justified by a balancing advantage. Environmentalists see dangers in this approach as tantamount to 'paying off' those who have to live with a polluting development rather than reducing the emissions (Cowell, 1993).

The important difference between rationale 2 and 3 is that, in the case of rationale 2, the development obligation is the means by which the development is made acceptable. This is the basis upon which the obligation on a developer may be justified. With rationale 3 the justification is not that the development will create social costs but that there is a duty on the developer to provide some of the profits derived from the development as a contribution towards community development objectives. In this respect, rationale 3 can be linked to what Loughlin (1980) described as the social needs model, where the planning system can be used to redistribute resources in favour of disadvantaged groups. However, we would suggest that the more significant argument in the present circumstances is that the private sector has a responsibility to contribute to a community's environmental and social objectives as an alternative to a strong public sector and high taxation. It is possible to square the circle, in the context of British law, if the absence of such contributions is seen as a material consideration and, as such, a reason for refusing planning permission for what is otherwise acceptable development. In this way, the test of acceptability in British courts can be extremely flexible. However, so far, while the courts have held that, in granting permission, regard can be had to contributions even if they are not strictly necessary to make the development acceptable in planning terms, they have not expressly held that development can be refused where the only objection is the lack of planning gain. Yet as, as we explained in Chapter 4, this can result in practice where there are two rival developers. Also, it would seem that, in the case of affordable housing, a failure to provide an element of affordable housing in a residential development may be taken to make the development unacceptable.

There is an area of overlap between rationales 2 and 3 or at least what can be described as a fuzzy distinction between the two concepts. The more the notion of 'impacts' is stretched, the nearer it becomes to a form of development charge. For example, while it can be argued that private housing developments can in certain circumstances create a need for affordable housing and that industrial development justifies calls for child-care provision and special training, the linkage is often very artificial. Even with infrastructure such as roads, where there may be a clear causal connection between the impact of the development and the obligation, the developer is sometimes called upon to contribute more than is strictly proportionate to the actual impact of the development. The Church Langley development in Harlow is a case in point (see Case 11 in Chapter 5). Secondly, when the contribution takes the form of a monetary payment based on the scale of the development (a kind of impact fee as in the **Crest Homes plc [1994]** case), it evolves into a kind of local development charge, though there remains in principle a critical difference between charges for adverse impacts and charges on developers profits. Indeed our own research suggests that all three rationales are jostling together in contemporary practice in Britain in the 1990s.

In this chapter, we explore that practice. We first examine how government policy has sought to clarify the justification for obligations. Government policy and its application in planning appeal decisions significantly frames the negotiative practices of local authorities and developers. We then examine how the local authorities in our case studies justified their policies and practices. This is followed by comment on the views of developers, drawn from those involved in the cases we examined and our general interviews. A significant trend was towards clearer statements concerning policies on obligations in development plans. We conclude with a review of the approaches used by our case study authorities in expressing their policies on development obligations in their plans.

6.2 GOVERNMENT POLICY AND MINISTERIAL DECISIONS

6.2.1 Tests of the reasonableness of obligations: Circular 16/91

British government policy since 1979 has always ruled out rationale 3 and been opposed to any form of local development charge. Circular 16/91 reaffirms this policy by ruling that

> Unacceptable development should never be permitted because of unrelated benefits offered by the applicant, nor should an acceptable development be refused permission simply because the applicant is unable or unwilling to offer such unrelated benefits (DoE, 1991b, para. B7).

However, as we point out above, the confusion and ambiguity as to what is acceptable and unacceptable development and what are related and unrelated benefits, both as a matter of law and policy, means that the issue is not as clear-cut as it might seem. Also the circular accepts that private developers should be prepared to pay for public facilities where the need for these facilities will be created by the development. This was made explicit by Sir George Young's statement in the House of Commons when steering the new clause 106 of the Planning Compensation Bill 1991 through Parliament. The Minister stated that:

> A planning gain would do more than merely provide facilities that would normally have been provided at public expense. It would provide facilities that the public purse could never have afforded ... members believe that there is no reason why the public sector should provide all the schools, community centres and infrastructure.[1]

The legal doubts about undertakings to pay for such facilities on land away from the site have largely been removed by the amendments to section 106 which provide for obligations requiring sums to be paid to the authority. As we pointed out in Chapter 4, the statute does not address the problem of the circumstances in which the private sector should be asked to provide such facilities, but Lord Justice Evans in the **Plymouth [1993]** case (see Chapter 4) appeared to accept that planning obligations could be used in this way when he stated that:

> The statutory provisions now reflect the political objective of permitting the greater use of private capital for what are described as 'off-site infrastructure costs' which formerly were borne by the public sector alone. Hence the increasing prominence of 'community benefits' and 'planning gain' (p. B86).

The old circular 22/83 (DoE, 1983) argued that planning gain should only be required where it was reasonable for the developer rather than the taxpayer to provide the facilities. This additional test of the need for private subsidy in determining whether a planning obligation is necessary has been dropped by the new circular. This test was probably otiose, as the need for private subsidy in substance turned on whether the need for public facilities would be caused wholly or substantially by the development. This restated the other tests of reasonableness. Yet the dropping of this test underlines the government's acceptance of the principle of private subsidy of public works.

As long as the private financing of public facilities can be seen as the means of making the development acceptable in planning terms, it stops short of rationale 3. The focus of circular 16/91, as with the earlier circular, is on the relationship between the benefits and the permission which is to be granted. Circular 16/91 sets out five tests as to whether it is *prima facie* reasonable to seek a planning obligation from an applicant for planning permission. These five tests of reasonableness are whether what is required:

(1) is needed to enable the development to go ahead, for example the provision of adequate access or car parking: or

(2) in the case of financial payment, will contribute to meeting the cost of providing such facilities in the near future; or

(3) is otherwise so directly related to the proposed development and to the use of the land after its completion, that the development ought not to be permitted without it, e.g. the provision, whether by the applicant or by the authority at the applicants' expense, of car parking in or near to the development, of reasonable amounts of

open space related to the development, or of social, educational, recreational, sporting, or other community provision the need for which arises from the development; or

(4) is designed in the case of mixed development to secure an acceptable balance of uses; or to secure the implementation of local plan policies for a particular area or type of development (e.g. the inclusion of an element of affordable housing in a larger residential development); or

(5) is intended to offset the loss of or impact on any amenity or resource present on the site prior to the development, for example in the interests of nature conservation. The Department welcomes the initiative taken by some developers in creating nature reserves, planting trees, establishing wildlife ponds and providing other nature conservation benefits. This echoes the Government's view in *This Common Inheritance* (Cmnd 1200) that local authorities and developers should work together in the interest of preserving the natural environment (DoE, 1991b, para. B8).

Tests (1) and (2) can be seen as coming within rationale 1 as the emphasis is on 'enabling the development to go ahead' and the focus is on the site or its immediate surroundings. The implication is that there exist clear criteria as to how the development is to be implemented. The examples given of access and car-parking also reflect traditional physical planning concerns about traffic and amenities.

In contrast, tests (3) and (5) are directly concerned with the impact of the development once it has been implemented and are therefore classic examples of rationale 2. Test (3) echoes the then planning minister Sir George Young's hope (Young, 1992) that the private sector will provide public facilities. On the one hand, it gives a wide interpretation of the social costs of the impact of development by including a wide range of community facilities in the examples of facilities which are so directly related to the development that the need arises from the development. The circular also makes clear that the facilities can be off-site. On the other hand, the test is only concerned with alleviation and does not extend to compensating for the impact of the development. Test (5), however, makes use of the language of compensation by holding that it is reasonable to seek to offset the damage caused by the development to any amenity or resource already on the site prior to development. Yet rather strangely it is only concerned with compensating for on-site damage. So together these two tests combine on-site and off-site impacts, and alleviation and compensation techniques.

Test (4) is the most enigmatic as it harks back to the old concept of mixed development which was one of the types of planning gain endorsed by circular 22/83. The way the test is drafted indicates that mixed development, such as offices with housing, can be sought not only when it is needed to secure an 'acceptable balance of uses' but also where it is needed to secure the implementation of local plan policies for a particular area or type of development. In the latter case, the circular appears to be stating that the obligation becomes necessary simply because it is a means of achieving a local plan policy. The only example given is the inclusion of an element of affordable housing in a larger residential development. As indicated already, this can be seen as a shift from rationale (2) to (3), in that the implementation of a large residential housing estate is likely to create the need for affordable housing only in very particular circumstances. It simply may not solve an existing need for that type of housing. Where permission is granted for housing on a site which is not designated for housing (the 'exceptions' approach), this can be seen as violating the principle that unacceptable development should not be permitted because of unrelated benefits offered by the applicant. Where the application is for housing on land which, according to the local plan, is suitable for housing, the seeking of an element of affordable housing could violate the principle that acceptable development should not be refused simply because the applicant is unable or unwilling to offer such unrelated benefits. Yet there is a clear physical relationship between the affordable housing and the development proposal, since both the affordable and the other housing are usually all on the same site. So on that count the provision of affordable housing is potentially a material consideration as discussed in Chapter 4. Also, permission for housing development which does not include an element of affordable housing could be refused on the grounds of competing needs; i.e. there is a need for affordable housing and granting permission for general housing reduces the amount of land available for affordable housing. However, it will not normally be possible to state with any certainty that, if permission is refused, the land will be used for affordable housing.

Even if the obligation passes one of the five tests of reasonableness, the circular also states that what is being required must be fairly and reasonably related in scale and kind to the proposed development. Otherwise, if developers' obligations go beyond what is needed to meet the impact of their developments, the obligation has aspects of a local development tax or even bribery.

6.2.2 Recent appeal decisions

While government policy undoubtedly leaves room for interpretation, the right of appeal from a refusal or conditional grant of permission to the minister, gives the minister and his/her inspectors the opportunity to set out how that policy is to be applied in practice. Only a few decisions go to appeal.

One of the primary purposes of negotiating obligations is, of course, to avoid an appeal. Nevertheless, these appeal decisions help to flesh out government policy and practice. A selection of the most important of these decisions are published in journals and in a series called *Planning Appeals Decisions*.[2] Inspectors cannot themselves make policy but they have to interpret and implement Government policy and are close to the current thinking of the Department of the Environment.

The provision of open space for public recreation on or near to a development site has been taken into account in several cases by inspectors. In one case, permission for housing was granted on appeal where there was a unilateral undertaking to create a new village green.[3] As is often the case, this could have been justified under several of the five tests but it is closest to test (4) as it represented a mixed development in accordance with the village plan which, although not a statutory plan, had been the subject of public consultation. Residential development has also been granted because the theoretical loss of amenity land was balanced by an undertaking to provide open space.[4] On the other hand, the inclusion of a country park in a large residential development, while accepted as reasonably related to the development in the light of the **Plymouth [1993]** judgement, was found not to provide for an appropriate balance of uses in line with the guidance in circular 16/91 or to justify the housing component of the scheme.[5] This shows that even when in law an obligation may be a material consideration, if it falls outside stated government policy, it will be given little weight. The main distinction between this decision and the village green decision would seem to be that the country park was not specifically designated in any plans.

The decisions also reveal a similar difficulty in determining when undertakings to restore or maintain listed building are sufficiently related to a development proposal to be taken into account. In granting permission for a golf course in the site of an old country estate, the inspector took into account an undertaking to use the profits to fund a 20 year programme of repairs to some nationally important listed buildings.[6] This last decision has since been upheld on a challenge in the courts (**South Oxfordshire CC [1994]**). In contrast, an undertaking to restore an old vicarage did not decisively influence an inspector's view of the planning merits of a case in determining an application to build a supermarket, as it was not seen to relate directly to any planning problems associated with the development.[7] There does not appear to be any way to distinguish the two decisions. It may be that some inspectors consider that the concept of **enabling development**, by which the profits from one development are used to carry out other desirable development, is separate from the policy towards planning obligations. This is dubious, as undertakings or agreements are usually employed to ensure that the development is enabled. The better answer is that obligations should not be sought in such circumstances, but that, if offered, they may nevertheless be material considerations (see the discussion in Chapter 4). The creation of new moorings has been held to be extraneous to applications to build houses even though a policy to seek new moorings was set out in the local plan.[8] Also it has been held that, where profits from a development would be used for a new building and a library for a university, this was not relevant as it was not a material consideration.[9] The funding of health care and/or future hospital permission in the health authority area has also been held not to be a planning matter.[10]

There are several ministerial decisions where undertakings to provide infrastructure have been found to come within the tests of reasonableness of circular 16/91 (DoE, 1991b). A striking example is where an outline application for comprehensive development included a new by-pass linked to a motorway.[11] There have, however, been cases where inspectors have held that local authorities have been wrong to seek contributions to infrastructure. In one case,[12] the Cherwell District Plan stated that contributions would be sought for the cost of dualling a road from developments which would significantly increased the traffic on that road which was already carrying traffic in excess of its design capacity. The council interpreted 'significant' as a 5% increase or more. The inspector concluded that 5% was an arbitrary, but not unreasonable, threshold and was to his knowledge used by other highway authorities. The council were only willing to grant permission for development if the applicant completed a section 106 agreement under which they would contribute to the cost of road dualling if the traffic generated from the site and adjoining land added more than 5% of traffic flows at the peak hour. The inspector on appeal concluded that dualling of roads was not so directly related to the proposed development and its use after its completion, that the development should not be permitted without it. Although he did not specifically refer to test (3), he was clearly applying it. He came to this conclusion on the basis that the traffic generated by the development which would use the road was small, the road was only overloaded at peak times, and in any case most of the traffic had been generated by other development which had largely not had to contribute to the proposed improvements. The inspector also concluded that the contribution did not fairly and reasonably relate in scale to the benefits from the proposed development, as the developers might have to pay for 9% of the cost even though the traffic likely to be generated from the appeal site itself would contribute only about 3% to the traffic volume. This case illustrates the difficulties a highway authority faces trying to get several relatively small developers to contribute where a road is already overloaded as the result of previous developments and the general expansion in traffic. Further, if the 5% trigger is used, contributions can be avoided by subdividing the land into small development sites which generate less than 5% of the traffic load.

Similar problems can arise when local planning authorities try to get developers to contribute to the cost of schooling. In a case concerning the

London Borough of Hounslow, the council had an informal policy that a deficit of 200 places in the borough triggered the seeking of planning obligations for the provision of additional school places from any development that would yield over 30 children.[13] In the case in question, it was agreed that the proposed development would yield at least 62 primary school children. The inspector concluded that it was legitimate to seek a contribution to infrastructure where a development would impose undue strains upon it. However he thought that the approach of the council was somewhat arbitrary and hence unfair. An approval before the 200-place trigger had been reached would escape having to make a contribution and it was unclear whether, if the deficit was made up, subsequent developers would be exempt. He therefore concluded that the decision did not meet the requirement of fairness emerging from circular 16/91 (DoE, 1991b). He was also concerned that the monies would not be used for the development of a specific school. The inspector stated that:

> A general contribution to the authority's capital budget, particularly in the absence of a formally and fairly applied policy, is not in my view, directly related to the development.[14]

In both this case and the Cherwell one, the inspectors considered that the strain on the infrastructure was not yet so great that permission should be refused. Yet, unless public money is spent on new infrastructure, future developments might have to be refused. This could be seen to penalize later developers unfairly and the strict application of circular 16/91 means that the problem will not be solved by the infusion of private money. Overall these cases show that while inspectors do their utmost to apply government policy, there is still confusion and inconsistency arising from that policy.

6.3 THE APPROACH OF THE FIVE STUDY AREAS

Local authorities and developers have to carry out their negotiations in the context of the latest court judgements on the scope of planning obligations, the government's latest policy pronouncements and a continuous flow of appeal decisions by inspectors. While this context constrains the outcome of those negotiations, its opaqueness gives all parties considerable flexibility. Our research shows how five local authorities operated. The period of our study ranges from the mid-1980s, when local authorities were still operating under circular 22/83, and extends to 1991, just when the more liberal circular 16/91 was published. As Chapter 5 suggests, some of our case study authorities were already moving towards and beyond circular 16/91 in their practice. Yet very few of these cases were challenged by way of appeal.

As noted in Chapter 5, the rationales adopted by the authorities varied considerably.

That adopted by Solihull closely resembled rationale 1, in that there was a deliberate policy only to use obligations as a means of enabling a development to take place. Their approach also paid close attention to government policy. Officers emphasized to us that they would not attempt to negotiate 'extraneous' benefits or what was termed 'planning gain'. The head of the planning section explained:

> My definition [of planning gain] is things that are not strictly necessary or related to a particular development proposal. So, for example, I wouldn't see improvement in the off-site drainage or off-site highway network that are geared towards the needs of the particular development – I wouldn't see that as planning gain. I wouldn't see it as planning gain if we construct a roundabout to produce a suitable access to a Tesco superstore. Although strictly that has to be done by a planning agreement, and therefore, in those terms some consider it to be planning gain. I would consider it to be planning gain if in return for granting consent to Tesco's, they would build us a nice indoor sports stadium four miles away – free, gratis and all part of the package. That's my definition.

Solihull's approach normally led to obligations related to the physical design and nature of the development itself. In cases where development would increase the amount of traffic on highways which had already reached saturation point, the authority would normally require certain improvements and contributions before allowing the development to go ahead. The precise amount of the contributions to highway improvements was geared to the amount of passenger traffic that the development was forecast to generate. This was calculated on the basis of the size of the development. Similar simple methods were used for other kinds of obligations.

The approach adopted by Solihull also had elements of rationale 2, in that they attempted to alleviate the impact which development would have off-site. In the case of the redevelopment of Solihull cinema site (Case 13 in Chapter 5), the developer was required to make commuted payments to cover the cost of additional car-parking which would be needed.

Tewkesbury had more consciously adopted an impact approach to development obligations and so fitted within rationale 2. They were particularly concerned to offset and protect the general impact of an accumulation of developments on the environment of their historic town. The concern was not only with the impact of development on infrastructure such as highways and drainage, but also the need for wider community and civic facilities. This was justified on the grounds that development ought to help create a better community and environment.

As the principal planning officer explained:

> We see development as having pluses and minuses. We don't see it as completely beneficial. It's got to be carefully assessed and steered and cajoled.

We see here a widening of planners' objectives. While they are still concerned with enabling development to take place, they are also trying to assess the overall impacts of the development and, if possible to minimize the costs to the community and increase the benefits. The principal planning officer argued that:

> Planning gain is not just strictly the infrastructure that is necessary – the roads or the drains. Without it, it would not take place. But it could also have wider consequences both in the terms of traffic flows generated elsewhere in the network, wider infrastructure consequences in terms of upgrading provision elsewhere or contributing to thresholds – also wider social and community implications as well. As regards the large new areas of housing, more pressure on facilities which are on their threshold anyway – in terms of sports centres, community facilities. Implications such as that which I think should be taken into account by planning gain.

It is significant that, at the date he was making this statement, this approach went much further than official government policy. Yet it very much foreshadowed the reformulation of government policy to be set out later in circular 16/91.

No precise method of calculation was employed in Tewkesbury and obligations and benefits tended to be tailored to particular developments, except in the case of social housing where there was an expectation that, in a housing development, there would be a one in ten ratio of social housing to the remainder of the housing development (see Case 18 in Chapter 5). Instead Tewkesbury employed a consultant to advise on what they could legitimately secure from developers and whether the proposed development would be able to bear the cost of the provision they sought

The Harlow planners also took an impact approach to obligations and similarly saw the role of the local planning authority as:

> to intervene in the market to ensure that the community benefits from the development ... and that any additional cost [to the community] should be offset in some way.

Harlow took a wide interpretation of the objectives and goals of the planning system and the scope of the obligations sought was accordingly broader and extended to socio-economic matters. For example, Harlow had a policy of expecting child-care facilities and training opportunities (see Case 17 in Chapter 5). This could be classified as a radical version of rationale 2. In the case of child care the Economic Development Officer argued that:

> An increase in [office] employment will increase the demand for child care, particularly among women returners – and employers should contribute towards providing that child care.

As with training, the justification was that the new developments would generate a need for employees with children and that the developer therefore had a responsibility to try and ensure that the local labour force could get those jobs:

> if there is a change from blue collar to white collar ... a trend caused by the private sector in an area. If we are not in the business of refusing changes of use from industry to office, then in order to enable that to happen we ought to be ensuring that they are contributing to training or retraining to assist the local labour force to get accessible jobs.

The connection here between the development and the obligation sought is stretching the concept of impact. In terms of circular 16/91, the local authority would have to argue that the need for training arose so directly from the development that the development ought not to be permitted without provision for that training, see test (3). Both the need for child care and training are also outside the traditional definition of **material considerations**. However the recent decision of the Court of Appeal in the **Mitchell [1994]** case discussed in Chapter 4 shows that the courts are prepared to extend the ambit of material considerations to social matters such as the need for affordable housing. In this respect, test (3) in circular 16/91 includes social, educational and other community provision among the needs arising from development which should be met. Child care and training could come within such needs.

Harlow planners did not generally employ any precise formulae for calculating the scale of obligations sought. Significantly they were considering trying to get developers to open up their books to enable them to assess the amount of profit that the development was likely to make in order to calculate the scale of the obligations.

Wandsworth, like Solihull, saw the primary justification for seeking obligations as the need to enable development to take place. However, they were also concerned with the impact of the development and the need to replace community facilities that might be lost if the development went ahead (see Case 14 in Chapter 5). In this regard, like Harlow, they took a broad view of planning objectives and used agreements to provide a wide variety of community facilities. For example, in the case of Battersea Power Station, they negotiated an employees' crèche and employment and training requirements (see Case 7 in Chapter 5). While they took a wide view of the scope of planning, the fact that the community facilities sought were incorporated into the development itself would suggest that they came within rationale 1. Rationale 1 is also suggested by their practice of preparing development briefs. These set out in advance the requriements needed in a particular area. In most cases which we examined, what was eventually negotiated did not depart substantially from that brief. There was however one important case concerning Roehampton Vale where, in a departure from the development brief, an undertaking to pay £30 000 to replace open space was negotiated (see Case 20). This showed some movement to towards rationale 2. Again there was no precise method of calculating obligations, what was required was set out in the development brief and tended to be based on the scale of the proposed development.

Case 20: Roehampton Vale, Wandsworth

Development type: retail

Developer: ASDA

Proposal: superstore

According to the development brief the site (owned by Smith's Industries plc) was to remain industrial. This reflected Wandsworth's concern to retain industry in the borough. It also reflected the engineer's view that any use which led to more traffic using the site would require major highways works. The superstore proposal contravened the development brief, though it was acknowledged that there was a need for retail facilities in that part of the borough. The agreement required that Smith's relocate to another site nearby. That part of the agreement was never fulfilled. The site was later sold to Kingston Polytechnic.

ASDA agreed to pay Wandsworth to carry out the major highway works. That payment covered the cost of design, supervision and construction of the temporary and permanent works listed in a schedule attached to the agreement. The total costs of the works was estimated at maximum to be £3 712 000.

Finally in the case of Newcastle, it seems that it is only recently that there has been much negotiation of obligations. This reflects the lack of growth pressure in the area. Most of the agreements which created positive off-site obligations related to highways and car-parking (see Case 21).

Case 21: Hollywood Avenue, Newcastle

Development type: Retail

Developer: ASDA

Proposal: outline application for erection of retail superstore and car-park

The developer was required to make highway improvements as the site was on a junction with the Great North Road.

The highway works included construction of two roundabouts, approaching arms to the roundabouts, filter lane, pelican crossing and guard-rail.

Newcastle were responsible for the design and construction of the highway works to be paid for by the developer. The agreement does not specify the cost of the works. Instead the developer is to pay all expenditure incurred by Newcastle City Council.

These conditions did not seem to be planned out in advance and the agreements appeared to be worked out on a case by case basis. This approach was described by the Newcastle city planner:

> As situations arise through the assessment of the development proposal and its impacts evolved through consultation, liaison, discussion.

So Newcastle's approach could be described as a modest version of rationale 2. However, in the early 1990s, Newcastle reviewed its approach, developing it to extend beyond infrastructure provision to social and community facilities and environmental benefits (Newcastle CC, 1993). The new policy states that, where highway improvements are needed, the developer has to pay the whole cost. This is justified on the grounds that the council could not provide the funds. This was so even though it seems likely that in such cases, other developers would benefit from the improvements. Newcastle were also aware that, in some instances, there was insufficient return on investment to cater for all these costs:

> The requirements for developers set out in this plan will be applied fairly throughout the City. However, there are some locations where land values and profit margins are low or indeed where public support

is necessary to allow development to take place. If a developer seeks to have normal planning requirements relaxed so as to make a scheme financially viable, then the City Council may request from the developer a financial assessment of the scheme and may also carry out its own assessment (Newcastle CC, 1993, p. 178).

It will be noted that none of the authorities studied justified the obligations negotiated solely as a charge on developers' profits, i.e. rationale 3, though it seemed to be generally accepted that the level of profit was relevant. However, the lack of precise calculations as to the level of obligations needed meant that, in several instances, in our research and in appeal cases, the obligation exceeded what was strictly necessary to enable the development to take place or to alleviate the impact. In such situations, it is arguable that obligations have the nature of a charge on the development for general community purposes (for example, the **Plymouth [1993]** case discussed in Chapter 4). It has already been noted that Tewkesbury expressly considered the profits to be made in calculating the value of an obligation.

The research commissioned by the Department of the Environment (Grimley J. R. Eve *et al.*, 1992) and the Scottish Office (Durman and Rowan-Robinson, 1991) was in both cases primarily designed to find out whether the scope, contents and terms of planning agreements were consistent with Government policy. The DoE research concluded that

Analysis of the requirement embodied in the survey agreements confirms that authorities are generally adhering to the policy guidance, as set out in the 'test' [of reasonableness in Circular 22/83 and Circular 16/91] (Grimley J. R. Eve *et al.*, 1992, para. 13).

The Scottish Office research equally concluded that generally planning authorities would seem to be observing both the spirit and letter of the circular, but the research significantly pointed to what it saw as:

a changing climate of opinion about the acceptability of recovering part of the betterment unlocked by a grant of planning permission for the benefit of the local community (Durman and Rowan-Robinson, 1991, para. 27.10).

In particular, the research concluded that benefits included in agreements did not always pass the necessity test, i.e. whether they were required in order to 'enable the development to proceed' and that in the case of collective infrastructure obligations, there were difficulties in ensuring that the developers' contribution was proportionate in scale.

In our own studies, all the authorities were quick to deny accepting what were generally termed 'inducements' and we equally found no evidence of obligations which could be seen as bribes or 'entry fees' to local authority areas, despite the fears noted in Chapter 1. However, like the research for the Scottish Office (Durman and Rowan-Robinson, 1991), our case studies and the appeal cases suggest that planning authorities are beginning to seek community benefits where they may not be strictly necessary in order to enable the development to go ahead and that there is only a limited attempt to work out the *scale* of contributions needed (see sections 4.6 and 6.5 and Chapter 5 on community facilities). In several cases, the contributions were made to provide facilities which did not arise wholly or substantially from the development itself. Certainly circular 22/83 (DoE, 1983) made no reference to the kind of community facilities which were commonly the subject of obligations by our authorities. The terms of the circular 16/91 (DoE, 1991b) are of course much more specific about the subject matter and expressly refer to roads and community facilities. Even so the new circular still leaves in doubt the propriety of negotiating for obligations to alleviate or offset impacts generated by development if the obligations are not directly related to the project in question, an approach which was taken by several of the authorities we studied. Also, the social policy obligations relating to crèches and training not only stretch the definition of material considerations, but can be seen as insufficiently related to come within the terms of the circular. So, while circular 16/91 can be seen as consolidating and legitimating established practice, we would argue that it still falling behind the actual practice of local planning authorities.

6.4 THE PERSPECTIVES OF DEVELOPERS

Our research found that developers generally regard planning obligations as the 'price' that has to be paid to secure a planning permission.[15] Though some developers interviewed argued that general taxation should be the source for financing physical and other infrastructure, most developers acknowledged the effect of central government restraints on local authority resources. As one stated:

> Fundamentally, the problem of local government finance is at the heart of the endeavours to maximise planning gain because certain authorities see it as a means of getting capital which they cannot get from this present central government.

In this context, some developers consider 'planning gain' as an informal development tax or as a 'price' to be paid. Thus

> We contribute because we need a planning permission. Every day is money.

So 'delay', as one developer commented, is the local authority weapon. For developers, delay in the granting of a planning permission can have two consequences. Firstly, an opportunity to benefit from a rising property market may be missed. Secondly, the overall cost of the development may rise because the period for which interest charges have to be paid is extended. Avoidance of delay becomes a primary objective for developers, particularly in rising property markets.

All developers and property consultants interviewed accepted that the provision of physical infrastructure directly related to a development would need to be paid for as part of the development costs. No objections in principle were raised to the provision of highways, sewerage, drainage or parking. Obligations relating to open space and landscaping were also uncontroversial. The primary purpose of entering into these obligations is to enable a development to go ahead. Such provision is made to meet the 'operational requirements' of the development in that without such planning obligations it would not be able to proceed. One commercial developer was succinct in his summation of such provision:

> The infrastructure – you ought to pay for it. If you want to carry out a development, you'll have to pay for it. That's yesterday's news.

A property consultant reinforced this opinion by observing that developer contributions towards the provision of physical infrastructure were a long-established practice:

> The stuff that developers are providing historically have never been provided by local authorities anyway. The provision of infrastructure off development, off new residential development – basic roads and drainage – is pretty well-established practice anyway. That goes far further back than ten years ago. And that's essential.

If most developers found the obligations relating to the provision of physical infrastructure to be acceptable, in a few instances developers viewed the scale of provision as excessive. Certain obligations were held to be beyond government guidance, in that they exceeded the requirement on local authorities to secure contributions which were in keeping with the scale of the development. A retail developer stated his willingness to provide obligations covering highway improvements necessary to enable a superstore development to go ahead. But he argued that a cash contribution to Solihull Council, to be used in the event that further highway improvements were necessary following the completion of the development, was 'excessive'. Instances of obligations of this nature were found in two other cases.

In the search for a permission, some developers are prepared to go further than merely providing physical infrastructure. Contributions for more than physical infrastructure were also made, as we have shown in Chapter 5. Harlow DC were able to secure 25% of the total cost of community facilities and sites for affordable housing from the consortium of developers on the Church Langley development of 3500 dwellings (see Case 11 in Chapter 5). Similar provision was supplied by developers at the Bishop's Cleeve site in Tewkesbury (highways, sewerage, drainage, open space, commuted sums for open space maintenance, footpaths, primary school site and playing fields (see Case 1 in Chapter 1). In Wandsworth developers of all types provided riverside walks in conformity with local authority requirements (for example, see Case 12 in Chapter 5). Child-care facilities were provided at three superstore developments in Wandsworth, for example, see Case 6 in Chapter 5. This follows a precedent set by the retail developer at Clapham Junction who offered these facilities. In Harlow again, the local authority secured provision of child-care and training facilities on a business park development (see Case 17 in Chapter 5). All of these planning obligations extend beyond the, albeit ambiguous, guidance of circular 22/83 and are not necessary to the progress of the development. This raises the question as to why developers agree to such provision.

What is critical in these cases was the need to secure a speedy planning permission to take advantage of a rising property market. A riverside walk was provided by Petmoor Developments for a residential development at Albert Wharf in Wandsworth despite the developer's general antipathy to 'planning gain' in order that the permission would not be delayed and the benefits of the housing boom of the late 1980s be secured. Similarly Sapcote and Co. refurbished a school hall on the redevelopment of the redundant Convent of Notre Dame school site in Wandsworth (see Case 14 in Chapter 5). ARC, the developers of Harlow Business Park, agreed to provide nursery and training facilities on site, though their provision was less than that sought by the local authority.

Developers did express concern at the legality of provisions. The developers of the Convent of Notre Dame site, when questioned about the legitimacy of Wandsworth's requirement for provision of the community facility, observed:

> We weren't very happy about it but the market in the 1980s was booming. We went along with it. We were happy to go along with it to get the permission.

These cases illustrate the willingness of developers to extend the scope of obligations provided in order to remove an obstacle to the granting of a planning permission. In these cases, the obstacles were the local authority's social policies.

For all of these developers, the securing of a speedy permission was the important consideration. The trade-off was between the costs of delay and an appeal and the costs of the obligation. Developers expressed an aversion to entering the appeals process even where they felt that the requirements were illegitimate. Inevitably, given the delays in the appeals process, it is more expensive to go to appeal than to make contributions to fulfil local planning authority requirements. As one developer observed:

> If the local authority ask for more than we are prepared to offer we have two choices. We just say no and forget the site or we go to appeal. We would go to appeal more often if we didn't have the planning system often stacked against us. So planning gain is often the result of us feeling unsafe with regard to the development plan system in terms of taking sites to an appeal. So it's a matter of minimising maximum losses – is a nice sort of way of looking at it.

There is no reason to doubt that the expense of an appeal can be exorbitant, particularly if the appeal is lost. The amount provided in planning obligations was in most cases less than the costs of delay.

In some of our cases, developers made offers that went further than simply seeking to 'ease' the granting of a permission. The objective here, as one property consultant stated, was to secure a permission on a sensitive site. Three cases came to light in our research, each with different planning considerations.

The first case was a proposal for a superstore development on a site adjacent to a residential area. The application was accompanied by an offer to provide a community centre to be included in a planning agreement. Newcastle City Council, the planning authority, considered that the proposed development was unsatisfactory in view of its impact on the surrounding environment – in other words it would constitute 'overdevelopment' of the site. This application was refused permission. A modified proposal was accepted, though no community centre was provided.

A proposal in Harlow for 3716 sq. m of office space by the side of the River Stort on the edge of the urban area was accompanied by an offer of contributions to child-care facilities at the rate of 50p per 0.09 sq. m (£20 000). Planners and members considered that the proposal represented overdevelopment of the area and the application was refused.[16]

Development of a superstore in an unnamed London borough led to a more satisfactory conclusion for the developer. The site identified was 20 acres in size and in use as a sports facility for London Transport employees. The developer proposed to purchase the site and use ten acres for the development. The remainder was to be refurbished as a sports/recreational facility and transferred to the local authority. The proposal was approved.

The developer detailed the thinking behind the strategy:

> There's a package, so perhaps what was just a muddy football pitch that London Transport Sports Club used every other Saturday – the public never had any access to – we now allow the public to use it six days a week. London Transport use it on the seventh day. And it can be used that way because it's now got all sorts of all-weather facilities – floodlighting etc. We get our store at the same time. So the public benefits. There is more intensive recreation use and the community-at-large gets something. Now that sort of proposal is us promoting it. We know we're never going to get planning permission for a super-store alone – let us think of a package which will appeal to a local authority and a local community.

Regardless of whether the community or the local planning authority secured benefits, development obligations such as these clearly constituted, in the developers' mind at least, inducements intended to secure a grant of planning permission which otherwise was unlikely to be secured. A commercial developer confirmed that the use of development obligations was considered a satisfactory way of securing a permission.

> I think the social conscience of the developer does have limitations if he can make a profit. You do need a system which controls his desires. That system is in place. All you've got to do is not stultify that develop-ment system in terms of developments taking place. That should take place to the benefit of the community and the individual concerned.

These examples illustrate how developers can use planning agreements and development obligations as a tool in advancing a project. Evidence from our research suggests three ways in which developers can use plan-ning agreements to advance their proposals.

- a means of making up the shortfall in local authority resources in order to enable a development to go ahead;
- a means of speeding up the granting of a permission;
- as an inducement to secure permission which otherwise would be refused.

From the developer's point of view, the rationale for the obligation was less important than its cost in relation to the benefits achieved, a speedy decision avoiding the costs of an appeal. They were therefore prepared in some instances to offer *inducements* even though the local planning authority might refuse to accept them as irrelevant to the planning issues or out of line with government policy.

Generally, developers were concerned to know in advance about what obligations were expected so that they could ensure that the costs were taken into account in calculating the profitability of the development. However as we will see, developers had mixed feelings about the inclusion of policies on development obligations in development plans.

6.5 THE USE OF THE DEVELOPMENT PLAN

Our research indicated that the policies on development obligations had usually evolved pragmatically. It was only after established practices had become settled that these policies were set out in development plans. It was significant however that all the authorities we studied included such policies in their emerging plans. Development plans help to give political legitimacy to the policies of local planning authorities as the plans go through public participation. They are usually scrutinized carefully by central government civil servants. The new status given to the plans by section 54A of the 1991 Town and Country Planning Act means that there is probably a legal presumption in favour of the plan (see Chapter 4). There are therefore good reasons for authorities to put their policies concerning development obligations into the now obligatory unitary and district-wide local plans that are at present being processed. Yet, in 'going public' with their approach to development obligations, local planning authorities risk having their development plan policies amended. Objectors to local and unitary plans have the right to a public inquiry to hear their objections and, although the local planning authority has the power to override the recommendations of the local plan inquiry inspector, the publication of an intent to flout an inspector's recommendations could result in the intervention of the Secretary of State. The government has the power to direct that a draft plan be modified or can call in all or part of a plan for determination. In this regard, the 1992 version of Planning Policy Guidance 1 (DoE, 1992a) states that:

> Since the commencement of section 54A, the Secretaries of State have been examining development plans carefully to identify whether there appear to be conflicts with national or regional policy guidance. They will continue to do so and will normally draw the attention of local authorities to those conflicts which do not appear to be justified by local circumstances. If necessary they will make formal intervention ... if no such intervention is made, local authorities may take it that the Secretaries of State are content with the plan at the time of adoption and will attach commensurate weight to it in decisions they make on appeals or called-in applications (DoE, 1992a, para. 29).

So, once the development plan has been formally adopted, in theory it should be the major determining influence on future decision-making in the area. In practice, as pointed out in Chapter 4, it is still unclear whether it authorizes the taking into account of what would otherwise be immaterial considerations.

All the authorities that we studied have used both non-statutory and statutory plans to set out their policies. Although most of their plan-making work precedes circular 16/91 (see Table 1.1), Solihull at first used non-statutory plans to identify what it required to be provided to enable development to go ahead. For example, the Cranmore–Widney Local Plan set out the developer provision which was needed to enable a large residential development to go ahead and also helped to co-ordinate the activities of several developers in the same area. In the case of the Solihull Unitary Development Plan, the policies on planning obligations are similarly closely linked to land allocations in the plan and indicate where development contributions are necessary to enable development to proceed. These policies are not set out in a special section, but the need for obligations forms part of certain key policies. Thus policies on highways and open space involve developers providing highway improvements, car-parking and the provision of open space. Where major development schemes are proposed, policies for contributions are included as part of the policies for the areas concerned (see Figure 6.1).

It is therefore not surprising that few developers objected to the substance of these policies. There were however objections to financial contributions to highway requirements and to the absence of limits on the scale of open space provision. This shows that developers were keen to retain their ability to negotiate with the authority. The local plan inquiry inspector substantially rejected these objections and, quoting circular 16/91 and Planning Policy Guidance 12 and 17 in support, in effect recommended that the scope of the obligations required should be broadened, while at the same time setting out more precisely the standards of car-parking and open space that were needed (Ennis, 1994).

In the case of Tewkesbury, the original practice of negotiating obligations emerged in a very pragmatic and un-coordinated way. There followed a concerted effort by officers to lay down a more systematic policy and a special statement on planning gain was produced. The Principal Planning Officer explained:

> We very much feel that we should give a proper framework to planning obligations and planning gain. As a council we should say this is how we approach it. This is how we relate to the county and other bodies. These are the people and this is the process. We think that we should set that down. There will be a planning gain policy thrashed out through the council. We will publish a booklet saying this is our

POLICY HH7 – COMMUNITY AND SOCIAL FACILITIES

The Council will expect developers acting in concert to provide sufficient social and community facilities as part of the new village to serve the needs of the new community ...

The council will allocate three acres of land on the south east side of Dickens Heath Road in the vicinity of Dickens Heath Farm for the purposes of a local centre ...

4.24 It is envisaged that the local centre might include:

(a) local shops
(b) medical facilities
(c) library
(d) other community facilities
(e) car parking
(f) business

POLICY HH8 – ADDITIONAL OPEN SPACE

The Council will require developers acting in concert to provide, as part of the new village, the area of open space designated in the Plan for recreational use to serve the needs of the new community.

POLICY HH9 – INFRASTRUCTURE

Contributions will be expected from developers to meet all or most of the costs of providing new infrastructure, road improvements and similar requirements generated by the new development.

Figure 6.1 Hockley Heath Parish: specifications for a new settlement (Solihull MBC, 1990)

approach because we think this is the right way to do it ... Our plans will have an implementation section ... The district plan will have a section on obligations that will go borough-wide. So we will properly thrash it out.

The implementation section of the draft local plan for Tewkesbury–Ashchurch justifies private developers having to pay for improvements on the grounds that, by law and government policy, developers have to pay for the direct consequences of their developments. Then a specific policy IMP 1 sets out that provision will be expected for infrastructure consequences in the form of both on- and off-site facilities. Contributions are expected from developers of residential, industrial and commercial sites. The facilities expected include, as well as highway and sewerage requirements, facilities such as sports halls, recreational facilities

and affordable housing. The plan then makes clear that there is no set formula as to how the scale of contributions is to be calculated. The inquiry
inspector concluded that the range of social and community benefits
included in Policy IMP 1 was inappropriate in view of the advice in Planning
Policy Guidance 12 (DoE, 1992b).

> Policies for non-land use matters should not be included in develop-
> ment plans (para 5.6).

In his view, Policy IMP 1 was a means of implementing infrastructure proposals and securing directly or indirectly financial support. He recommended that Policy IMP 1 be deleted and replaced by a statement that
Tewkesbury Council seek voluntary agreements for the provision of necessary infrastructure in accordance with central government policy and
advice. Recognizing that there were substantial infrastructure requirements
necessary for the implementation of the plan, he recommended that the
local authority include a list of requirements, the agencies responsible for
provision, any thresholds which might be exceeded and any problems
which might arise from lack of provision.

Harlow's policy represented the most a priori and deliberate attempt to
use development obligations to achieve wide-ranging planning objectives.
These policies were consolidated in their draft local plan which was put on
deposit in 1990. As we have seen, the policies were intended to secure
cross-subsidization for community benefits from development activity. The
Harlow plan therefore looks for environmental benefits and social benefits
as well as contributions to infrastructure. In this regard, the policies make
an interesting distinction between **planning gain** where developers are
required to enter into agreements and **community benefits** which are
only *expected.* In the case of training and child-care facilities, obligations
are only *expected* (see Figure 6.2).

This suggests that Harlow was aware that they could have been on weak
legal ground in holding out that an application could be refused because of
the lack of community benefits; though it now seems that such benefits
could nevertheless amount to a material consideration if they were offered
(see the discussion in Chapter 4 and particularly the **Plymouth [1993]**
case).

Developers objected to the above policies on the grounds that the training and child-care contributions related to non-land use matters and that
the other obligations conflicted with government policy as they did not
have to relate to the development. The inspector who examined the
Harlow plan agreed with the objectors that the policy on child care and
training was invalid as it did not make clear that contributions were only
expected when they were necessary for the development to proceed
(Ennis, 1994). The inspector, however replaced this and the more general

---

TRAINING AND CHILD-CARE FACILITIES

E12   Due to the increasing demand for child-care facilities and to the changing skills and work patterns generated by new commercial developments, Harlow Council will expect all developers to make a contribution towards the provision of child-care and training in Harlow, or other appropriate benefits, on all proposals which create new employment and enter into agreements under section 106 of the Town and Country Planning Act 1990 accordingly.

IMPLEMENTATION POLICIES

IR2   The District Council will require developers to enter into agreements under section 106 of the Town and Country Planning Act 1990 or other relevant status, for relevant works or other related matters as determined by the District Council, to be undertaken or funded by a developer where they are required as part of a planning permission. Wherever they are prepared, development briefs will indicate the nature of any planning gain.

IR3   Developers are expected to enter into agreements with the District Council to provide facilities, as determined by the District Council, which will provide general community benefits. Wherever they are prepared, development briefs will indicate the nature of any community gain.

Figure 6.2   Harlow Local Plan: Harlow District Council (1990).
Policies on obligations for community facilities

policy on obligations with policies that expected facilities including training and child-care facilities, but only when these were *directly related* to the development as set out in circular 16/91 (DoE, 1991b). While this shows that the government still rejects rationale 3, an inspector is nevertheless prepared to accept that developments can create a need for training and child care and so come within the parameters of circular 16/91. In both cases, the wording the inspector recommended was that contributions were only *expected* rather than *required* and this would seem to apply even to physical infrastructure (see Figure 6.3).

Wandsworth, like Solihull, has incorporated its long-standing practices into its plans and treats these policies in the plan as part of the implementation of development control. Policy DP11 lays down the principle that development will be expected to provide local improvements and additional facilities and then sets out a list of facilities and improvements which in particular will be expected from large developments (see Figure 6.4).

These policies are then spelt out in more detail in the form of development briefs for particular sites and areas. These policies were not issues of contention in the Inquiry into the plan.

For Newcastle, the Unitary Development Plan in its deposit version

POLICY E12 – TRAINING AND CHILD-CARE FACILITIES

5.3.5 I recommend that Policy E12 be deleted and replaced with the following:

E12   Where a commercial development will generate requirements for training and child-care facilities, directly related to that development and not provided for as part of the proposals, the local planning authority will expect the applicant to make a contribution of such facilities in accordance with the terms of Circular 16/91.

POLICY IR1 AND IR3 – PLANNING OBLIGATIONS

11.1.3   I recommend that Policies IR2 and IR3 be deleted and Policy IR2 replaced by:

IR2   Where a development will impose requirements for facilities which cannot be met by means of conditions and which are directly related to that development and not provided as part of the proposals, the local planning authority will expect the applicant to make a contribution to the provision of such facilities, in accordance with the terms of Circular 16/91.

Figure 6.3   Harlow Local Plan: Inspector's recommended modification to policies on community facilities

(NCC, 1993), provides the opportunity to prepare policies on development obligations which centre on proposed greenfield residential development to the north-west of the city. In this area, an allocation for 2500 dwellings, a range of community facilities is to be funded by developer contributions, either within the development area or in surrounding communities. Developer contributions towards 'extensive outdoor recreational facilities' for both the new development and more general needs 'might be appropriate to compensate for losses elsewhere' (p. 193). Developers are expected to contribute to highway works and the provision of environmental assets. The plan then goes on to stress that:

> for such a major scheme, a development and management agreement under Section 106 of The Town and Country Planning Act will be necessary. It will ... establish financial arrangements to secure, manage and maintain the open spaces and recreation facilities created. Parties to the agreement will include the developers, landowners and the City Council ...

Developer contributions will be required to meet directly all capital costs of necessary highway works and to fund other mains services and drainage in accordance with normal practice. Some of these works may fall outside the

---

Policy DP 11

Development will be expected to provide local improvements and additional facilities related to the Plan's policies and appropriate to the location, scale and nature of the development. In particular large
developments should provide, where appropriate:

(a) pedestrian access, amenity space and open areas for the use of the
    public (including a riverside walk) ...
(b) crèches for employees, visitors and shoppers ...
(c) other community facilities ...
(d) public toilets ...
(e) recycling facilities ...
(f) public transport improvements ...
(g) conservation of historic buildings ...
(h) shoppers' car parks...
(i) positive action policies on employment ...

Where appropriate the Council will require the submission of an
Environmental Impact Assessment, or a traffic, retail or other impact study
to accompany proposals for large-scale development.

Figure 6.4   Wandsworth UDP 1991: Development Plan Principles.
Wandsworth LB (1991)

Development Area. Developers will also be required to provide any necessary
social, recreational community facilities, including schools, and to make provision for the continuing revenue costs of management and maintenance of
open space and countryside management (NCC, 1993, pp. 195–6).

This in effect writes a development brief into the development plan as in
the example quoted from Solihull (Figure 6.1). To give added support, the
plan also has a specific policy for the whole Unitary Development Plan area
on *Planning obligations and developer contributions.* This is phrased in
terms of rationale 1 ('requirements to meet the ... consequential needs of
development'), but its content suggests a wider remit.

Our five case study authorities thus reflect in their plans an increasingly
explicit approach to the negotiation of obligations. They show clearly both
the tendency to broaden the range of obligations considered, to stretch the
relation between a development and obligations arising from its impacts, and
to consider the impact of obligation requirements on project viability. There
was a marked shift beyond rationale 1 into rationale 2 in these plans. By 1991,
government policy too had made this shift. However, because of the need to
keep within boundaries set by government policy, the justification for policies
was phrased to avoid straying too far beyond rationale 2. Inspectors, however,
were uneven in their approach to the widening range of policies on

---

POLICY IM5

DEVELOPERS MAY BE REQUIRED TO ENTER INTO PLANNING OBLIGA-
TIONS WHERE IT CAN BE SHOWN THAT THIS IS NECESSARY TO THE
GRANTING OF PLANNING PERMISSION. DEVELOPER CONTRIBUTIONS
MAY BE REQUIRED TO MEET THE INFRASTRUCTURE OR OTHER CON-
SEQUENTIAL NEEDS OF DEVELOPMENT. EXAMPLES OF SUCH NEEDS
INCLUDE:

(a) transport infrastructure, including public transport, highways, car
     parking and facilities for pedestrians and cyclists;
(b) foul and surface drainage and other mains services;
(c) social, recreational and community facilities;
(d) open space and access to countryside;
(e) community woodland;
(f) affordable or special needs housing;
(g) training;
(h) protection and enhancement of the natural environment;

Figure 6.5   Newcastle CC (1993): Requirements for planning obligations and
developer contributions (Policy IM5)

obligations. Some argued for a clear limitation to physical infrastructure.
Others supported the inclusion of social impacts. They, too, suffered from the
lack of clarity in government policy.

6.6 CONCLUSIONS

Government policy has moved substantially towards rationale 2 in that it is
now accepted that developers must contribute towards the cost of providing
infrastructure such as highways and schools, the need for which is created
by the impact of the development. What is still confused is the exact scope
of the community facilities which developers will be expected to provide and
whether it extends to social facilities such as crèches and training. Further,
the policy does not make clear how far environmental impacts must be alleviated or whether they can merely be compensated by the provision of other
facilities. The justification for requiring affordable housing has not yet been
fully spelt out. In consequence, inspectors have difficulty applying the
policies; especially the test of securing an acceptable balance of uses and
its relationship to the legal principles of 'enabling development'. Similarly,
inspectors have problems determining thresholds above which developers will be required to contribute and the scale of contributions. This is of
course compounded by the confused state of the law on these issues
(see Chapter 4).

With this background, many local planning authorities are adopting some form of rationale 2. Others are pushing at its limits both in their plan-making and in their practice of negotiating planning obligations. With the new status of the development plan, most of the dialogue between local planning authorities and the government on these issues now takes place through the process of adopting plans. The new status of plans combined with the powers of the independent inspector to make recommendations and of the government to intervene, mean that this process is crucial in fixing the limits of development obligations.

In four case study authorities for which inspector's reports have been received, support for planning obligations policies has been provided, though inspectors have modified the local authority proposals in line with their assessment of the limits of government guidance.

In Chapter 7 we examine in detail how local planning authorities negotiate and manage development obligations.

NOTES

1. See Hansard Standing Committee F, 16 April 1991, col. 116.
2. These are published by Sweet and Maxwell and are cited as PAD.
3. See [1993] JPL 192.
4. See [1993] PAD 162.
5. See [1994] PAD 150.
6. [1994] JPL 479.
7. [1993] JPL 884.
8. See [1992] PAD 588.
9. See [1994] PAD 293.
10. See [1993] PAD 634.
11. See [1993] PAD 404.
12. See [1993] JPL 969.
13. See [1994] PAD 293.
14. [1994] PAF 293, para. 4.9.
15. We interviewed developers involved with a sample of our cases and included some developers in our general interview survey (see Appendix 1).
16. At the subsequent appeal, the developer argued that the child-care contributions were requirements beyond government guidance.

7

THE NEGOTIATION
AND MANAGEMENT
OF OBLIGATIONS

7.1 INTRODUCTION

As we have shown in previous chapters, there has been considerable discussion and some research on the incidence of agreements and their justification. In this chapter, we consider the issues which arise in relation to the practices of negotiating agreements and their subsequent management. This requires attention to both the micropolitics of negotiation, and a range of technical and administrative matters raised by the challenge of drafting, recording and enforcing agreements. These considerations are important, not merely with respect to administrative efficiency. If negotiating practices are unsophisticated, or legal drafting inept, and if the management of agreements is neglected, then the effectiveness and accountability of the negotiation of obligations through agreements will be called into question. Few studies have given much attention to these issues. Nevertheless, research commissioned by the Department of the Environment (Grimley J. R. Eve *et al.*, 1992) and the Scottish Office (Durman and Rowan-Robinson, 1991) contains some discussion of the way agreements were negotiated.

This chapter is based primarily on our own case study research, along with analysis of recent statutes and case law in sections 7.5 and 7.6. Because of its qualitative nature, our research was able to explore negotiative practice and management questions in some depth. We discuss the main 'players' in the negotiative process, their relative strengths, the sequence of the negotiation process, the legal issues involved in drafting agreements, the oversight of agreements once signed and the issue of accountability. In conclusion, we emphasize the need for a more systematic approach to the management of the negotiation of obligations and make some suggestions about the elements of such an approach.

7.2 THE MAIN PLAYERS

Local Authority: District
Planning Department
Housing Department
Engineers Department
Parks/Landscape Department
Estates Department
Legal Department
Economic Development Department
Equal Opportunities Department
Leisure Services
Politicians

Local Authority: County
Planning Department
Highways Department

Local Interests
Parish Councils
Amenity Groups
Other Local Special Interest Groups

Special Interest Groups
Nature Conservancy Council
English Heritage

Utilities Companies
Water companies

Development Industry
Developers
      development sections
      legal sections
      planning sections

Landowners of sites
Developers/Landowners of related sites
Financial Institutions
Planning and legal consultants to any
      of the above

Figure 7.1   Agencies involved in negotiating agreements in case study districts

The range of agencies potentially involved in negotiating a planning agreement is very wide. Figure 7.1 includes all the agencies encountered in our case studies. Obligations may derive from the interests of different sections of a local authority, from the utility companies, from government departments, special interest groups and parish councils. Within a local authority, several departments may be involved. Developers themselves may be in a complex 'negotiative net' involving other developers, landowners, financiers and sometimes future occupiers. Local authority planning departments may in their turn be faced with competition between development groups offering different packages of obligations. The management of the negotiative process is thus a challenging task, involving many more players than merely a planning official and a developer.

There were significant variations between our case study authorities, and among developers, in how these complex relations were addressed. These variations partly related to the nature of specific development projects. They also varied with the experience, skills, interests and local connections of developers. However another factor was the skill and organization of the local authority negotiators. Further significant factors producing variation were the way the different local authority departments and the utility companies co-ordinated with each other, how officers related to politicians, and the roles available to community groups, parish councils and other 'third parties'. Our case studies show that public and private sector and community negotiators improved their skills in negotiation and their demands over time.

Solihull provides an example of a well-developed technical approach. The Council did not have a strongly integrated corporate organizational structure, but had many years experience of negotiating with developers over large projects. Solihull also benefited from being a unitary authority, able to deal with all highway matters. It also acted as agent for the Severn Trent Water Company. Within the local authority, it was the planners and engineers who were the key negotiators, co-ordinated through the Deputy Director of Technical Services. Politicians' concerns were kept in mind but there appeared to be few direct links made between developers and council members. Parish councils and other interest groups were kept at arm's length. Solihull MBC thus acted as something of a 'one-stop shop' for developers. The only areas of difficulty encountered within the authority related to landscape issues. The Council's landscape architect believed there should be a strategic landscaping brief to give a stronger policy base for negotiating landscape issues. In negotiation, Solihull appeared to take a facilitative, enabling role with respect to development, in some cases acting to assist developers in co-ordinating with each other and with landowners. For the large sites, small area local plans were used to co-ordinate the various claims for obligations. (This approach is illustrated by Case 8 in Chapter 5 and Figure 6.1 in Chapter 6.)

The authority was responsive to developers' timing priorities, moving quickly if necessary. Within the authority, the Legal Department and the Treasurer's Department were only brought in once the policy contents of agreements had been concluded. This caused few problems, since the parties were fully aware of the legal and financial implications of their negotiations. Solihull thus offered a skilled and experienced 'negotiating service'. Its approach was well known among developers working in the area and was clearly stated in its Unitary Development Plan, Solihull's informal policy plans and its development briefs. However, as discussed in Chapters 5 and 6, its agenda of planning objectives pursued through agreements was confined to physical infrastructure and landscaping issues.

Wandsworth provides an example of a seasoned approach to the negotiation of planning requirements. The Adopted Plan of 1984 had required developers of riverside sites to provide riverside walkways through the mechanism of a planning agreement. Like Solihull, Wandsworth benefited from being a unitary authority, able to deal with highway matters. The key negotiators were planning officers. They were able to negotiate the scope of obligations on the basis of advice received from officers in other departments. Wandsworth, too, also thus provided a 'one-stop shop' which informed developers of local authority requirements.

Wandsworth's requirements were set out in a series of development briefs which provided the basis for negotiations. Most requirements related to the provision of physical infrastructure necessary to enable a development to proceed, for example, highways, car-parking, but the planning authority aimed to facilitate development. One developer praised Wandsworth for its approach which, in comparison with other London authorities, was considered 'businesslike'. The agenda for negotiations was broader than that of Solihull covering community benefits as well as physical infrastructure (see Case 22).

Case 22: Clapham Junction, Wandsworth

Development type: Mixed

Developer: Charterhall Properties Civil and Public Services Association (CPSA)

Proposal: superstore, offices, station shopping centre

The core of this development was the St John's Hill site in front of the BR station. Over a period of years a number of proposals had been put forward to develop this derelict site.

Initially Charterhall proposed a superstore development (3716 sq. m) for the site with associated car-parking. The land price meant that the scheme was not viable.

The problems associated with the site development led to the involvement of a second site nearby.

This site – Lavender Hill – was part owned by the CPSA and part owned by British Rail. The CPSA had bought their site with a view to erecting new headquarters. Their difficulty was that they had agreed to relocate the vendor – the London Electricity Board (LEB).

Charterhall's strategy was to take an option to buy all three sites operable only if all three were purchased. The aim was to do a land swap so that the superstore was built on the Lavender Hill site and the CPSA HQ on the St John's Hill site. The LEB were to be relocated in the station approach shopping centre.

The agreement contained obligations covering highway works, crèche provision, public toilets, open car-parking space and management and maintenance obligations.

The defining feature of **Newcastle's** approach to negotiation was the lack of development pressure in the region. This is reflected in the small number of obligations negotiated. Though Newcastle is a unitary authority and the planning department acted as a focus for negotiations, the approach to negotiations was *ad hoc* and reactive during the period of our research. The requirements were not specified in advance and agreements were worked out on a case by case basis. With the exception of obligations covering community facilities negotiated as part of landscape restoration following minerals applications, the agenda for negotiations was limited. However, the planners changed their approach in the early 1991, partly in response to development interest in the green belt between the northern edge of the city and the expanding airport. This location was made more attractive by the completion of a Western bypass round the conurbation, now the A1, with a dual carriageway link to the airport. In response to developer interest, particularly from European Land, a developer-trader company, the city consolidated both its approach to negotiations on projects in this area, and to development obligations generally, into the polices included in the deposit draft of its Unitary Development Plan, as discussed in Chapter 6.

Tewkesbury's approach contrasts with these cases. Many more participants were actively involved in making claims and sometimes negotiating over individual cases. This was compounded by the council's position as a second tier authority, highway matters being dealt with by Gloucestershire County Council (see Case 1 in Chapter 1). After losing an appeal in the early 1980s and with it the possibility of contributions to highway impacts, the county's policy has been to negotiate independently using section 33 powers. The county's engineers visited Tewkesbury Borough Council once a week to review applications. However, the borough found their negotiating position constrained by the demands for contributions made by the county. Tewkesbury had a further problem; the power of the parish councils. The authority's councillors were primarily independent and gave considerable weight to local opinion. Councillors were also concerned to act legitimately and avoid inducements unrelated to planning issues. This allowed some parish councils to take the initiative in promoting community benefits sought from developers as compensation for accepting development. In a few cases, involving both large developers and local landowners, there were direct negotiations between developers and the parish councils. In addition, community members sometimes expressed views at odds with those of the parish councils. Tewkesbury officers (and members) were thus caught between the county engineers and parish pump politics. They also faced pressures from bodies such as the Nature Conservancy Council, which pressed for obligations to be placed on developers, although these arose as a by-product of concern about specific applications.

The council's work on a planning gain policy and an infrastructure planning strategy, combined with its approach to the Tewkesbury–Ashchurch Local Plan (see Chapters 5 and 6), reflected an attempt to sort out these complex relationships. Within the Borough Council, several departments had an interest in negotiations over planning agreements, reflecting the council's various policy concerns. The key players were the planners, engineers, the Housing Department and the solicitors. All were involved in negotiating over principle; with the solicitor responsible for drafting the final agreement. Applications came into the planning department and were then circulated to other departments. The authority was small, and people knew each other well, which facilitated co-ordination. The effort to produce a more coherent policy towards development obligations was in part motivated by a concern to improve co-ordination and in part by an attempt to 'capture control' of negotiations from the County Council and the parishes. The aim was to clarify both what could legitimately be demanded and to establish co-ordinated procedures for negotiation. Nevertheless, both the engineers and the Housing Departments sometimes negotiated directly with developers, the latter with respect to affordable housing.

The engineer's concerns were with landscaping and, most particularly, drainage issues. The engineer acted as agent to Severn Trent Water Company and had responsibilities under Land Drainage Act powers. Until the Water Act 1989, local authorities acted as agents for Water Authorities. Since that Act, Water Companies have used 'management contractors'. Management contractors may be individual local authorities, a consortium of local authorities or a private contractor. Effectively, according to the principal solicitor of Thames Water Utilities, management contractors, chosen by tender, are agents of the Water Authority. The effect of this change was mixed, according to Tewkesbury's Drainage Engineer:

> In terms of actual power ... to discuss and liaise with developers it does affect us strategically but it doesn't take us out of strategic considerations because as agent for Severn Trent we are still involved in the mechanics of assembling or assessing what the sewerage needs are. It just takes away the financing.

Given the frequency of flooding in Tewkesbury, the engineer had produced an *Infrastructure Planning Strategy* in 1985. This was later incorporated into the Tewkesbury–Ashchurch District Development Plan (see Chapter 6).

Despite these efforts at formalizing policy, and the informal 'corporate' tradition within the authority, the co-ordination of claims for obligations in Tewkesbury was not easy to achieve. This situation allowed developers to play one claim off against another. This became very obvious in the debate over the Tewkesbury–Ashchurch Local Plan. While this proved a useful vehicle for clarifying policies and stabilizing community demands within a legitimate framework, it also led to disputes with developers, one of whom took a case to appeal offering unilateral undertakings, because his site had not been included in the plan (see Case 23).

Case 23 Tewkesbury–Ashchurch Local Plan

Development type: residential

Developers: J.S. Bloor Ltd and Bovis Homes Ltd, and Robert Hitchins Ltd

Under the First Alteration to the Gloucestershire Structure Plan (1987), Tewkesbury BC had to meet a residential allocation of 2700 dwellings between 1986 and 2001. A local plan was drawn up to cover the allocation. When the deposit draft was approved in October 1990, this allocation (taking into account windfall allowances and modifications to the First Alteration) had shrunk to 1129 dwellings. That allocation was to be satisfied using three sites adjacent to the Tewkesbury urban area. Two of these sites were under the control of Bloor and Bovis.

Robert Hitchins, the third developer, found that its sites, some distance from Tewkesbury, were only allocated for residential development post-2001. Hitchins made applications to develop both sites. When appeals were launched for both sites, Hitchins submitted unilateral undertakings to cover highways, landscaping, community facilities and social housing. A contribution of £400 000 was made to Ashchurch Parish Council.

Hitchins also objected to the residential allocations at the Local Plan Inquiry offering an alternative strategy to meet the Structure Plan requirements which incorporated his sites to the exclusion of those preferred by Tewkesbury.

Bovis and Bloor agreed to provide highways, provision for nature conservation, landscaping and open space (and maintenance), recreational, neighbourhood and community facilities, drainage, sewerage and plots for affordable housing (see Case 18). As with Hitchins, a gift of £400 000 was made to Ashchurch Parish Council

This situation is still unresolved (November 1994). Following the Local Plan Inquiry, the Inspector added a further 300 dwellings to the Stonehill–Wheatpieces allocations (see Case 18). Tewkesbury have accepted this as a modification to the plan, but Hitchins will object. The Borough Council is faced either with holding a second inquiry or facing judicial review.

Harlow, with its radical politics, had a clear strategic approach to its wide-ranging planning objectives. The District Development Plan (1990) included the council's policy principles regarding 'planning and community gain'. But these were not developed into a corporate strategy or into a system of development briefs for major sites, or principles for what should be provided on individual sites. As a result, each case was negotiated on its merits. Because of the Council's broad policy orientation, a range of interests within the council were involved in negotiations over planning agreements.

The practice of negotiation often involved initial pre-application advice. Once an application was received, the developer and planning officer negotiated over 'heads of agreement'. At this stage, the planning officer referred applications to other departments, notably the Parks Manager, the Economic Development section, the Equal Opportunities section and the Housing Department. There then sometimes followed direct negotiations over these issues with the relevant officers. Councillors took a strong interest in negotiations, seeking to pursue social objectives while avoiding inducements which could not be justified in planning policy terms. As one planning officer commented:

> I think it's fair to say that the council members to a fair degree don't like to ... feel they are being manipulated by developers in terms of having developments thrust upon them which they don't particularly agree with. They like to feel they control the development of the town.

In one instance, in the later 1980s, an application from the retail chain, Sainsbury, was refused despite 'inducements' as it was seen to threaten the vitality of the town centre. The council's decision was overturned on appeal.[1] Reflecting councillors' priorities, as much attention was given to social housing, economic development and equal opportunities issues, as to landscaping and infrastructure issues. Harlow involved its legal advisers in negotiations at an early stage, a necessity given that they were often seeking contentious contributions. The council acted as agents for Thames Water and for Essex County Council with respect to highways, which gave the council a stronger control over the total package of contributions than was available to Tewkesbury. In theory, the county identified what needed to be provided, and the district negotiated the details. However, problems sometimes arose in these county–district relations. One issue of contention related to who would carry out the works.

Harlow's preference was for the work to be done by its Direct Labour Organisation (DLO), Essex County Council preferred to put the works out to private contractors. The turning point for Harlow was the Edinburgh Way project (see Case 25 below). Until then Harlow had been able to secure highway work for their DLO. Now the county highway authority requires developers to undertake all works.

In Harlow, therefore, a strong policy orientation to the practice of planning gain had not led to a stable, consistent approach. This was partly because the council was pushing at the margins of what it was legitimate to negotiate under current legislation and national advice, and partly because a number of benefits negotiated were called into question due to the economic recession, notably those relating to child care. It also reflects the council's approach. Harlow viewed physical development within the context of its overall social and economic development strategy. It did not have a clear strategy for what it wanted to see on particular sites, in terms of development quality and specific facilities. Taken together, the result was some uncertainty for developers, as well as for the council. The council lost appeals on contentious cases (see Case 17 in Chapter 5); and several agreements did not survive the property slump.

Meanwhile, as public expenditure constraints bit still further, other departments in the council began to look to developers' contributions to help pay for community facilities; leisure services were cited as an example. Yet despite the council's commitment to the community, there was no indication that community interests were involved in negotiations over developers' contributions, in contrast to Tewkesbury, although community consultation was a feature of local plan preparation. This in part reflects different social and geographical circumstances, with Harlow being a compact town without parish or town councils.

The relations between the various **players** in the negotiation process thus varied from authority to authority. Faced with the complex co-ordination which negotiating an agreement often requires, certain parties tended to emerge as **mediators** or **brokers**. Planning officers, consultants and developers were all candidates for this role. In our case studies, this role was typically played by planners and engineers (for example, in Solihull, Wandsworth, Gloucestershire County Council, Harlow) (see Case 2 in Chapter 3). The efforts directed at developing a planning gain policy in Tewkesbury can partly be understood as an attempt by the planners and engineers to take over such a strong brokerage role. Tewkesbury planners argued that, in producing an internal report on planning gain to assess the requirements entailed by the residential allocations included in the revised Gloucestershire Structure Plan, they set the agenda for developers (see Case 23 above). But examples were also found where developers acted as brokers (for example in Bishop's Cleeve where developers co-ordinated 31 landowners during the negotiations of the agreement (see Case 1 in Chapter 1) and Clapham Junction (see Case 22 above)).

7.3 THE POWER RELATIONS OF NEGOTIATION

Who then 'controls' the negotiation process? Power and the potential for control lie in the parameters of the negotiation process, the 'rules of the game', and the specific resources which each party brings to the negotiating table. Many of the national representatives interviewed in our study described the negotiation of agreements as a time–cost bargain, within which a negotiated settlement was preferable to an appeal. This was implicit in discussions with the case study authorities. As a result, very few agreements or negotiations in which agreements were discussed went to appeal. Thus while national policy and legal judgements set general parameters of reasonableness in the bargaining process, developers and local authorities could negotiate whatever was convenient to them.

In negotiating development obligations, developers are trading-off the time spent in negotiations and the cost (both direct and indirect) of the obligations against the time and cost of going to appeal, and the benefit to them of the planning permission. Durman and Rowan-Robinson (1991) found that some developers complained about the delay involved in negotiating obligations. Our studies showed that the time taken, and the relative advantage of a negotiated solution over an appeal varied between projects, developers and time periods. Generally, our interviews with developers suggested that the burden of obligations was considerably less than the cost of time lost, particularly where interest payments on loans to finance projects had to be met. This was acknowledged by the director of a financial institution whom we interviewed. He observed that:

> The balance of power depends on market conditions. It favours the local authority in a boom. Delay is the local authority weapon. The developer's power lies in the option to disinvest.

Those parties making claims for obligations bring regulatory resources to the bargaining table, while developers bring financial resources. The extent of these resources varies with market conditions and a developer's particular circumstances. This point was well understood by a chief planning officer of an inner London Borough interviewed in our research:

> I think the main reason we are so effective is the DoE are so badly organised through the Inspectorate and take so long to organise appeals. Quite honestly, I think most of what we achieve would be killed off overnight if the developer knew they could get an appeal decision within two or three months. But as you can't get an appeal decision inside a year most of what we achieve is based on the cost to the developer of waiting a year. And, of course, the uncertainty of not knowing whether they'll get consent at the end of that ... we are benefiting from the system working imperfectly.

It has sometimes been suggested that obligations could only be expected and demanded in buoyant market conditions. The problems in Harlow with developer liquidation in 1990/92 appear to support this point, as does the low level of agreements negotiated in Newcastle until the late 1980s. However, if, following rationale 2, it is established that developers should pay the full cost of the impacts they generate, and if market conditions do not allow this, then it is clear that, where permission is granted without alleviating or compensating for all impacts, a developer is receiving a form of subsidy. In the example from Newcastle (see Case 3 in Chapter 3), a normal requirement for car-parking paid for by the developer was relaxed, as part of the package of subsidies for a scheme.

Three specific resources can increase the power available to the negotiating parties. These are: negotiating skill and knowledge, good contacts and clear, well-grounded strategies. We found that neither side had a monopoly of skill and knowledge. In Solihull and Wandsworth, local planning officers were highly skilled negotiators, with a good grasp of both the political and commercial dimensions of the development process. In Harlow, expertise was being rapidly built up through 'learning on the job'.

Inter-personal networks and contacts were very important in this context, spreading knowledge about expectations and procedures among the parties. Solihull had built up a long-standing working relationship between local authority officers and a number of developers. A similar pattern appeared to be emerging in Tewkesbury although one developer felt left out, and is now challenging the authority (see Case 23 above). But officers could be fobbed off, because of the lack of knowledge about a developer's behaviour in other areas. For example, Harlow was persuaded against requiring child-care provision in a superstore scheme, on the grounds that this would set a precedent, while just such an obligation had been secured in Wandsworth (see Case 6 in Chapter 5). But in many instances, planning interests and commercial interests worked in the same direction (for example in Church Langley, Harlow, with respect to social housing (see Case 11 in Chapter 5), and Clapham Junction in Wandsworth (see Case 22 above)). This inevitably facilitated negotiation.

Where there are two or more developers in competition, this strengthens the hand of the local planning authority; see the **Plymouth [1993]** and **Tesco (Witney) [1994]** cases described in Chapter 4. Two developers were in competition in a case concerning the Tewkesbury–Ashchurch Local Plan (see Case 23 above). However in this case, because Tewkesbury favoured development at the Stonehill–Wheatpieces site, the developers were concerned to get parish council support. Both promised £400 000 for recreational facilities. More significantly, it was the inspector at the local plan inquiry whom they sought to influence. The beneficiary in terms of development obligations would be the local authority and the parish council. The involvement of parish councils in such negotiations is not uncommon. The Grimley J. R. Eve *et al.* (1992) study notes similar tendencies:

Many larger sized development companies are now recognising the importance of involving the local community and other third parties at the pre-application stage in order to secure their support for the proposed development. Inevitably, success in obtaining such support will depend, in part, upon demonstrating that certain obligations can be provided (para. 6.21).

For planning authorities, the power relations of negotiation were not confined to the exercise of regulatory versus commercial power. They were also faced with an increasing number of competing claims for obligations from different parts of the public sector and from the utilities companies. How these claims were prioritized was rarely systematically discussed.

Prior to the preparation of the Tewkesbury–Ashchurch Local Plan (see Case 23 above), Tewkesbury's approach was *ad hoc* and reactive. This was a common feature of all the case study authorities. While development plan preparation allowed the formalization and systematization of practices relating to development obligations (see Healey, 1991b; Durman and Rowan-Robinson, 1991), this did not necessarily lead to the establishment of administrative structures to match.

Solihull's internal organization was informal. Prioritization of claims was achieved by personal contact. As the highways engineer stated:

We all know each other and we talk to each other and if we've got any problems we'll address each other. This is all very informal.

The planning division set the pace for negotiations. Within that division there was considerable variation from case to case and from officer to officer. Solihull's approach was a reactive one in that the council saw itself as an 'enabling' authority, according to the solicitor:

Developers come along and say they want to do this and we say 'All right. We'll look at it and make sure it's done properly.' That's the kind of role we take.

Solihull, as discussed earlier, had taken on a co-ordinating role in the case of the Cranmore–Widney and the West Midlands Renaissance Area developments. This followed from its focus on bringing forward development rather dealing with the broader impacts of development.

Harlow approached development obligations with a strategic orientation focused on negotiating community benefits from development. Councillors took a keen interest in individual negotiations, and several departments came forward to make claims. Though the Harlow Local Plan (1990) had a clear policy on planning and community gain, this had not been worked through into development briefs for key sites which could have created more co-ordination of expectations. The prioritization of claims was unstructured. Applications for development were circulated to officers who returned comments. As a consequence the Head of Planning explained:

> The identified need so far is coming from those departments which came forward first – child care and training ... and the whole of the available money has been directed towards that.

Prioritization in Harlow was achieved on a 'first come, first served' basis. Harlow planning officers recognized that there was a need for a corporate approach:

> We really need a working group which is going to sit down and work out a practice paper on how we are going to treat different types of application – what we are looking for corporately. There's no one place where it is all set down ... We all have a good idea as individual officers what we are looking for but nowhere is it in one place.

The co-ordination of claims for development obligations had, in the past, been a reactive process with local authority departments competing for developer contributions. Items such as highways, sewerage and drainage, landscaping and open space, deemed by the local authority and developer to be necessary to the development, absorbed the major share of obligations provided. Other items were secured inconsistently. This was a reflection *inter alia* of the lack of prioritization by local authorities.

Newcastle had given little consideration to the prioritization of claims until the early 1990s, since their approach had been *ad hoc* and reactive. In the more systematic approach adopted in the 1993 Deposit Draft Unitary Development, the Council indicate all requirements, and then consider how to help out if these cannot all be met in a viable project (see Chapter 6).

Wandsworth used a *de facto* form of prioritization, as a result of the evolution of its approach to contributions. The requirements for the provision of a walkway on riverside sites and off street car-parking were long-standing. To this were added child-care provision in superstore developments (see Case 22 above), employment and training (Case 7 in Chapter 5 and Case 20 in Chapter 6), and then community facilities, linked to the loss of facilities caused by hospital and school closures. However, this process extended the list of requirements. It did not indicate whether some were more important than others.

Thus there was generally little attempt in our authorities to prioritize claims for obligations in advance, although it was understood that highways obligations and water authorities (now water companies) tended to take 'first cut'. Payments to the water authorities are now formalized into statutory development charges since the 1989 Water Act. Beyond this, the different claims in effect competed for attention. Development briefs, if available, provided a baseline for negotiation, rather than a prioritized list. They helped to clarify what was required. As the Wandsworth's borough planning officer observed:

> if there is to be ... bartering (if that is the word), then it ought to be established at a distance in the development brief. It's perfectly clear what the council's seeking and the developers know it.

Our case study evidence tends to reinforce this point. A local authority's negotiating position was greatly strengthened firstly by long-standing and well-established strategies and policies towards obligations; secondly by a clear view on the relative priority of different claims; and thirdly by strong market conditions. Developers, whose objectives relate to making a profit on a specific project and to smoothing the path for future negotiations in an area, have to balance the increasing scale of claims from the regulatory authorities with project costs and likely returns, and their position in relation to their financiers and to landowners. Our interviews showed that whatever their rhetoric, many were quite accustomed to negotiating practice, treating the negotiation of obligations as part of the necessary costs of obtaining planning permission.

7.4 THE NEGOTIATION TIMETABLE

An agreement moves through three main stages:

1. pre-application discussions between a developer and the planning authority;
2. formal submission of the planning application to planning committee approval, subject to agreement;
3. drafting and signing the agreement.

In each of these stages, the agreement is developed further by the parties involved. In general terms, the objectives of the main parties to the negotiations – developer and planning authority (or highway authority) – are to secure, respectively, a planning permission and an agreement. An agreement, when concluded, will be detailed, specifying the obligations imposed on the parties. Each stage involves further 'fleshing out' of the terms of the agreement. As the agreement is developed, the number of actors involved in negotiations can increase significantly – particularly on a large scheme.

7.4.1 Pre-application discussions

Such discussions are normal on major projects (Grimley J. R. Eve *et al.*, 1992) and can take a number of forms. A developer may contact a planning department prior to submission to discuss the proposed application with planners. Then the developer will be informed of any requirements which the local planning authority is likely to make. These contacts cannot properly be termed negotiations in that they tend to involve merely the dissemination of the local authority perspective. Yet, as Glasson and Booth (1992) note in their survey of planning decision times, this stage may be very important, setting the agenda for subsequent negotiations.

Sometimes an outline application will be submitted to 'test the water' as in a case in Wandsworth where an application was refused, but a subsequent application approved subject to agreement. Sears, developers of an office site in Solihull (see Case 19 in Chapter 5), valued pre-application discussions highly. The application received committee approval within a month of submission. The agreement was concluded six months later. In Newcastle, a project on a city centre site with sensitive conservation issues was in pre-application discussion for three years, with the content of an agreement arising quite late in the process.

Where a development brief exists, or where pre-application discussions have clarified the issues, the principle of an agreement and its contents, or heads of agreement, are likely to be well-defined. The brief thus structures developers' expectations. Sometimes an approach by a developer may lead to the production of a development brief to clarify the requirements for obligations. Developers expressed a preference for producing the development brief themselves, arguing that they were more aware of the commercial realities of the market. In general their view was that local authority briefs could be out of date or not relevant to the development proposed One example from our research concerned a hospital site in Newcastle, where the development brief was produced through negotiation with the landowners, but we found no cases where developers had independently produced a development brief.

In large schemes, developers will normally have anticipated some requirements before contacting the planning authorities, either informally or when submitting their application. This is specially so with respect to highways and sewerage matters.

7.4.2 The application stage

When an application is received, it must be formally considered by the local authority. Whatever pre-application discussions have taken place – whether informal or formalized by a local plan or a development brief – this stage involves discussion about the obligations to be secured from a developer. In cases where a local plan or a development brief exists, the developer will know what the range of a local authority's requirements are. In other cases, the planning authority needs to inform the developer of those requirements. At this stage the application is normally circulated to the relevant departments of the local authority, the county council, if relevant, and the utilities companies and other agencies for their observations.

This stage focuses on developing the principles governing the contents of an agreement. Engineers and other technical officers become involved, though their involvement was typically confined to indicating general requirements. Rarely at this stage will such officers be involved in detailed negotiations with developers. Alternatively, the need for an agreement will be identified during discussion of the application.

If requirements additional to the development are identified, they will be expressed by the officers concerned in general terms. Thus the need for highways improvements, for sewerage, drainage, landscaping etc. may be raised. It will be the planning officer responsible for the application who informs the developer of those requirements and the need for a planning agreement. The planning officer then has to secure agreement in principle by the developer to make the necessary provision. The planning officer, or relevant technical officer, will indicate the nature of the provision and provide some indication of likely cost. When agreement is secured in principle, a committee report will be drawn up with a recommendation that the committee be 'minded to approve subject to the conclusion of an agreement'. The report to planning committee will normally include the *heads of agreement* finally reached, with the planning officer's recommendation.

7.4.3 Post-approval negotiation

A planning committee decision will give planning permission subject to an agreement. Negotiation now moves into a new phase, focusing on the details of obligations and legal drafting. However, this stage may involve complex discussions with the various parties who made claims for development obligations, and with the developer. A Wandsworth planner described the negotiating process for the Clapham Junction development (see Case 22 above):

> because of the complexity of the agreement, several aspects were being negotiated at the same time involving planners, engineers, parks managers and social services in a minor way. A lot of co-ordination had to be done. Mostly by me.

Solicitors for both the local authority and the developer played a central role at this stage. In Wandsworth, this stage was expedited by a standardized agreement schedule. Newcastle solicitors maintained a list of what needed to go into an agreement. Developers expressed criticism of local authority practice – complaining that it was too slow. A Newcastle solicitor argued that often developers lost interest once committee approval had been secured. Some developers sent first drafts to local authority solicitors in order (they claimed) to reduce the time for this stage. Local authority solicitors were generally wary of this practice. A Newcastle solicitor explained:

> I prefer to do the drafting because I know what is to be achieved and how to do it. I try to avoid giving the agreement to developers for drafting as they will draft it from their point of view. That means the agreement can be difficult to amend.

On the other hand, the Grimley J. R. Eve *et al.* (1992) study (section 6.25) found that developers considered that delays are caused by the reluctance of local authority legal departments to allow the applicant's solicitor to take the lead in drafting agreements. In Wandsworth the solicitor stated that he was willing to allow developers to draft agreements once a precedent had been established. In Solihull, the solicitor who drafted agreements said that most agreements were based on precedent:

> There is over the years the building up of the system of precedents. We know ... the basic terms for incorporation in the agreement from the legislation. That's OK. And we know what we have to incorporate to make sure that the provisions are effective to do what the legislation says they could do.

Local authority solicitors acknowledged that shortages of staff created problems for them. They also felt, in some cases, that the absence of standardized procedures within local authorities for providing instructions for the drafting of agreements caused delays.

Local practice in our case studies varied as to how far solicitors were closely involved in negotiations from the start. This had the benefit that legal issues could be clearly identified early on. In Newcastle, the solicitor's section tended not to be involved until the final stage. The subsequent negotiations were often protracted as a result. Both Solihull and Harlow reported problems where legal issues had arisen late in the process. Problems arose when a developer's approach to the terms of an agreement raised questions about the validity of the heads of agreement. The Harlow solicitor stated that developers' solicitors sometimes argued that what had been agreed in principle (i.e. the heads of the agreements) went beyond the requirements of government policy:

though the developers and developers' agents invariably will come round and agree, the haggling that then goes on between the various branches of my profession are quite horrendous, It's often very difficult at the end of the day to get the solicitors that are acting for the developer to accept that what the developer has undertaken to do is reasonable and proper. So we are dealing with that problem as well as making sure that the form of words actually reflects what has been agreed between the parties.

What this meant was that the drafting process was slowed down by the retracing of old ground. In Tewkesbury, legal advisers were involved both in negotiating the heads of agreement and in detailed drafting. The planning officer nevertheless maintained overall responsibility, though claiming not to understand the legal document fully. The Tewkesbury solicitor described her role in the negotiating process:

> My primary role is to advise on legal matters and to couch the agreements so that it expresses exactly what has been agreed by the parties, which is why I need to be involved in the discussion so that I can understand what the intention is. I think that my role in the negotiations is sometimes, if I can see what the arguments are on both sides, I might be able to suggest some sort of compromise.

This solicitor described her role as a mediator between the local authority and the developer. Other solicitors perceived their role more narrowly, as merely providing legal opinion and technical drafting skill. Most solicitors, however, thought it would be helpful to be involved in the process earlier. The Grimley J. R. Eve *et al.* (1992) study pointed out that developers considered that much of the delay in drawing up agreements was caused by lack of communication between the planning and legal departments of local authorities.

The negotiation process thus moves through exploratory stages, to bargaining, the striking of a deal, and then to drawing up a technical contract. It is always possible for broader issues to be raised late in the process, and principles of agreement may be shifted over time as a consequence. This raises difficult issues of accountability, especially as it is rare for the contents of an agreement to be formally reported. Negotiations can also be protracted, with considerable delays between the granting of planning permission subject to an agreement and the final confirmation of the permission. This usually takes place at the same time as the agreement is signed.

7.5 DRAFTING THE OBLIGATIONS

7.5.1 The choice of statutory basis for the obligation

Our study revealed a significant variation in the statutory bases for agreements (see Table A1.1 in Appendix 1). As would be expected, all the authorities studied most commonly used section 52 (now section 106) of the Town and Country Planning legislation. This was usually used in combination with section 33 of the Local Government (Miscellaneous Provisions) Act 1982 and section 111 of the Local Government Act 1972. This combination was employed because of the doubts over the legal scope of section 52 and the need to ensure that obligations ran with the land and were enforceable against successors in title. For similar reasons, up to early 1986, Tewkesbury used section 19 of the Gloucestershire County Council Act 1956. Wandsworth almost always relied on section 16 of the Greater London (Special Powers) Act 1974.

In the case of off-site highways, section 278 of the Highways Act 1980 (now as amended by the New Roads and Street Works Act 1991) provides an obvious alternative for local planning authorities who are also the highway authority. However it is significant that this section was often not used or was used in combination with section 52 (now 106). This is probably because there were certain drawbacks with using section 278. Firstly it remains the case that it can only be used by a local planning authority which is also the local highway authority, though a planning authority who is not a highway authority can be authorized to negotiate a section 278 agreement on behalf of the highway authority. Secondly there was no statutory provision that any obligations run with the land and are binding on successors in title. The new version of section 278 still does not expressly provide that the undertaking specifically binds successors in title. However, if any amount due under the agreement is not paid, the authority now has draconian powers to direct that facilities provided by the works, such as means of access to a highway, should not be used, and to recover the costs from any person having an interest in any land which has benefited from the works. Further the authority can declare the amount owing as a charge on such land and register the charge as a local land charge. Nevertheless it is significant to note that these powers are directed at land which benefits from the works. Therefore difficulties in recovering the costs could still arise where there was no direct connection between the works and the land being developed. Therefore highway authorities will still normally seek a bond or guarantee from the developer as security to ensure that the costs are met (as described in Chapter 5). Thirdly there used to be a restriction on the use of compulsory purchase powers to acquire the land needed for the works. We were told by Solihull that this was one reason for preferring the planning legislation. This restriction has now been removed and section 278(4) expressly states that:

> the fact that works are to be executed in pursuance of an agreement under this section does not effect the power of the authority to acquire land by agreement or compulsorily for the purpose of the works.

The main advantage of using section 278 is that, as well as being very specific about the costs that can be charged by the highway authority (this includes all the costs of making the agreement and related orders; including administrative expenses), there is an express power for the agreement to provide that the developer shall pay for the subsequent maintenance of the works. There is no such express power in section 106; though this would be covered by the provision in section 106(1)(d) under which obligations can be created requiring 'a sum or sums of money to be paid on a specific date or dates or periodically'. In this regard, circular 16/92 advises that:

> The costs of subsequent maintenance and other recurring expenditure should normally be borne by the authority or body in which the asset is to be vested and the planning authority should not attempt to impose commuted maintenance sums when considering the planning aspects of development (see para. B10 of Annex B (DoE, 1991b)).

Another advantage to the local planning authority of using section 278 is that there is no provision for the discharge of such agreements, in contrast to the position with section 106 obligations. A limitation of using section 278 is that it only provides for the payment of the costs of the works and so the agreement could not provide for the developer to carry out the works.

The reforms instituted by the Planning and Compensation Act 1991, by providing for positive obligations enforceable against successors in title in section 106 and by closing off section 33 as a mechanism for negotiating development obligations, have done much to clarify the choice of statutory authority. What still remains confused is the relationship between section 106 and section 278. There is a substantial overlap between the two provisions and it is hard to justify there being a choice between two legal mechanisms, with different forms and legal consequences. This confusion is compounded where the highway authority is not the local planning authority granting the permission. Circular 16/91 gives no guidance on the choice of instrument but does state that, insofar as section 278 arrangements are made in connection with the grant of permission, the general guidance in the circular is relevant. This raises the question of whether such overlap is desirable, or whether the legal authority for each obligation negotiated should be kept separate.

7.5.2 The parties and the land

A section 106 obligation must be entered into by an instrument executed as a deed and must state that it is a planning obligation for the purposes of section 106 and identify the land, the person and the interest in the land and the local planning authority who can enforce the obligation. In this regard it should be noted that the deed could make an obligation enforceable by both the District and the County Planning Authority and that the obligation can be made conditional on the person retaining an interest in the land which is the subject of the obligation.[2]

Such a planning obligation can only be entered into by a person who is 'interested in land'. It is not clear whether this includes only persons who own, at the time, legally recognized interests in the land in which title can be passed. The Court of Appeal in **Jones [1974]** took the view that prospective developers were not 'interested in land' and so could not enter into a planning agreement under section 52. On the other hand in **Pennine Raceways [1982]**, Lord Justice Eveleigh argued that to be 'interested in land' for the purposes of section 52, you did not have to own a transferable interest and so technically persons who own non-transferable interests in land such as licences may be able to enter into obligations. Prospective developers who do not have an interest in the land could enter into binding contracts with a local planning authority under section 111 but if the authorities seek to ensure that the obligation is enforceable on all future owners of the land, they will wish to ensure that all present landowners, tenants and mortgagees are made parties to an obligation under section 106. One implication is that, where unilateral undertakings are proffered by applicants at planning appeals, it will be particularly important for the authority to get the inspector to ensure that all the necessary interests in land are made parties to the agreement. In this regard circular 16/91 states that if a unilateral undertaking is proffered at an inquiry, the local planning authority should be given the opportunity to examine the document and the inspector may wish to seek evidence of title.

Section 106 only provides for the obligation being enforceable by the designated local planning authority. This means that, if undertakings are given to other authorities such as parish councils, they will not be enforceable by them under section 106, though if they are made under deed they should be enforceable against the undertaker, but will not run with the land. Which local authorities are designated in this context will depend on the terms of the obligation. For example, where undertakings are made which relate to schools the county may wish to be designated.

7.5.3 The terms

When the obligation is to take effect

It is important to make clear when the obligation will take effect. If it is to be on the grant of permission, the deed should specify precisely which planning application is relevant (there could be several) and what are the terms on which it has to be granted for the obligation to bite. Developers might wish there to be a clause dealing with the possibility of the permission being quashed on judicial review. In this case, it would be stated that the effect of the permission being quashed would be to annul the obligation. In some instances, an obligation may stand even though a permission is not taken up. This led to a threat of legal action in one of our cases (see Case 24). In many cases it may be appropriate to delay the obligation taking effect until after the development has been commenced or completed. Indeed the deed may be drafted so that different obligations arise at different times as the project advances.

Case 24: Wandsworth Gas Works, Wandsworth

Development type: mixed

Developer: Carroll Business Parks Ltd

Proposal: Area A: business accommodation (32 515 sq. m) with 600 car-parking spaces; Area B: residential (1100 habitable rooms); A1, A3 leisure uses; 450 parking spaces; Area C: business accommodation (5585 sq. m) with 100 parking spaces; highway improvements; riverside walk, access

The application was made in 1989. At this time, Carroll held an existing planning permission dated 1985 for the site. An agreement was attached to this permission requiring a riverside walk to be constructed by 1988. The permission had been partially implemented though no riverside walk had been provided.

Consequently under the agreement negotiated in relation to the 1989 application, Wandsworth required provision of the riverside walk within two years of the agreement date.

Carroll did not implement the 1989 permission. Nor did they construct a riverside walk within the two-year period. Wandsworth threatened legal action to secure fulfilment. Carroll provided a temporary riverside walk.

The exact nature of the obligation

It is obviously crucial to ensure that the terms are expressed clearly. However, in **South Oxfordshire [1994]**, a challenge to the validity of an undertaking made under section 106 on the grounds of uncertainty was rejected. The undertaking was to carry out repairs to specific listed buildings. The income for the works was to come from the letting of land as a golf course; the purpose of the undertaking being to persuade an inspector on appeal to grant planning permission for the golf course use. The undertaking provided that the trustees would use 'all reasonable endeavours' to dispose of the site and to utilize the income for the repairs. It was therefore argued that the requirement was contingent upon matters of manifest uncertainty. The Deputy Judge, however, held that the essential question was whether the inspector judged that the undertaking would work. This indicates that an obligation made under section 106 is valid if it comes within the terms of section 106 and is enforceable. It does not matter if the undertaking is dependent on steps being taken by the developer which may not be successful. Nevertheless, if works are to be carried out or land transferred, the extent and nature should be clear. It may be noted that there is no provision in section 106 for the transfer of land as such but obligations can be entered into wider section 106 which involved the transfer of land as part of the restriction or regulation of that land: see **Crest Homes plc [1994]**. Where undertakings involve the payment of money, especially on a continuous basis, careful thought will have to be given to the method of calculation and the need for subsequent variation. Sometimes authorities may try to insist on a bond being provided or a commuted capital sum, as previously discussed.

Duplication of planning conditions

Planning authorities sometimes try to insist on a 'belt and braces' approach by which the developer undertakes through an agreement to carry out any conditions that are attached to the permission to be granted. Circular 16/91 advises against the use of such a clause. Developers will usually prefer the obligation to take the form of a planning condition. This is because once permission is granted an application can always be made to have the condition removed and an appeal made to the Secretary of State should this be refused. In the case of planning obligations, an application modification can only be made after at least five years have elapsed. Our case study authorities continued to prefer the duplication of planning conditions, even after circular 16/91's advice.

7.6 RECORDING, MANAGING AND ENFORCING OBLIGATIONS

7.6.1 Registration and recording of obligations

The first step in any system of monitoring must be to have an effective system of recording and filing the agreement so that it is easily identifiable and retrievable. With the exception of Wandsworth, the authorities whom we studied did not maintain formal records of agreements signed. Wandsworth had a list of agreements reached from 1984 onwards, with information on obligations negotiated and type of development. This was reported regularly to the Planning Committee. Completions, however, were not recorded. Solihull and Harlow maintained informal lists in the planning department, and in Newcastle, the legal department maintained such a list. Since 1968, as noted in Chapter 5, there has been no central record of agreements. Otherwise the main way of recording an agreement is in the minutes of the planning committee and the agenda for that committee. The statement of grant of planning permission itself may refer to an associated agreement. In fact, as Grimley J. R. Eve *et al*. (1992) found, it was not easy to get comprehensive information on all agreements in an authority.

Otherwise the only place where there should always be a record of an agreement is the register of local land charges. A planning obligation whether created by agreement or by unilateral undertaking is registrable as a local land charge.[3] This is an effective way of ensuring that prospective purchasers of land are made aware of any obligation affecting land title when making the normal pre-contract searches. However, the register is not a convenient method of finding out what obligations have been made as it is organized by way of land parcels. This means that all land parcels in the jurisdiction of the local authority would have to be searched in order to find out the number of obligations entered into for that authority.

It is clear that the present system of recording obligations is unsatisfactory both at a formal and informal level. This creates problems with respect to accountability and monitoring. We return to this issue in Chapter 8.

7.6.2 The monitoring and management of obligations

None of our case study authorities systematically monitored compliance with agreements. For negative obligations, authorities relied on complaints raised by local people, and, in Tewkesbury, by parish councils. Tewkesbury's principal planning officer described the approach typical of all our case study authorities:

> We tend to have an approach where if anything goes wrong we hear about it and we chase things up. If nobody complains, then nothing is done.

Much more attention was paid to compliance with positive obligations. Where the developer undertakes to carry out works, the local authority needs to assure itself that works are completed to agreed standards and timescales. This could be linked to a **Grampian** condition under which the development could not commence until the works were completed to the satisfaction of the authority (see Chapter 4 for a discussion of **Grampian** conditions). In our case study authorities, the procedures were most developed with respect to highway works. Agreements typically required the approval of designs prior to commencement of works, and supervision of works during construction (see Case 5 in Chapter 5). Developers are often required to maintain highways for 12 months after completion prior to adoption. Performance bonds may be lodged with the local authority in case of default or bankruptcy. Similar arrangements are normal in relation to sewerage and drainage obligations although less detail is usually provided, given the separate arrangements which will be made with water companies. For landscaping and open space obligations, local authority officers required submission of designs prior to commencement of works. Developers typically carried out the works. Where payment for maintenance was required, this was secured at the time of land transfer to the local authority. A similar practice operated with respect to community and recreational facilities. Where the developer was to manage the facilities on completion, as in Wandsworth's child-care facilities and public toilets in shopping schemes, obligations specified management requirements.

It was normal practice for a case officer in the planning department to be responsible for monitoring major schemes. This might include regular visits to sites to check progress on agreed works or on working conditions during construction. The extent of supervision depends on the size of the works. On the Bishop's Cleeve development (Case 1 in Chapter 1), the works, which included improvements and the construction of new highways, were supervised by a Gloucestershire County Council engineer who was installed on-site. One schedule of the agreement specifies details of the accommodation for him or her to be provided by the developers. Typically a local authority will issue an interim letter certifying satisfactory completion allowing the development to be used.

Sewerage and drainage obligations were monitored by local authority engineers or by the water companies themselves.

The most complex tasks which local authorities faced once agreements were signed related to the management of financial payments. There was no consistent pattern in the treatment of financial payments. After some earlier experiences with staged payments in times of inflation in the 1970s, authorities generally required payment on the signing of an agreement. These might be staged on larger schemes (as in the Roehampton case, see Case 2 in Chapter 3). Some authorities were very careful to ring-fence funds acquired through obligations. For example, in Harlow, payments for landscape maintenance were placed in a special interest-bearing account, with the interest used for maintenance. Another strategy was to earmark funds but pay them into a general account. In Solihull, amounts were credited to the highways department but paid into the local authority's general account, to gain investment returns prior to use. In Wandsworth, financial payments were kept in the authority's general account. Commuted car-parking payments tended not to be ring-fenced in any way, and could be deflected to related purposes (for example, to redesign a bus station to provide more car-parking as in a Harlow case). Developer contributions were most likely to be recorded in a general category in local authority accounts. This meant that the tracking payments made through to works undertaken was not always easy. This fuels charges that payments represent an informal tax, even though, within the authority, it may be possible to identify the route which connects the payment to actions related to the development in question.

Only one authority, Harlow, had a systematic system of monitoring obligations. This operated by appointing a specific officer for each project whose job it was to achieve performance. That officer had the job of bringing in other officers when the project involved their interests. This would seem a useful device and superior to the other authorities who relied on the operational clauses bringing defaults to the attention of the authority.

7.6.3 Enforcement

The legal powers

If the obligation is not registered in the local land charges registry, this does not make it unenforceable. However, the purchaser of the land who has searched the register is entitled to compensation from the authority who looks after the register for any loss suffered by the virtue of the failure to register. This will normally be the same authority who should have registered the charge. If it is not, the authority who should have registered the charge will have to reimburse the registering authority.

In the case of section 106 obligations the new wording inserted by the Planning and Compensation Act 1991 makes clear that all the types of obligation are enforceable against successors in title. The main remedies available are:

1. injunction;
2. civil debt for monetary obligations; and
3. carrying out necessary works and recovering costs.

In Chapters 5 and 6, it was pointed out that all the authorities felt more confident about the enforcement of agreements as opposed to conditions. This appeared to be due in part to a belief that developers were less likely to break agreements to which they had committed themselves. Another factor was undoubtedly that the private law remedies of damages and injunction, which arise in the case of a breach of a contract, were considered to be more speedy and effective than the cumbersome methods of enforcing planning conditions. The changes to the enforcement of development control introduced by the Planning and Compensation Act 1991 mean that planning conditions can now be much more easily enforced. Apart from the new breach of condition notices, there is now an express statutory right to enforce all kinds of breaches of planning control by injunction both in the High Court and in the County Court.

Problems over the fulfilment of obligations sometimes cropped up in our case study authorities. Failure to comply occasionally led to the threat of legal action to enforce obligations (see Case 24 above), but this was very rare. In Harlow, developers failed to comply because of bankruptcy (see Case 25).

Case 25: Edinburgh Way, Harlow

Development type: Retail

Developer: Citygrove plc

Proposal: 23 225 sq. m retail

The application was for a development on local authority-owned land. That land was the site of a council depot. Prior to the development commencing the developer re-located the council depot to a new site.

The agreement related to the provision of both on- and off-site highways works. The highways works involved construction of an access road, an exit only highway and a roundabout. The work was to be carried out by Citygrove's contractor. The developer provided a bond of £660 000.

The developer and the contractor both went into liquidation and the work was finished by Harlow's Direct Labour Organisation.

Though the bond was sufficient to cover the cost of the highways works, the Finance Department estimated that overall Harlow suffered a financial loss because of necessary associated works not covered by the bond.

7.6.4 Modification and discharge of planning obligations

Prior to the 1991 Planning and Compensation Act, the only ways by which agreements entered into under sections 52/106, or indeed under any of the other statutory mechanisms, could be varied or discharged were either to get the authority to agree to the variation or discharge, or to apply to the Lands Tribunal for modification or discharge of the covenant. The Lands Tribunal only had jurisdiction with respect to restrictive covenants and the grounds for modification or discharge were very limited. This has now been replaced by section 106B which creates a specific mechanism for the modification or discharge of planning obligations.

These new provisions are similar to the provision by which an application can be made to develop land without compliance with conditions previously attached.[4] The main points to note are:

1. *The time limits.* An application can only be made after five years from the date on which the obligation was entered into or such period as may be prescribed by regulations (currently five years as well). This is a crucial provision, as the earlier the application can be made, the more the right to apply resembles a right of appeal. The present five-year period means that it will normally only be applicable to restrictive obligations as positive obligations will usually be completed by the time the right to apply arises. However it could be manipulated by developers who might delay the start of developments in order to avoid obligation commitments.

2. *The grounds.* No express grounds are set out, but the authority may discharge the obligation if it no longer serves a useful purpose or it may accept the modifications in the application where the obligation still serves a useful purpose but it would equally serve that purpose as modified. This could lead to the same problems as arose in **Martins [1988]** (see Figure 7.2), where an obligation still served a useful planning purpose but there were planning reasons for discharging it. It may also be noted that an authority has no jurisdiction to impose its own modifications and so if it is dissatisfied with the modifications in the application it must reject the application. This seems unnecessarily rigid.

3. *Appeal to Secretary of State.* This is in the standard form, but again the Secretary of State has no power to impose his own modifications and is stuck with the terms of the application.

4. *Restrictive covenants.* Even if the obligation is in the form of a restrictive covenant it will no longer be possible to apply to the Land Tribunal for its discharge.

A difficult question is whether this statutory right to apply for discharge or modification can be excluded by agreement. It could be argued that such

Re Martins Application

An agreement had been entered into under section 37 of the Town and Country Planning Act 1962 that land 'should not be used for any purpose other than as a private open space and that no building, structure or erection ... shall be placed thereon'. Years later the Secretary of State upheld an appeal against a refusal to grant planning permission to build a dwelling on that land but the local authority were not willing to release the owners from the covenant as they still considered that it was in the interests of the amenities and environment of the area that the land remained undeveloped. The Lands Tribunal rejected an application for the covenant to be discharged and this decision was upheld by the Court of Appeal. The court held that the fact that the Secretary of State had granted planning permission (which, if implemented, would involve a breach of covenant) was a factor to be considered but it did not prevent the Tribunal from concluding that the covenant was not obsolete as it was still achieving its original purpose.

Figure 7.2 The durability of covenants entered into through an agreement: The Martins [1988] case

a clause would be invalid as contrary to public policy. However from the Court of Appeal decision in **Fulham Football Club [1992]** there would appear to be nothing to prevent parties agreeing to their own system of discharge or modification by reference to arbitration. This could get around the five-year period. It is always possible for an agreement to be varied by a later agreement entered into between the same parties.

However, even before these changes it was quite common for applications to be made for the modification or discharge of obligations. Discharge requests occurred most frequently where a development had not proceeded and a new application was initiated. Our case study authorities appear to have been reasonably accommodating if they considered developers were in difficulty (see Case 26).

7.7 ACCOUNTABILITY

Our case studies showed that normally very careful consideration was given to the planning policy issues involved in negotiations over planning agreements. However, this is insufficient guarantee for a properly accountable process where practices have the potential, if not carefully used, of contravening agreed planning policy and undermining the integrity of the system.

The point at which an agreement is normally available for public consideration is at the end of the second stage of the negotiating process (see

Case 26: Osborne Avenue, Newcastle

Development type: Residential

Developer: N. E. Construction Partnership

Proposal: Nine flats and four houses

The agreement required that four of the flats should be occupied by persons over 55 years of age. Newcastle insisted upon this provision to prevent over-development. In consequence the development required a lower standard of car-parking provision.

The developer subsequently applied to have the section 52 agreement relaxed as he could not sell the flats with the occupancy restriction. This first request was refused.

A further application was made later. The developer argued that the situation had not been foreseen when the agreement was signed. On the basis that the flats if unsold could be subject to vandalism and blight and that the developer was likely to suffer financial hardship, the City agreed to the relaxation of the agreement but stipulated that this was not to be considered as a precedent for other developers.

section 7.4 above). Then the application together with the heads of agreement reaches the planning committee. Wandsworth's borough planning officer describes a typical situation:

> The committee see the potential heads of agreement. Then the officers conduct the negotiations. The members have little interest in agreements.

The limits of accountability in the process are shown here. In Wandsworth, as in Harlow, Newcastle and Solihull, there was no formal process for consultation over planning agreements outside this brief appearance at the relevant committee.

Wandsworth consulted with interested parties over the preparation of large development site briefs, but not on the legal agreement which might result. Only in the case of Battersea Power Station (see Case 7 in Chapter 5) was there an ongoing involvement with community groups.

While Harlow had an established and expanding mechanism for consultation with the public at large using neighbourhood committees, public meetings and questionnaires, there was no specific remit to consult over planning agreements. One council officer expressed concern about the value of these consultative mechanisms:

We are not arguing for less consultation. We are just arguing that more of the same thing isn't necessarily better. Perhaps if we need more consultation we need a different approach, a different type of consultation. Personally I think there's a big gap in the council's consultation in that they don't consult interest groups. They consult an amorphous public – I don't mean that in a derogatory way. But the public – who is the public? It's just the people who happen to turn up on the night. ... It's only a public-type consultation ... when an organisation is formed – usually unfortunately opposing things. I think you should have people supporting things ... It's only when an organisation like that appears ... then things really become ... focused. ... We need further analysis of type of consultation.

In general, the research showed that protests focused on opposition to the development itself, not to lack of consultation over the negotiation of planning agreements. An example of the involvement of an interest group in the negotiative process occurred in relation to a proposed development at the National Exhibition Centre in Solihull (see Case 16 in Chapter 5). Such consultation was rare in Solihull. One parish council chair observed:

There are two developments in the parish in which we are extremely interested ... but we are kept at arm's length ... Our parish wish to be a party to agreements ... At [one site] we have land. We are interested in getting involved in development. ... At [another site] we want to get involved in the management of a country park.

The attitude of local authorities can be explained by the fact that most feel that the issue of accountability is adequately dealt with by existing arrangements – i.e. by approval of the deal by elected members. This is a view supported by developers. 'Elected members', one argued, 'represent the community.' Developers have an interest, acknowledged by some, in restricting the number of parties to the negotiations as this would lengthen the process. The parties to the negotiation of most agreements remained the ultimate signatories, reflecting the private contractual nature of a planning agreement.

In Tewkesbury, on the other hand, there was a definite attempt to involve the parish councils. In part this was a reflection of the political structure of the council which was in Independent control. Further the need to co-ordinate the management of the development process in Tewkesbury necessitated the incorporation of parish councils in this process to prevent fragmentation (see section 7.3 above). The Borough Planning Officer outlined the council's aims:

The links with the community [are] to make sure that legal agreements aren't things struck behind closed doors. That's not our council's intention. Effectively town councils and parish councils – are involved in the process of negotiating what goes into the legal agreement. In fact all the elements that are involved in Tewkesbury [see Case 23 in Chapter 6] have been debated by the committee and both parish councils for a couple of years now. They've been part of the plan process. And I think that would be part of planning gain work – whether it's the local plan-led planning gain or whether it's the opportunistic – related to an application.

Local authorities are now encouraged by government advice to bring their deliberations on planning agreements to public attention. Circular 16/91 (DoE, 1991b) states that:

Authorities are reminded that planning obligations must be registered on the local land charges register. Members of the public should be given every assistance in locating planning obligations which are of interest to them. Planning obligations and related correspondence should be listed as background papers to the committee report relating to the development proposal (see section 100D of the Local Government Act 1972). Authorities would need a very strong case either to exclude the press and public when discussing a planning obligation or to determine that connected correspondence should be kept from public view (para. B14 of Annex B, DoE, 1991b).

Yet there is no statutory requirement to publicize the contents of proposed obligations and the courts are reluctant to imply such a duty. The issue arose in the case of **Daniel Davies [1994]** where the validity of a grant of a planning permission was challenged by an objector on the grounds that the details of the proposed agreement had not been put before the planning committee which had determined the application. The argument put forward by the applicants was that where planning permission is being granted subject to a planning agreement being entered into, it is necessary that the 'gist and essential terms' of such an agreement should be known in advance of the decision of the authority. Otherwise it was argued that the members of the authority will not be able to consider the application properly and it will be impossible for the public to have meaningful participation. The Court of Appeal, in upholding the decision of Mr Justice MacPherson, held that, when the agreements to be entered into are 'merely regulatory' with respect to how the premises are to be occupied or used, objectors are not entitled to see the terms of those agreements. The meaning of 'regulatory' was not defined but it would appear that it was referring to an agreement which in some way restricted or regulated the development being proposed and therefore did not fundamentally change what was being originally proposed. Lord Justice Neill giving the judgement of the Court, however accepted that

> There might be an extreme case where there was such a departure from the original planning permission that an exception would have to be made but in the ordinary way it seems to me that the terms of the agreement are not matters which have to be brought to the notice of objectors.

This kind of reasoning is similar to that employed by the courts to determine whether a planning application can be modified or a condition imposed without there being a fresh application.[5] This approach ensures that a planning permission cannot be granted for something substantially different from that originally set out in the planning application. However, it does not ensure that, where there are planning objections to a proposed development, there is genuine public discussion of whether the proposed agreements meet these planning objections.

As was pointed out earlier, the need to register a planning obligation as a local land charge is not a very practical way of ensuring that the contents of obligations are made public. It is only when the charge is registered (which will normally be after the related planning permission has been granted) that a third party can find out the contents of the agreement and then only if they know the identity of the land which is subject to the obligation. So a local planning authority can keep the contents secret for some time. This is well illustrated by the **Crest Homes plc [1994]** decision (see Figure 4.3). There the applicants for judicial review, who were rival developers, wrote to the council asking for information concerning legal agreements which had been entered into by other developers. The council replied that, until these agreements had been completed, the information sought was confidential. At this date permission had not yet been granted for development in connection with the agreements though the judgement sets out that some agreements had already been executed. The facts of the case illustrate how delicate the negotiations prior to the granting of permission can be when the local planning authority is dealing with several developers and is trying to get a series of agreements signed before the approval of the local plan. Mr Justice Brooke commented that the council's district secretary was being 'less than frank' when she said that the agreements were still subject to negotiation when, at the time, three of the six agreements had been executed. However Mr Justice Booke concluded that this did not excuse the applicants for not themselves searching the Local Lands Charges Register. So it would seem that if the local planning authority are not willing to be open, the only remedy is to search the register on the assumption that the agreements will be registered promptly.

Two procedures were generally considered to increase the accountability of the process. The first was to establish in advance clear policy statements in the development plans and in subsequent development briefs. The second was to ensure that the general contents of an obligation are given the same publicity as the application for permission, which the obligation is intended to release. In most cases our study authorities provided well-reasoned reports to Planning Committee, indicating the heads of agreement. But these were not made available to the general public.

There has been some discussion of more radical ways of making negotiative processes more accountable. One proposal, used at the Kings Cross development project in Islington, London, is for 'open book accounting' by which the developer would have to set out the likely profits that would flow from the development. Harlow gave some consideration to this approach. This would require legislative change and engender considerable opposition from the development sector. It also implicitly treats the negotiation of obligations as a form of tax. A second proposal is to enable challenges to be made to planning permissions, particularly where plan policies are not followed. All parties to a negotiation would in this case have to ensure that their reasoning and practices stood up to scrutiny in an inquiry, as now happens with respect to planning refusals. We discuss these issues in more detail in Part Three.

7.8 CONCLUSIONS

As with much of development control practice in England, the management of agreements has developed in an *ad hoc* way in each of the four case-study authorities. If, as we argue, the negotiation of developer obligations and the use of agreements has a strategic significance in the planning system, then a more systematic approach is desirable. Local authorities need good information for monitoring, management and enforcement purposes. Local communities need to be confident that an authority is following through decisions made in line with policies. Developers will want to be reassured that they are being treated fairly as compared with competitors. We discuss in Chapter 8 in more detail what such a systematic approach could look like. In the light of the discussion in this chapter, we suggest its main elements would be as follows:

1. It would cover the whole negotiation process and any post-agreement management issues.
2. It should include a public statement as to how the various claims for obligations are to be co-ordinated, providing as far as possible a 'one-stop shop' for developers, with advice and cross-referral where claims from different agencies are involved.

3. It should provide clear advice, based on plans and development briefs, as to the range of claims for obligations to be expected prior to discussions about individual applications. The objective should be to specify the quantum of obligations a developer should expect, with an indication of the circumstances in which any may be relaxed. (This is particularly important with respect to rationale 2.)

4. There should be clear advice on how any post-agreement monitoring of works or provision of services is to be carried out.

5. Heads of agreement reached should be reported to the Planning Committee and objectors, along with the decision recommendations, supported by reasons explaining each one, in relation to plan policies and relevant development briefs, including reasons why indicated obligations have not been sought.

6. The maintenance of a readily available public record of agreements and their contents should be required, supplemented by (a) regular monitoring of compliance and (b) visible accounting of any financial transactions, to ensure that funds received are deployed in a way which is reasonably related to the specific obligation.

Such an approach, we believe, would help to ensure efficiency, effectiveness and fairness in the practice of negotiating and managing agreements. It would mean that both local authorities and developers would need to ensure that planning and legal staff are knowledgeable and skilled in such work and are involved throughout the negotiation process.

NOTES

1. Recent changes in government policy might have led to a different conclusion (see DoE, 1993).
2. See subsections (9)(d) and (4) respectively.
3. See Local land Charges Act 1975 and the Local Land Charges Regulations 1977.
4. See section 73 of the Town and Country Planning 1990 Act.
5. See **Wheatcroft [1980]**.

PART THREE

IMPLICATIONS

8

REGULATION THROUGH NEGOTIATION: A SYSTEMATIC APPROACH

8.1 NEGOTIATIVE PRACTICE IN THE 1990s

The evidence presented in Part Two describes a practice of negotiating development obligations which had become routine across most local authorities in England by the 1990s. Although the numbers of actual agreements negotiated remains small in relation to the total number of planning decisions made, agreements are frequently used for larger and more complex applications with diverse impacts. Local authorities increasingly recognize their importance in their development plan policies. Even more significant has been the extension in the scope of agreements and the scale of obligations negotiated. There seems little sign of this tendency abating, despite the more difficult development conditions of the 1990s. Packages of obligations often represent sophisticated 'deals' covering compensation and mitigation for adverse impacts, co-ordination among different developers, and arrangements for organizing who will pay for what infrastructure. Obligations relate increasingly to positive actions which developers are to undertake, to social and economic impacts as well as infrastructural ones, and to sites at a distance from the development site. Similar tendencies are recorded in the United States (Delafons, 1991a, b; Callies and Grant, 1991; Nicholas *et al.*, 1991; Bailey, 1990; Wakeford, 1990).

Much negotiation is *ad hoc*, relating to the specific circumstances of the project in question. However, faced with the routinization of negotiating agreement packages, several authorities and the utilities companies have developed policies which require the payment of standard charges or contributions, with respect to infrastructure hook ups, or payments for landscape maintenance. This begins to look like a form of 'proto impact fee', as has developed in the US, or the urbanization fees often required in continental European planning systems (see Davies *et al.*, 1989). These latter have the advantage that they 'capture' all applications in a relevant category, whereas the British negotiation of obligations affects relatively small numbers of applications. Our research also illustrates the variability in development projects, in their sites, in the situation of the developers involved and in the impacts which a project generates. This makes it difficult to determine in advance what social costs a project will impose on the community, of an area and to ensure that these are mitigated appropriately.

These days, many local authorities recognize the strategic importance of the practice, in relation both to issues about the financing of community, social and physical infrastructure and the balance between development activity and conceptions of environmental quality and sustainability. The negotiation of agreements is no longer treated as a minor support for a planning permission. Generally, local authorities rationalized their practice explicitly in terms either of enabling development to proceed, or dealing with the adverse impacts of development. However, many authorities clearly saw the profit to be made from a development as a relevant consideration. In some cases, obligations went further than was strictly necessary to counteract the immediate impact of a development project, as we have illustrated in Chapters 4 and 5.

We also found that the evolution of negotiative practice around planning agreements was drawing on, and leading to, new techniques of economic, environmental and social impact assessment, the identification of mitigation measures, and the translation of impact mitigation measures into pro rata charges. This methodological evolution was being fostered by the constraints on public finance, the role of the private sector as the primary initiator of land and property development activity, and the increasing policy recognition of the complex interconnections of economic and social life and environmental quality.

Developers were generally prepared to accept the practice. It helped to co-ordinate the various parties in the process of development through negotiating commitments to actions necessary for a project to proceed. It also helped to overcome policy or political difficulties which their projects may encounter. Many developers, nevertheless, made complaints about the practice. However, these complaints were primarily focused on the 'boundaries' of the practice. What seems to have happened is that developers have by and large accepted that making contributions is an accepted part of current planning practice. Their criticisms serve to limit the increases in expectations from the regulatory bodies and public agencies, and constrain an 'upward ratchet' in demands. The debates and controversies in the professional and political press about the practice are thus essentially about the limits of the practice, not about the practice itself, although this reality has often been masked by the ideological terms in which debate has been conducted. There has also been a significant shift in the terms of discourse about development obligations. The concept of 'planning gain' helped to construct debate in terms of a struggle over the capture of the benefits or 'betterment' from development. In contrast, the language of 'development impacts' focuses attention on the social costs of development projects.

Yet while some projects can cope with their impacts by mitigation measures without extra cost, in most cases, the costs of obligations and their negotiation add to project costs and thus eat into profitability. In the 1980s, the development boom made many projects very profitable. But in the more sober conditions of the 1990s, easy development profits are not likely in the foreseeable future except in particularly favourable locations. If development projects are required to pay for their infrastructure demands and their environmental impacts, the projects which will succeed through the regulatory hurdles are those near to infrastructure with spare capacity and on large, greenfield sites where cross-subsidy and the sharing of costs is possible. Where market conditions make it difficult for the costs of obligations to be passed forward to consumers, the pressure will continue to build costs back into the land price. This will favour situations where the land price can bear such costs. Elsewhere, some form of subsidy will be needed to enable development to proceed. The waiving of obligation requirements could be one such subsidy.

There are thus major problems in squaring the promotion of development projects which can afford to pay for their 'obligations' and impacts, with the concern to promote specific social and environmental objectives through the negotiation of obligations, as in the case of low-cost social housing and safeguarding environmental resources. The practice of negotiating obligations favours development on larger greenfield sites in profitable locations. This can be no substitute for investment out of general and local taxation revenues to promote community development and environmental improvement.

Meanwhile, there is a great deal of confusion in public policy debate about how to think about the practice of negotiating obligations and its legitimate boundaries. While there has been a slow shift in both government policy and legal judgements to accept a wider range of impacts and a looser relationship between a project and the location of its impacts, legal interpretations are often inconsistent. Government policy, though now much more positive about the practice, is riddled with inconsistency, and trails behind current practice. Local authorities are producing policy statements to outline their practices, but these are open to challenge at public inquiry and in the courts and are thus affected by the above inconsistencies.

The management of the negotiation of development obligations and subsequent actions reflects its origins as an *ad hoc* support for development control. It is not well-recorded, or well-monitored. This has consequences for the accountability of the practice. If bargains struck are not held to, their credibility to a public increasingly cynical of public actions, and to other developers who have lost out through not being able to provide obligations, will be called into question. If the negotiated packages do not lead to the anticipated mitigation of adverse effects, then the legitimacy of the whole regulatory process is affected. As Lichfield (1989) observes:

> We have a fuzzy concept (planning gain) as the tip of the iceberg in fuzzy practice (development control) linked to fuzzy law at the borderlines of exacting contributions to infrastructure costs for new development and of planning and other development controls (p. 69).

In the next section, we outline our views on what can de done to move beyond this confusion, inconsistency and erratic management practices.

8.2 OUR POLICY PROPOSALS

8.2.1 An impact–alleviation approach: our approach in outline

At the conclusion of the research upon which this book is based, we made the following recommendations:

- government policy should be expanded to include both the on-site and off-site impacts of development projects;
- development plans should specify the scope of impacts and what measures to alleviate or compensate for impacts are expected, linking explicitly such measures to the impacts concerned;
- a systematic and plan-based approach to identifying obligations is to be preferred to the general use of impact fees, though there may well be a case for standardized charges in some instances;
- clear arrangements should be introduced for reporting, registering and monitoring agreements.

We argued that such an approach:

> should provide a stable and accountable framework so that community concerns and commercial interests can negotiate mutually beneficial and effective solutions to local development problems (Healey *et al.*, 1993a, p. 4).

In making these recommendations, we firmly advocated the adoption of the second of the three rationales we discussed in Chapters 1 and 6. In seeking contributions from developers in the context of the regulation of land use change and development for planning purposes, local authorities should focus on identifying and negotiating ways of *alleviating or mitigating the adverse impacts*, that is, the social costs, which projects may generate. The objective should be to ensure that the external costs of a development project are born by the development. In this way, local authorities would be able to 'enable' development to proceed, while at the same time keeping the adverse impacts of developments to an acceptable minimum. As we argued in Chapter 2, we consider that the taxation of *profits* of development projects is a separate question. Measures to achieve this should not be allied to the requirement that developers mitigate the costs they impose on a community. We therefore would agree with current British government policy that it is inappropriate to confuse the alleviation of the impact of schemes with taxation. While there is a strong argument for taxing the profits which are often made from development projects, there is a fundamental distinction between requiring community benefits to make a project acceptable in planning terms, including mitigating its adverse impacts, and requiring community benefits because the development is profitable. As a recent report on the potential use of impact fees in Britain points out (Goodchild and Henneberry, 1994), there is not always a correlation between the level of the impact costs of a development and the profits to be made from their development. The report concluded that:

> There is a dichotomy between the financial characteristics of schemes and their infrastructure impacts. The two are not closely related. The scheme with the highest unit construction cost, the central London office development, and the most valuable and profitable scheme, the high street shop development, impose minimal additional demands on existing infrastructure. A scheme with a relatively low unit building cost, the greenfield housing development, would have the greatest additional infrastructure requirements. In other words, some high value/high profit schemes may pay a very low impact fee burden (p. 51).

As the report recognizes, this has implications for the fairness of uniform or flat-rate systems of impact fees. So, while the lack of profitability of a project may be a reason for not seeking to recoup all the social costs that the project will cause, the profitability of the project should not be a justification for seeking community benefits from a project which will have only a small impact in terms of social costs. We similarly reject notions such as auctions of planning permission (see for example, Curry 1991). This would distort the planning system. Planning decisions should be made on the grounds of the overall quality of the use and development of land and not on financial gain *per se*.

In our view, a decisive shift to an impact–alleviation approach would achieve such a clear separation. It would shift policy and legal discourse to focus on the language of impact. Core concepts in this language are establishing the **scope of impacts** to be considered, **specifying the causal relationships** between projects, their impacts and measures to alleviate them, and assessing the scale or **proportionality** of the impact created and means to alleviate it. Already, in technical fields and in legal judgements, principles are being articulated to develop this approach. We discuss the analysis of impacts further in section 8.3. Legal debate is fast adjusting to the logic of an impact–alleviation approach. This is important, as the assessment of impacts and measures for their alleviation are matters of judgement as much as technique. Legal decisions thus serve to define what it is acceptable in terms of constraints on developers' rights.

The scope of impacts

The legal determination of what is a legitimate impact to alleviate turns in substance on the extent to which the potential impact of a development can be used as a reason for a refusal of planning permission. This is a difficult issue as the boundary between what is and what is not a **material consideration** in development control law is continually moving. It has been seen how local planning authorities such as Harlow have been pushing at that boundary by seeking obligations relating to child-care facilities and training obligations. Until recently such socio-economic matters would have been considered by many to be outside the scope of the Town and Country Planning legislation. The courts have not yet had to rule directly on whether they come within the term **material considerations**. However, since the Court of Appeal's decision in **Mitchell [1994]** which argued that the need for affordable housing is a material consideration, it is likely that the courts would hold that such considerations legitimately come within the scope of planning.[1]

We would support an interpretation of what constitutes a legitimate adverse impact which encompasses both on-site and off-site impacts and extends to social, economic and environmental impacts. Development projects can have fundamental and far reaching effects on communities. It is therefore important that in considering whether to grant permission, the local planning authorities should be able to take a comprehensive view of the desirability of those effects. The government would appear to take a similar broad view of the kind of impacts that can be taken into consideration. Circular 16/91 (DoE, 1991b) states that it is reasonable for local planning authorities to seek social, educational, recreational, sporting or other community provision the need for which arises from the development (para B8(4) of annex B).

However it is still left rather unclear what is meant by such 'community provisions' and whether they extend to facilities such as child care and training.

Whatever the exact scope of material considerations, we would argue that the local planning authority should be able to show that the 'needs' identified will be created by the impact of the development. It is the creation of such needs by a project, through an adverse impact of some kind, which causes it to be unacceptable in planning terms without some alleviation measures. This raises the issue of whether the absence of the community benefit is sufficient to make the development unacceptable and so justifies requiring the benefit. As we pointed out in Chapter 4, the High Court has recently held that permission for housing can be refused on the grounds that the proposal does not make secure provision for affordable housing which would be appropriate for the site (**EEC Construction [1994]**). While it is now established that the need for affordable housing is a material consideration, neither the inspector or the deputy judge who upheld the inspector's decision in this case explained why the failure to provide the need meant that the development project would cause 'demonstrable harm'.[2] The fact that there is a need or shortage of a facility, for example a park or a theatre, should not justify refusing an application to carry out a development which will not cause or increase that need. Of course, it is possible to argue that the granting of permission for residential development without an element of affordable housing will reduce the land available for affordable housing and thus cause harm, though it may be hard to demonstrate this causation. It would also be different if the site had been selected in the development plan as particularly appropriate for affordable housing. The important matter of principle is that the local planning authority should be able to show that the development will have an adverse impact.

A sufficient causal relationship

Having established the impact, the next step is show a link between the adverse impact and the obligation which is being sought. Circular 16/91 makes clear that there should be a 'direct' relationship between the development and the obligation. In other words, there must be a clear nexus between the development and the need for the action and provision the obligation requires. We support this approach as it is again important that local planning authorities should have to justify imposing the burden on the developer. There has been a similar discussion in the United States. The United States supreme court has termed this the 'essential nexus' test. This still leaves considerable interpretation with respect to how direct the connection has to be. A narrow view was taken in the **Nollan [1987]** case. Here, it was accepted that permission for the expansion of a seashore cabin could be refused on the grounds that it would restrict the public's view of the beach. However the Court held that any requirement imposed on a permit had to further the end advanced as the justification for the prohibition. In other words, the requirement had to make the development acceptable. On the facts of the particular case, the supreme court held that there was not a sufficient relationship between a requirement that the public should be able to walk alongside the sea wall of the property and the objective of protecting the public's view of the beach. On this interpretation, some of Wandsworth's negotiated obligations for their riverside walkway (see Chapter 5) might have been held to be invalid. While it is important that there should be a sufficient and reasonable relationship between the obligation and the planning objective, we consider the **Nollan [1987]** case takes too rigid an application of the principle of an 'essential nexus'. It would seem reasonable to consider the opening up of the beach alongside the shoreline as compensating for and so making acceptable the loss of views of the beach from the shore road.

This, however, opens up the question of how far local planning authorities can seek and developers can offer obligations which will compensate for, rather than alleviate, the adverse impacts of development projects. This is a key issue in environmental debate, where compensating for environmental loss is seen as less satisfactory than reducing the scale of the loss (Jacobs, 1991; Cowell, 1993). Circular 16/91 does not fully address this aspect of planning obligations. Test (5) in the circular accepts that it is reasonable to seek obligations which are intended to off-set an adverse impact on the development site and would seem to accept that damage to wildlife on one part of the site can be off-set by creating new nature reserves. Further, the concept of mixed development in test (4), under which an element of affordable housing can be sought in a larger residential development, may be viewed as a form of the compensatory principle, where the impact of the residential development would normally be considered unacceptable. Otherwise the circular is silent on whether it is legitimate to seek to alleviate adverse environmental impacts which arise off-site and avoids the issue of compensating for the impacts of development. This is perhaps understandable, as the main focus of the circular is on what can be required to alleviate the impacts of development. The trading or balancing of one planning advantage against another planning disadvantage (which is what the compensatory principle involves) is a different, if related, issue.

This raises the issue of the validity of the compensation principle. Compensation in a 'balance of account' approach to alleviating impacts is certainly a logical strategy. Some environmentalists encourage it. As Chapter 4 explains, the concept of compensatory obligations is endorsed by the courts, and by the policy of unilateral undertakings. Such an approach can be defended on the grounds that it should be left to the planning authorities to determine whether such a deal is in the public interest. However, a compensatory approach may make it too easy for developers to escape pressure to *reduce* their impacts, as other environmentalists argue (Jacobs, 1991). The main planning objection is that the encouragement of developers to offer extraneous community benefits would tend to subvert agreed planning policies and lead to developers 'paying off' adverse environmental effects rather than preventing them from arising. Our conclusion is that it should only be justifiable to allow the planning benefits from development obligations to be weighed against the disadvantages of the proposed development where there is a *sufficient causal relationship* between the benefits and disadvantages. Compensation measures, we argue, should relate in scale and kind to the impacts in question, and be such as to encourage developers to reduce the adverse impacts they generate.

It is difficult to lay down precise rules as to what constitutes a sufficient relationship. There will clearly be a sufficient relationship when benefits and disadvantages are the inevitable, direct consequences of a development and are intrinsic to the development. A sufficient relationship is also likely to be obvious when there is a composite development on one physical site. However, physical proximity is an inappropriate proxy for a sufficient relationship where it is clear that there is no functional relationship between two different developments on a site even though they are physically adjacent.

For example, if a superstore would normally be refused on a particular site as a result of adverse impacts on a town centre, it should not be possible to obtain permission by, say, adding on a swimming pool or art gallery next door to the superstore. A sufficient relationship can of course be established if the development obligation alleviates the impact of the development proposal, even though the obligation relates to land far distant from the main site. It would equally be clear that there would not be a sufficient relationship if the development obligation is some distance from the site and has no relationship to the impact of the development. Thus a local planning authority should not grant permission for development in a site of special scientific interest on the grounds of an undertaking to solve outstanding traffic problems elsewhere. On the other hand, there could be a sufficient relationship if the road improvement would help to protect the site of special scientific interest even if there is not a complete fit between the benefits and disadvantages to the site of special scientific interest. There could also be a sufficient relationship where the benefits and disadvantages are in the same policy field and are not too physically distant.

These examples show the difficulty of providing general principles about the relations between projects and their impacts. The sufficiency of a relationship in causal terms will depend on the particular project in question. Therefore in our view, the locus of responsibility is establishing a reasonable and sufficient causal relationship should lie with local planning authorities, subject to appeal to the Secretary of State. Such appeals should be assessed on the basis of argumentation about the specific causal relationship. While the courts should lay down guidance as to what constitutes a sufficient relationship, they should only intervene if the decision-maker had come to a clearly unreasonable decision or had made a misdirection in coming to a judgement.

The 'proportionality' of impact–alleviation measures

Finally, there is the question of the scale of alleviation required to deal with an adverse impact. The United States Supreme Court has held that a public authority should not require a lot more than is necessary to meet the policy objective on which basis the permit could be refused, even where an 'essential nexus' exists. In **Dolan [1994]** the US Supreme court held that there must be a 'rough proportionality' between the obligations and the impact of the development. Chief Justice Rehnquist, giving the judgement of the majority, laid down that:

> No precise mathematical calculation is required, but the city must make some sort of individualised determination that the required dedication is related both in nature and extent to the impact of the proposed development.

This test of 'rough proportionality' would seem to be equally appropriate in the British context. It is similar to Mr Justice Brooke's view in **Crest Homes plc [1994]** that:

> Even if the proposed benefit is of a type which can be properly be regarded as material, it must not be so disproportionately large as to include a significantly additional benefit over and above that which could properly be considered to be material (p. 947).

This view has been upheld by the court of appeal. Lord Justice Henry, who gave the only judgement held that:

> A benefit disproportionate to the adverse planning impact of the development to which it was linked would not fairly and reasonably relate to that development.

On the other hand, the English courts take a far less strict approach to what is disproportionate in practice, compared to the US Supreme Court. In Crest Homes plc, the Court of Appeal upheld a formula based on a percentage of the increase in development value, on the grounds that it was a *bona fide* attempt at working out development costs. While we agree with the less exacting approach of the English courts, we consider that the kind of formula used in Crest Homes should be avoided as it is too arbitrary.

Of course it could still be in the interests of developers to offer a disproportionate amount if this was the only way of getting the necessary road or facilities, since the impact that the development would have on the roads could be a reason for refusing permission. Those developing in the early stages of a large scheme may need to install a substantial part of the scheme infrastructure from which others may later benefit, in order to get started. However, local planning authorities should not set out to require more than a proportionate contribution. Further, if there are other reasons for refusing a planning application, any surplus contributions offered should not be taken into account in coming to a decision.

8.2.2 Negotiated contributions or impact fees

An impact–alleviation approach thus emphasizes the making of systematic, but reasonable and proportionate connections between a project, its adverse impacts and measures to alleviate them. This involves difficult judgements on a case-by-case basis. One way to simplify this process is by developing formalized systems of charging for impacts generated. This implies that a generalized calculation in some form can replace the assessment of the actual impacts of specific projects. Several commentators have argued that the United Kingdom should consider introducing a form of impact charge or fee similar to the impact fees found in the United States (see Delafons, 1991b; Callies and Grant, 1991). The Department of the Environment recently commissioned research into the economic costs of impact fees (Goodchild and Henneberry, 1994). A good precedent is the fee at present charged for a connection to the water supply and sewerage networks under the Water Industry Act 1991, and a precedent is set by the *Berkshire Schedule of Infrastructure Charges*, which specifies infrastructure contributions for different types of project (Berkshire CC, 1989; Barton Willmore Planning Partnership, 1991). The terms **development charge** and **impact fee** are used with considerable flexibility, however.[3] Any contribution aimed at alleviating the impact of a development could be described as an impact fee but the term is usually reserved for a formal set of charges based on objective criteria. As we have shown in Part Two, there are already examples of formalized charges for a variety of impact alleviation measures, particularly with respect to infrastructure and landscape provision and

maintenance. This suggests that charges and fees could be introduced without too much difficulty into the British system.

The main difference between impact fees and the present practice lies
not in the justification for seeking to alleviate the impact but in the process
by which the fee/contribution is exacted and in how the level or amount of
the fee/contribution is calculated. An extreme version of an impact fee
would be one that was mandatory on all developments and was levied at
the same flat rate nationally. From the point of view of central government,
such a fee would have the advantage of being simple and easy to collect.
From the developer's perspective, it would have the advantage of being
open, predictable and consistent. It would also be likely to cover more
developers than currently negotiate development obligations, in particular
drawing in smaller projects and schemes with very small impacts. The disadvantages of such nationally fixed fees would be that they would be perceived as unfair by some developers as the charges would not reflect the
actual cost of the impact. They could also prevent development taking
place where it was most needed. As such a system would have many of the
characteristics of tax, there would be both practical and political difficulties
in ensuring that the income was actually used to provide the necessary facilities needed to alleviate the impact.

In contrast, an extreme version of negotiated contributions would apply
where it was left to the local planning authority to decide, on a case-by-case
basis, whether to seek to negotiate a contribution and how to determine its
scale and scope, with the potential for this to be based on very wide general
principles. This would reflect the diversity of development conditions and
the real impacts which specific developments generate. As a result, it would
be seen as fairer as between developers, in that the contribution could be
varied to reflect the real impact of the development. It would also be more
flexible as the authority could determine both the incidence and level of
contributions according to particular local circumstances. The fact that the
contributions would be negotiated could make the process appear more
legitimate. The disadvantage to developers would be that it would appear
arbitrary and unpredictable and the process of negotiation could be time-
consuming and costly. From the public's point of view, the process of negotiation would seem secretive and potentially corrupting.

The challenge is therefore to devise a system which is sufficiently predictable and simple to be efficient to operate but which is also flexible
enough to be fair and likely to achieve planning objectives. Goodchild and
Henneberry (1994) sum up the difficulties well:

> The typical preferences amongst both planning practitioners and
> developers is for a structure which is simultaneously simple to admin-
> ister, predictable in its financial impact and sensitive to variations
> between different sites and areas. Simplicity and predictability are

related one to another. However, neither simplicity nor predictability is easily reconciled with the desire for an impact system which is sensitive to the variations in costs and in local policies (para. 6.2).

Our view is that the best approach to this difficult combination is to try to build into the present flexible structure more openness, clarity and predictability. The important principle would be that local planning authorities should have to set out in advance the basis on which they would be requiring contributions. Where (as in the case of the need for highways infrastructure caused by development on green field sites) the cost can be routinely predicted, detailed scales and tables of charges could be devised, as in the case of the *Berkshire Schedule of Infrastructure Charges*. However, there should always be room for deviation if this can be justified in relation to well-constructed arguments about a 'sufficient relationship', relating a project to particular adverse impacts and measures for alleviating them. We consider it important to retain this flexibility because of the extensive variation in both the type of project and in the local circumstances which is to be found in the British context. As we argue in Chapter 3, project variability means that physical, social and environmental impacts and requirements of projects differ and the value of projects in particular locations can outweigh their costs. It is significant that all the commentators who are in favour of introducing some form of impact fees into the UK recognize the need to keep an element of flexibility. Indeed, Goodchild and Henneberry (1994) argue that:

the lesson of impact fees in USA and France is that there are always exceptional cases that require exceptional negotiation solutions (para. 5, 37).

Goodchild and Henneberry, whose study concerns physical infrastructure considerations only, favour retaining the use of section 106 agreements under planning legislation to deal with the provision of infrastructure that cannot be incorporated within an impact fee regime. Instead, we would argue for the introduction of a systematic and accountable approach to the negotiation of development obligations using the section 106 format, without introducing a legally separate system of impact fees. Grounding policies and principles in the development plan, supplemented by development briefs and schedules of charges where appropriate, could provide such a systematic and accountable approach.

As we indicated earlier, an impact–alleviation approach of this kind cannot be considered as a substitute for a programme of capital funding for local infrastructure or financial measures for alleviating social problems. These should remain a charge on national and local taxation. Otherwise within the context of clear and stable policy frameworks, developers and planning authorities should be able to negotiate contributions to community concerns which balance the need for a development project and its impact on the community. In this way, negotiated planning can proceed as an effective and accountable partnership between regulatory and commercial interests within the context of the land use planning system. We set out, in section 8.4, some of the legal and management issues which need attention for such an approach to work effectively. In the next section, we examine how our approach fits into wider questions about the consideration of impacts in the planning system, and the overall evolving form of the planning system itself.

8.3 SOME GENERAL IMPLICATIONS OF THIS APPROACH

8.3.1 The analysis of impacts

An impact–alleviation approach turns the spotlight on the way impacts are identified. It emphasizes the explicit construction of a causal chain linking a project to its impacts, to the people and places who experience those impacts, and the likely effectiveness of measures to alleviate them. Constructing a 'sufficient relationship' would appear to be a technical question, to be resolved by expert analysts. However, both what is considered an impact and what is seen as an appropriate measure to deal with an impact are likely to be contested, among expert communities and among all those with an interest in the issues in question. Disputes over the reasonableness of arguments have, as we have seen, ended up in the courts for resolution. This potential for dispute makes it clear that the discussion of impacts is as much a technical as a political question.

The particularity of impacts

We have argued that development projects, those promoting them and the impacts they produce, are highly variable phenomena. Further, the connection between a project and its impacts may be conceptualized in different ways. In the past, 'blueprint' approaches to spatial planning dealt with development impacts within models of urban structure, while goal-oriented planning processes dealt with impacts by analysing tendencies in relation to goals (Healey, 1994a). Such models assumed relatively simple functional relations between work and home, economic base and service requirements and between people and nature. Projects were assessed in terms of their impacts on **policy principles**, such as the hierarchy of centres, or the restructuring of road systems, or urban containment through green belts.

These models now seem not merely flawed. The search for a comprehensive grasp of urban system relations itself seems inappropriate to the more diffuse and fragmented forms of the contemporary economic and social relations of urban regions. Places are now more likely to be understood as locales within which a whole range of social and economic relations co-exist, without any necessary connections with each other, except that the activities of one group may get in the way of another, and the activities of everyone may harm the long-term condition of the biosphere.[4] Further, there is a strong contemporary awareness of diversity and particularity, in the characteristics of people, of firms, of neighbourhoods and of environments. Each household combines within itself different dimensions of class, culture, gender, race, ethnicity, physical and mental ability. Firms organize their production and distribution processes in very different ways, even for the same product. The natural environment is no longer seen just as a source of resources to support human activity and a backcloth to urban life. We are now aware of the delicate fragility of ecological, geological and hydrological systems. As Beck argues, we are preoccupied with the risks which our actions may create for our future life (Beck, 1992). As a result, it is no longer possible to imagine that an urban structure model or a set of strategic goals has taken care of the impacts which may concern us. The impacts of a development project seem to spread out across the diffuse relationships of localities, taking unique forms in time and place and potentially affecting a wide range of economic, socio-cultural and environmental relationships.

Current planning practice is struggling with these issues largely on an *ad hoc* basis, as they arise in relation to specific projects. New types of impact are thrown into the arena for consideration as they are raised by national policy or local pressure group politics. Local authorities negotiating development applications are sometimes overwhelmed with the mass of claims for attention which a project raise. Planning officers typically turn to government advice, precedent or the development plan for criteria to help them sort through what it is legitimate to consider and why. The criteria that emerge in individual decisions are then consolidated into specific policy criteria the next time plans are revised. The result is an accretion of criteria derived from custom and practice as much as systematic review.

Identifying impacts

Influenced by planning law and procedure, planning regulation in Britain tends to emphasize arriving at a *qualitative judgement*, within which various considerations are balanced. This recognizes the difficulty of identifying and quantifying that the causal chains linking projects and consequences. Professional judgement, based on experience and precedent, becomes the basis for assessments. Infrastructure, visual environmental impacts and effects on 'amenity' are highlighted in this tradition (see for example, Cullingworth, 1988). A major problem with this approach, however, is that it can deteriorate into an uncritical application of tradition, making it difficult to recognize and attribute either the nature of the causal relationship between a project and its impacts or the proportionality of any impact mitigation measures.

Planning practice is also strongly influenced by political considerations as translated into the policies of central and local government. This serves to highlight particular attributes of projects and fields of impact which deserve consideration. The policies and practices of the planning system are for this reason fine-tuned in their sensitivity to impacts on the visual environment. There is also a considerable tradition of attention to distributive impacts, introduced into planning discourse in the 1970s, and to impacts on developers and businesses, introduced in the 1980s.

These professional, legal and policy discourses which have dominated the planning system in the post-war years are now being challenged by the practices of economic evaluation and environmental appraisal. Economic evaluation is particularly strongly developed in the field of urban policy, where funding regimes emphasize the achievement of particular output criteria. These may emphasize a range of desirable outputs, from jobs and training places to numbers of trees planted and kilometres of streets improved (Hambleton and Thomas, 1995). The introduction of such performance criteria has led to extensive discussion on the relevance of policy objectives. This is in effect a debate over the scope of impact and ways of measuring a 'sufficient relationship'. Despite the criticism of this approach, it has the merit of introducing a more systematic, more carefully reasoned and disaggregated vocabulary to the discussion of impacts than that of the traditional planning judgement.

The emphasis on systematic disaggregation of impacts in relation to the scope of impact is even more clearly evident in the techniques of policy appraisal and evaluation. These have been introduced into the planning field from two directions; economic evaluation and environmental appraisal. Economic evaluation has expanded the technique of cost–benefit analysis to encompass disaggregated impact fields. Cost–benefit analysis identifies impacts as costs, to be offset against benefits. These are aggregated up to obtain an overall calculation of the general welfare contribution of a project, using the concepts and vocabulary of welfare economics (see Chapter 3). Others have sought to break out of this aggregative straitjacket by laying out clearly not merely the types and forms of costs, but the impact of these costs on different objectives (as in Hill's **goals–achievement matrix**) or different groups (as in Lichfield's **planning balance sheet**).[5]

In the field of environmental appraisal, economic techniques of this kind are combined with the techniques and concepts of natural and physical science, to identify the type and scale of impacts on biospheric conditions. These appraisal practices are influencing both development control decision-making in Britain, and the assessment of development plans, as increasing attention is given to the *Strategic Environmental Appraisal* of plans and policies (Glasson *et al.*, 1994). A key conceptual idea in environmental appraisal is the significance of the initial **scoping** of the fields of impact affected by a project or a plan. Appraisal then focuses on establishing the causal chains of connection between project and impact, and the scale of impact generated and its consequences. There have recently been interesting attempts to combine the economic and environmental traditions in developments of Lichfield's **planning balance sheet** (Choudhry and Lichfield, 1993; Lichfield, 1989, 1992).

The discourses of science and economics are given a privileged emphasis in government discussions of environmental appraisal in relation to achieving sustainability objectives (DoE, 1993, p. 10). This suggests that identifying impact fields and measuring impacts are matters of technical calculation based on objective scientific principles. However, it is clear from the debates on environmental policy as well as public discussion of specific projects that the scientific community is divided within itself about cause–effect relationships in many cases, and about the appropriateness of particular measures. Further, what constitutes an adverse impact is a matter of individual perception and cultural judgement as much as technical calculation. As Owens (1994) argues, there are limits to the extent to which technical calculus can and should replace public judgement on environmental questions, since these raise issues of moral significance and cultural values. Further, technical calculation does not itself assess exactly how particular individuals and agencies are likely to be affected by adverse impacts. Yet, in calculating alleviation measures, it is impacts on individuals and agencies which are the critical factor.

At the present time, in the field of impact assessment, there is substantial contestation among different traditions. Environmental regulation, through the work of such bodies as the National Rivers Authority and the Health and Safety Executive, emphasizes systematic calculation using the discourses of economists and scientists. Within the planning field, professional and legal judgement, in the context of policy statements, emphasizes **balancing judgements**, in the vocabulary of legal and policy acceptability. The first recognizes the value of systematic laying out (**scoping**) of impact fields, causal chains and scales of impact. The second accepts that there are rarely hard and fast technical answers to the questions raised, and that such questions in any case involve much more than technical dimensions. As a result, a politically accountable judgemental capacity is essential, to weigh up the relative merits of technical calculation against other considerations.

What this suggests is that an impact-driven approach to the negotiation of development obligations would benefit from the introduction of more systematic approaches to laying out the reasoning behind what impacts are identified, what and who are affected by these impacts, the assessment of the scale of effect and how might this be mitigated. But such **scoping of arguments** cannot rely solely upon economic and scientific analysis. It will need to draw in other dimensions of social science which address questions of moral and cultural perceptions, and involve the various parties, interest groups and 'stakeholders', whose perceptions are involved. It was also need to recognize that, in the end, **judgements balancing the various arguments** will have to be made. An impact-driven approach thus leads on to consideration of the nature of the **argumentation** of the planning system.

Arguments about impacts

This conclusion reinforces our view that it will be difficult to convert development obligations into standardized development charges or impact fees. Not only are projects variable in the impacts they generate and the way these are distributed at particular times and in particular places. There will also be variation in the weight which particular political communities will wish to give to impacts and measures to mitigate them. Much of the attraction of standardized impact fees at national level and of nationally accepted technical and scientific calculations must be understood as an attempt to limit local interpretations of what impacts are important and how they should be addressed. Yet it is people and environments in local communities who bear the brunt of most impacts.

The analysis of the impacts of development projects and measures to mitigate them leads, thus, both to more systematic **scoping** of the causal chains between projects and impacts and attempts at assessing the scale and distribution of impacts, and to the potential for conflict over the scope, the sufficiency of the relationship, the scale of the impact, its distribution and appropriate mitigation. If this is so, then the argumentation surrounding any particular development project could prove extremely complex. The task involves moving from scoping the arguments about impacts, to sorting through the significance of the arguments and developing ways of ameliorating them. The conclusions of this process must stand up to political scrutiny and legal challenge. Any interest group could challenge decisions, through lobbying and media campaigns as well as through formal processes. Formalized challenges could then end up in the courts, where arguments would be subjected to detailed legal examination. The resultant process could be time-consuming and politically complex. An impact-driven approach centred around appraising every project *de novo* would thus be impracticable.

There are various responses to this dilemma. One is the traditional *ad hoc* balancing judgements which remain common in much of the development control arena. But these are in reality constrained by past policies, legal judgements and plan statements. The emphasis on grounding regulatory decisions in plans is an attempt to ensure that development control judgements are based on relevant policy considerations produced in publicly accountable ways. A second response is to limit the range of impacts which can be considered, through limiting the scope and the 'reach' of impacts which can be considered. The attempt to confine development obligations to matters primarily related to the development site is one such limitation. The US **rational nexus** test also aims to constrain the reach of the causal chains of impact arguments. The attempt to limit 'material considerations' in development control to 'land use' matters, and exclude social and economic impacts, is another example. None of these seems likely to stand up against current concerns about development activity and its consequences.

A third option is to develop local policies about the scope and range of impacts which will be considered, the way arguments will be made about projects and their impacts, and the forms of mitigation measures which are considered appropriate. The development plan, with its formal procedures of preparation and approval, provides both the arena for discussion and debate about such policies and a legitimate and accountable statement of what has been agreed. We believe that an impact-driven approach to development obligations grounded in development plans could combine the value of systematic argumentation about impacts with the flexibility to recognize the specificities of individual projects and places. The argumentation of the plan would then provide not merely a store of reasoning through which to define the relationship between projects, their impacts and mitigation measures. It would define the terms of discourse through which the courts could establish what a 'sufficient relationship' between a project and its impacts could be. Plans, policies and individual regulatory decisions would stand or fall by the quality of their argumentation. Development projects in turn, would stand or fall by the quality of the 'package' (see Lichfield, 1989), both the project itself and the measures to mitigate adverse effects as identified within the context of the plan arguments. Negotiation would be undertaken within the context of these parameters.

8.3.2 The regulatory form of the planning system

Our emphasis on the importance of a 'plan-led' approach to the regulation of land-use change assumes that this approach will continue. Yet the past history of the planning system shows that support for plans within the system has been uneven. The discretionary nature of the planning system allows central government to change the weight given to plans, and the balancing of policy considerations, with relative ease. Section 54A of the 1990 Town and Country Planning Act, with its emphasis on regulatory decisions being 'in accordance' with the plan only provides a marginal shift in this position (Purdue, 1994). This could mean that our approach to the treatment of development obligations will be overtaken by changes in government policy as to the status of the plan. However, there are several reasons which make it likely that government will continue to support a plan-led approach.

A planning system which emphasizes locally articulated and approved development plans as the key source of policies, policy arguments and criteria upon which to base regulatory decisions gives priority to the **territorial integration** of considerations of projects and impacts. It also allows land use and development decisions to be set in the context of the economic, social and environmental relations which give rise to development activity, through which impacts have their effects and agencies get involved in mitigation measures. It provides an arena through which the spatial interrelations of activities can be identified and policies to deal with interconnections articulated.

But there are currently, as in earlier periods, considerable challenges to this activity. At the present time, there are tendencies which could lead in different directions. One is a retreat to the practices of the 1980s, when powerful players negotiated individual deals with local planning authorities. As we have argued in relation to the negotiation of development obligations, these practices are now widely recognized as unfair as between other developers and landowners. They are also likely to ignore significant impacts, and may be inefficient, where developers end up paying much more for projects which unlock development opportunities for them than they would have to with more strategic policies. The impetus for the present book was the adverse reaction to *ad hoc* negotiation as a way forward for the regulation of land-use change and development.

A second possibility is that the locus of the articulation of regulatory criteria could move away from the local level, and focus instead on nationally developed policy criteria. This would fit well with the traditional sectoralism of British government (Francis, 1993). The planning system would become merely a set of regulatory criteria to be applied to development anywhere. It would be clearly separated from other regulatory systems, which deal with matters such as environmental pollution, health and safety, and national heritage. It would also be distinct from policies to promote development, such as urban regeneration policy, or economic development policy. There are considerable tendencies in this direction at present, not merely in the role of the various *Planning Policy Guidance* notes produced by the Department of the Environment, but the emergence of new regulatory systems in the environmental arena. Such a management-by-criteria (Healey, 1994a) limits the consideration of the relationship between projects and impacts, particularly as regards the distributive impacts of projects in time and place. It also allows national lobby groupings to dominate the articulation of policies, rather than local ones. Yet the direction of government thinking on planning matters was tending in this direction in the 1980s.

The re-emphasis on the plan at the end of the 1980s gave renewed force to the development plan, because government recognized the significance of territorial impacts and the political concern with the quality of local environments. Conflicts over land-use change and development projects arouse often intense local feeling. The array of interests with a stake in a particular issue is very difficult to predict and allow for in national legislation and policy criteria. Pushing responsibility onto the development plan, and onto local planning authorities in approving their plans, helps not merely to respond to this reality. It also pulls central government back from the weight of political and legal lobbying and challenge which a national criteria-based system would produce. There are also many other pressures giving more weight to local policy articulation, particularly European Union pressures for territorially articulated regional and local development strategies as the basis of bids for EU regional development funds.

But a strong locally based, plan-driven approach can take several forms. It could be driven by the argumentation of professional and expert groups. At present, this would mean a procedural and legalistic discourse built up from the experience of planners in defending policies against developer challenges and in accommodating to central government policy directives. But in future, the expertise informing planning work could shift to take on the discourses of urban economics or environmental appraisal. Or it could be driven by local political alliances, pursuing self-interested policies. Current examples include those authorities with strong economic development agendas, often these days in alliance with business interests. This could lead to plans with a fairly narrow scope of impact arguments. Or the process of plan preparation could reflect a broadly based involvement of stakeholders in framing the issue agendas, the strategy and the implications of the plan. Such a process would be likely to reflect the pressure to make complex connections between elements of the plan, reflecting the diversity of stakeholder interests and points of view. This would be likely to lead to a broad and carefully argued approach to the scope and reach of impact arguments.

There are signs in contemporary British practice of all these approaches to plan-making (see Healey, 1993, 1994c). Our approach could have a place in them all. But if the adverse impacts of development projects are to be adequately identified and mitigated, our preference is for the third of these plan-based approaches. The development plan within the British planning system is distinctive as a public policy instrument because it provides an arena where complex, spatially interconnected issues of interest to many stakeholders in localities can be discussed and policies developed, challenged and agreed. If, as the Labour Party and others propose (Labour Party, 1994), third parties are given the right to challenge development control decisions which are not in line with plans, plan-making will be pushed vigorously to attend to all those who could raise such a challenge. Narrow issue agendas and narrow arguments would be unlikely to survive such a change. This would be a welcome development for all those who believe, as we do, that Britain would benefit from a more effective contribution by citizens and all affected stakeholders in public policy, more openness in public decision-making, and real 'subsidiarity', that is, devolving decisions down to those most affected.

8.4 THE IMPLEMENTATION OF OUR PROPOSALS

The approach set out in section 8.2 above would raise a number of practical issues which need careful attention if effective implementation is to be achieved. These relate to the legal mechanisms through which development obligations are created, the relation of development obligations to **material considerations**, how much of the specification of obligation can be contained in the development plan, the efficiency and accountability of the negotiation process and the management of obligations, once agreed. Many of these need attention in any case, as we have indicated in Chapter 7. Most can be dealt with in the framework of current British law and policy. However, in some instances, changes in law and policy will be required. We therefore make it clear when this would be necessary.

8.4.1 The legal mechanisms for creating development obligations

At present there are two main statutory instruments for creating development obligations, section 106 of the Town and Country Planning Act 1990 and section 278 of the Highways Act 1980, with section 111 used as a sweeping-up provision. The new wording of section 106 (see Chapters 4 and 7) means that it can be used to create a wide range of on-site and off-site obligations which would be effective in the alleviation of the impacts of developments. The main gap which has been identified by the courts is that there is no provision for the transfer of land. In particular, it is doubtful whether a binding unilateral undertaking could be made transferring land to a local planning authority. The Court of Appeal in **Crest Homes plc [1994]**, has helped to close this gap by upholding the validity of agreements where the transfer can be considered as part of the restrictions or positive steps which are being imposed. Nevertheless, we consider that section 106 should be amended so that the owners of land should be able to bind themselves to transfer land to the council free of charge. Of course, where this was done by a unilateral undertaking the council should be able to decline the offer if it was considered to be too burdensome.

As we pointed out in Chapter 4, many of the obligations which take the form of a section 106 obligation could be equally well, and often are, imposed by way of a planning condition attached to the grant of permission. It would therefore be possible to replace the negotiation of obligations by amending the statutory power to impose conditions. If it was made clear that conditions could be validly imposed which required an action to be undertaken to alleviate the impact of the development (including the payment of moneys and the free transfer of land), this would substantially remove the need for a separate legal mechanism for creating development obligations. Such a solution has its attractions. It would simplify the system and reassert the traditional regulatory model of development control with its virtues of openness and participation. Nevertheless, we conclude that it is necessary to retain the extra dimension of negotiated obligations. The medium of the agreement is a much more efficient way of dealing with the complex arrangements that are necessary to deal with the full range of impacts. Although the consensual element of agreements can be exaggerated, as developers only volunteer the obligations because of the need to obtain planning permission, the fact that obligations are agreed or offered helps to underpin their legitimacy and the willingness of developers to implement the undertakings. Also, agreements are sometimes used to duplicate clearly valid and appropriate conditions just to give the authority extra control over the development. While this 'belt and braces' approach is not strictly necessary, we consider it should be left to developers to determine whether to enter into such agreements in addition to the conditions imposed on the grant of planning permission.

The relationship between sections 106 and 278 of the Highways Act is particularly difficult to resolve. It raises the wider issue of whether every agency which might need to ensure that an adverse impact is addressed would need a separate legal power to authorize a contribution. Alternatively, the planning legislation could act as a general co-ordinator of the various claims, through section 106 agreements. Our research showed that highways and planning powers are often used in combination to ensure that developers contribute to the creation of new highway infrastructure. The option of consolidating section 106 as the sole mechanism for creating development obligations has the merit of simplicity. It would also be logical in that it is the grant of permission which both requires the actions needed to ameliorate the impacts and which unlocks the means by which the private developer undertakes what has been agreed. The section 106 format is also more flexible in that it allows for works to be carried out by the developer as an alternative to the developer paying for the highway authority or other agency to undertake the work. The main disadvantage would be that, where the local planning authority was not the agency with responsibility for the activities which the obligation involves, for example, if it is not the highway authority, or in charge of managing public landscape, the agency concerned would have to rely on the planning authority to act as its agent. Yet this already happens in practice and highway authorities no longer have power to prevent the grant of permission for developments which will increase the amount of traffic on their highways. We would suggest that the best solution would be to retain the power for highway authorities, and other affected agencies, to enter into agreements under legislation specific to them but to amend all such legislation and section 106 so that there is a more uniform approach. Then in most cases obligations requiring contributions to highways and other matters should be created through section 106. But agency-specific legislation could still be used by other authorities in cases where planning permission was not at issue.

8.4.2 Development obligations as 'material considerations'

This is the most fundamental issue as regards the offer of obligations as it is only where development obligations are seen as making an unacceptable or marginal development acceptable that developers will offer them and local planning authorities feel justified in seeking them. Despite the fact that the courts have in most cases insisted that they alone can determine whether a consideration is material enough to justify the refusal or the granting of permission in contrast to the US courts, they have been reluctant to spell out what is the required relationship between the obligation and the grant of permission. They have generally been content to endorse the approach of the Department of the Environment. The present loose legal framework means that the main safeguards against local planning authorities pressuring developers into providing unnecessary contributions or the 'buying' of planning permissions by the offer of unrelated planning advantages, is the right of appeal and the power of the Secretary of State to call in applications. This allows, as in the **Tesco (Witney) [1994]** case, the decision to be made by the Secretary of State or his inspectors and the policies of the Secretary of State to be made to prevail. Much could be achieved by a further clarification of the government's policy towards development obligations on the lines that we have proposed in this chapter. This would require a more express endorsement by the government of the types of impacts which need to be alleviated and a limited acceptance of the compensatory principle where there is a close association between the development and the obligation.

There would remain the difficulty that, as the law presently stands, the courts appear reluctant to ensure that, where permission is granted by a local planning authority on the basis of a development obligation, there is both a sufficient relationship and rough proportionality between the harm which would otherwise be caused by the development and the obligation. So developers could still find it convenient to agree to obligations to obtain permission, even, if according to government policy, those obligations or part of them should be disregarded by the local planning authority in the determining the planning application. On the other hand, the courts have held that government policy as to the weight that should be given to material considerations is itself a material consideration. Therefore the courts could be expected at least to ensure that local planning authorities justify any violation of that policy. Of course, the Town and Country Planning Act 1990 could be amended so as to require what we have termed a sufficient relationship between the obligation and the development. However, as we indicated earlier, this would be hard to spell out in statutory language and a new statutory formulation could itself cause more difficulties in raising new issues of interpretation. It is preferable to leave it to the courts to lay down consistent and authoritative guidance as to what constitutes a sufficient relationship. While we have been critical of the courts' record on this in the past, the courts are now clearly aware of the issues. The appeal at present going to the House of Lords give them an opportunity to clarify the law. Once this is clearly laid down, most local planning authorities would not deliberately evade such an approach and the remedy of judicial review would be available to challenge cases where the guidance had been clearly flouted.

The enactment of third-party rights to appeal against the granting of planning permission would further help to prevent the undermining of established planning policies in return for development obligations. The present government is unlikely to look with favour on such a change and it would certainly be opposed by most developers. Yet some Conservative MPs have expressed support for the idea, and it is already Labour Party policy to introduce third-party rights of appeal against permissions which are contrary to development plan policy (Labour Party, 1994). The introduction of such a right is in any case a logical consequence of the increased status of the development plan under section 54A (see Chapter 4).

8.4.3 Formulating and publicizing policies and criteria relating to development obligations

The need for predictability means that as far as possible both the basic policies regarding the alleviation of the impacts of development, and the detailed criteria as to their application, should be set out in advance. It is equally important for the legitimacy of the process that interested parties should be able to participate in the preparation of the policies and criteria. It is for this reason that we argue that policies towards development obligations should be grounded in approved development plans. Our research has already shown that there is a trend towards local planning authorities setting out clear strategies for development obligations in their development

plans. The practical issue, however, is how far should the detailed specification of the terms of negotiation and any charges required be contained
in the development plan, which is supposed to last as a policy frame-work
for 5–10 years, and how far should there be some form of supplementary
planning guidance? There are several advantages in using the mechanism
of the development plan as the main vehicle for setting out local planning
policies regarding development obligations. First, the procedures are
already geared towards ensuring a substantial amount of public participation
and scrutiny. Second, the powers of the Secretary of State to make directions
and to call in plans enables some consistency to be imposed on the
approach taken by local planning authorities. This is an important accountability mechanism. Third, the enhanced status of the plans should ensure
that the policies are not lightly disregarded and that departures are properly
justified.

More problematic is the extent to which the detailed criteria and scales of
contributions should be set out in the plans. Delafons, in discussing the
possible introduction of a system of impact fees into the UK, has argued
that the standards of provision and scales of payment should be published
separately from the development plan, since the plan approval process is
already slow and complex and it might well be necessary to revise the scales
more frequently than the normal quinquennial review (Delafons, 1991a,
1991b). Similarly Goodchild and Henneberry (1994) argue that, if a system
of impact fees were to be introduced, the role of the development plan
should be confined to setting out the broad framework for the application
of different types of impact fees. They propose that:

> Specific standards for community facilities, for instance the provision
> of public open space, could be included in a development plan, at the
> discretion of the planning authority. However, other forms of policy
> statements should be avoided. District-wide lists of desired facilities
> should be avoided because they are too vague. Lists of site-by-site
> requirements should be avoided because these are likely to become
> obsolete (para. 5.47).

Our proposals are not so dependent on the existence of set scales of contributions, though we consider that charges should be standardized where
this can be done fairly. While we accept that the development plans should
not contain detailed costings, we believe that development plans should
make clear, drawing on the issues raised in section 8.3, what kind of impacts
the local planning authorities will normally require to be alleviated before
permission is granted and the standards and criteria which will be applied.
This should deliver the right mixture of certainty and flexibility, while the
existing development plan procedures would ensure the necessary public
participation and accountability.

We therefore do not consider that it is necessary to introduce a separate formal procedure for the publication and approval of standard charges and the application of the policies and standards to particular sites and areas. Our research suggests that this could be achieved through supplementary development guidance, development briefs, area-specific programmes and schedules of infrastructure requirements. What might be appropriate would depend on specific local circumstances. It would of course still be important that all interested parties should be properly involved in the drawing up of these documents. This would be indispensable in the case of large projects where several different developers could be involved.

8.4.4 The efficiency and accountability of the negotiation process

One of the main objections to negotiating development obligations is that the drafting of agreements and undertakings is time-consuming and costly to all the parties involved. A lot of these costs should be avoided by clarifying in advance what contributions will be expected and the quantum of those contributions. However, as we pointed out in Chapter 7, it is also desirable for the local planning authorities to systematize the way the various claims for obligations are to be co-ordinated. Developers should have one main contact point with the authority and should not have to be referred back and forth to different agencies. It should also be possible to standardize the form of the heads of agreement which will form the basis of the agreement contract.

While the actual negotiation of obligations cannot be conducted publicly, it is important that interested parties should be consulted if there is likely to be any substantial change from the published policies and standards. This would become more necessary if third party rights of appeal against permissions out of line with plan policy were introduced. It has been pointed out in Chapter 7 that, while there are statutory requirements for publicizing planning applications, there are no requirements for publicizing the development obligations which are proposed as a pre-condition of the granting of permission. We therefore argue that there should be a requirement that the heads of any proposed obligations should be made public before a decision is made. These in turn should clearly relate both to the nature of the project and its impacts, to the scope of impact considered important in the development plan, and the reasoning connecting the project and its impacts to the measures negotiated for alleviation.

8.4.5 The recording and management of obligations

As we set out in Chapter 7, the present system of recording of obligations is very unsatisfactory. We would argue that all obligations linked to the grant of planning permission should be required to be entered on the existing planning register. This would ensure that the general public could easily find out just what obligations have been created. This would make for open accountability. At the same time, local planning authorities should follow the Wandsworth practice of keeping a separate record of all obligations to ensure subsequent monitoring and management.

Our research shows that once planning permission is granted, there is no certainty that either the developer will comply with the obligation or that the authority will ensure that the contributions are used to alleviate the impact. Grant has argued that:

All funds collected should be placed in a special trust account administered by the local planning authority but with additional trustees appointed from outside the authority, and applied solely to local infrastructure improvements. Whether developers would be entitled to refunds of unexpended contributions would depend upon whether the scheme was designed as project-specific, or collective. But as a minimum requirement of public accountability the trust would be required to publish its investment plans and its annual accounts (Grant, 1991, p. 83).

Our case study authorities were aware of this issue, and most took care to ensure that there was a clear accounting link between payments made and what they were to be used for. The problem was that this was not always visible, even to councillors and other officers. It is unclear at present whether a local planning authority would be acting 'contrary to law' in spending money contributed for specific projects on extraneous matters. We therefore agree that a mechanism is necessary to ensure that moneys are used for the purposes intended by the recipient. However, we doubt whether it is necessary to set up a special trust. It is already open to the developer to write into the agreement a clause that the moneys will be returned if they are not used as required by the agreement. Otherwise, present local authority accounting mechanisms could be modified so that contributions have to be kept in separate accounts for which public accounts are provided. It could also be made clear that the improper use of the moneys was contrary to law. This would make the members and officers responsible subject to being surcharged. In respect of the developer's side of the bargain, the present powers of enforcement are generally adequate and the need is for authorities to set up regular monitoring of obligations.

8.5 CONCLUSIONS

This book has argued for a decisive shift in the treatment of development obligations within the context of the planning system. This shift focuses attention on the adverse impacts of development and ways of mitigating them. This has always been a core concern of the British planning system. But the treatment of adverse impacts in the system has become embedded in government and legal practices which have obscured rather than revealed the way projects generate impacts and how these impacts are then dealt with. This leads to problems of legitimacy and accountability. These undermine confidence in the planning system at a time when public confidence in governance processes is low and awareness of wide-ranging adverse social, economic and environmental impacts is high.

Our objective is to re-focus the approach to development impacts. This would help to tidy up a messy area of planning practice, the negotiation of development obligations. But it could also spearhead a more general reconceptualization of both development control law and practice, and the argumentation of the planning system in general. An impact–alleviation emphasis within the planning system would encourage much greater attention in policies to determining the scope of impacts to consider, and the 'sufficiency' and 'proportionality' of the relationship between projects, impacts and measures to mitigate them. It would focus on the quality of the 'reasoned justification' behind policies and proposals. It would also help to link the various dimensions of planning policies, through tracing impacts in one policy field in relation to others.

Our approach emphasizes the importance of systematic reasoning. We, however, anticipate that the processes of debate over policy content will draw upon various modes of reasoning, from scientific and social scientific fields, to legal discourse and moral arguments. This reflects the reality of contemporary public reasoning about projects and impacts. It is for this reason that we favour a plan-based approach to defining the scope and scale of impact–alleviation measures, rather than a general system of a priori standardized charges.

Our approach also allows sensitivity to the diversity of development projects and the local particularity of their impacts. We believe it offers a way of providing the flexibility to reflect this diversity, with the predictability needed to ensure efficiency and accountability in the regulation of development. This combination has been a major strength of the British planning system over the years, and is a quality even more required in planning systems these days than in periods when urban growth was more assured and public finance more substantial and predictable.

The planning system plays a valuable role in providing a local focus for negotiating how to promote, enable and regulate the transformation of local environments. It provides an arena for articulating the concerns of a wide range of stakeholders, with direct interests in sites and projects, and less direct interests in the qualities of places. If used well, it provides policy parameters through the development plan-making process, which can serve to frame the ideas, projects and actions of many parties. The policy parameters provide a framework within which negotiation over the precise balancing of claims for attention can be undertaken with respect to specific projects.

We consider that our approach contributes to the evolution of the British planning system into an effective tool for an enabling regulatory regime for addressing public concerns about land use change and development. It should help to make the practice of negotiating obligations more efficient, effective, fair and relevant. It should also help to make the planning system more open and accountable, and contribute towards ensuring that it evolves towards a form which facilitates development while bearing in mind the varied dimensions of the community interest.

NOTES

1. See Chapter 4 for a discussion of the scope of **material considerations**.
2. In British development control law, applications for planning permission must be permitted unless they would cause 'demonstrable harm to interests of acknowledged importance' (DoE, 1992a).
3. The report on impact fees for the Department of the Environment (Goodchild and Henneberry, 1994) illustrates this, using a very broad definition initially ('any contribution towards the cost of a public service necessary to sustain a development or to ensure that development accords with usual environmental standards', para. 1.2), and later limiting the term to a fee based on a schedule of charges levied on a developer.
4. See the introduction to Healey *et al.* (1995) for a discussion of recent trends in approaches to urban and regional change.
5. See Cowling and Steeley (1973) for a review of these evaluation methods.

APPENDIX 1: THE STUDY APPROACH

Reflecting the increased awareness of negotiated planning in the 1980s, there has been a recent burst of research interest in the issue of planning agreements. There have been surveys to establish the scale of the practice (Grimley J. R. Eve *et al.*, 1992; MacDonald, 1991; Durman and Rowan-Robinson, 1991); assessments of the role of planning gain in large new settlement projects (Elson, 1990a); exploration of the use of planning agreements to pursue environmental conservation and ecological objectives (Whatmore and Boucher, 1992) and social housing objectives (Barlow and Chambers, 1992; Williams *et al.*, 1991) and studies of the role of agreements in relation to infrastructure provision (Rowan-Robinson and Lloyd, 1988).

The aim of the research reported in this book study, funded by the Joseph Rowntree Foundation, was to:

1. review the *arguments* being used to justify negotiating obligations from developers, both their general rationale and the problems of applying arguments to specific cases; the objective was to explore ways of clarifying policy principles and decision criteria;
2. explore the *form* and *content* of planning agreements, and their relation to the arguments used to *justify* them; and their *significance* in relation to the overall amount of development activity, to public, private and community sector roles in managing environmental change, and to the accountability and legitimacy of the planning system;
3. examine the practice surrounding the negotiation of obligations to identify the *operational challenges* arising and the way these were being addressed. This involved intensive case study research, as called for by the survey for the DoE (Grimley J. R. Eve *et al.*, 1992).

The research started in January 1991 and was completed by the end of 1992. It involved the following stages:

1. Review of the literature to identify the various arguments, and hypotheses as to practice. This led to the identification of three broad *rationales* for planning gain (Healey *et al.*, 1992b), and a discussion of the relations between British and American legal arguments, particularly with respect to the **rational nexus test** (Purdue *et al.*, 1992).
2. Interviews with representatives of key interest groups, i.e. planning officers, developers, planning and property consultants, solicitors and environmental interest groups. These were undertaken in spring/summer 1991.
3. Review of the treatment of the planning gain issue in recent local plans (Healey, 1991b; Healey *et al.*, 1992a).
4. Intensive case studies with the following local authorities; undertaken in 1991 and 1992:
   - Solihull Metropolitan Borough Council, West Midlands;
   - Tewkesbury Borough Council, Gloucestershire;
   - Harlow District Council, Essex;
   - London Borough of Wandsworth;
   - Newcastle City Council, Tyne and Wear.

Each study involved interviews with planning officers, officers in other departments, council members, developers, and some interest groups; review of planning case files, collection of information on agreements, and selection of cases for detailed investigation. For each case, a report was prepared and discussed with officers in the case study local authority.

The period covered in the case studies was from 1984 to 1991. It therefore precedes the amendments made to the law on planning obligations and the status of development plans by the Planning and Compensation Act 1991 and the subsequent change in government policy with respect to developer obligations (circular 16/91). It also largely pre-dates the water charges introduced in the 1989 Water Act. Our interviews were also conducted before circular 16/91 was published. Our research can therefore only provide comments on how those interviewed generally and in the case studies viewed the new legislative provisions. Our research thus records the evolution of practice during the 1980s and people's views as to the development of practice in the early 1990s. In preparing this book, we have made every effort to update information on the projects and policies discussed.

For information, we provide a list of legal sources cited in agreements reviewed in our case study authorities (Table A1.1), and the full classification of developer obligations used in producing the summary tables in Chapter 5.

Table A1.1   The legal sources cited in agreements in the study
(Note: Not all of these are strictly powers authorizing agreements)

Section 16 Public Health Act 1936

Section 18 Public Health Act 1936

Section 87 Public Health Act 1936

Section 52 Town and Country Planning Act 1971

Section 111 Local Goverment Act 1972

Section 120 Local Goverment Act 1972

Section 123 Local Goverment Act 1972

Section 19 Local Government (Miscellaneous Provisions) Act 1976

Section 24 Highways Act 1980

Section 25 Highways Act 1980

Section 35 Highways Act 1980

Section 37 Highways Act 1980

Section 38 Highways Act 1980

Section 41 Highways Act 1980

Section 62 Highways Act 1980

Section 64 Highways Act 1980

Section 72 Highways Act 1980

Section 177 Highways Act 1980

Section 239 Highways Act 1980

Section 251 Highways Act 1980

Section 252 Highways Act 1980

Section 278 Highways Act 1980

Section 296 Highways Act 1980

Section 33 Local Government (Miscellaneous Provisions) Act 1982

Section 8 Housing Act 1985

Section 9 Housing Act 1985

Section 106 Town and Country Planning Act 1990

Private Acts

Section 19 Gloucestershire County Council Act 1956

Section 27 Greater London Council (General Powers) 1969

Section 16 Greater London Council (General Powers) 1974

Section 40 Severn-Trent Water Act 1983

Table A1.2   Full classification of development obligations identified in agreements in our case study authorities

Negative obligations

Development control administration
prior permission not implemented
personal permission

Controlling development
phasing of development
controlling development
development to be completed

Post development control
restrictions on site use
conditions of use
building use restriction
cessation of use – on-site
cessation of use – off-site
reversion of use
controls over use
agricultural use restriction

rights of way
rights of access
access to water
riverside access

agricultural occupancy restriction
age occupancy restriction
occupancy restriction
ownership restriction

negation of CDO
restriction of development rights
demolition option

noise control

Affordable housing

Management and maintenance
developer to maintain
LA to maintain
management/control specified

Employment and training

Modification
agreement renewed
agreement varied
release from agreement

Other
remove mobile home from site
increase horticultural holding

Positive obligations

Highways
on-site highways

Recreational facilities
playing fields

off-site highways
footpaths

Sewerage
on-site sewerage
off-site sewerage

Drainage
on-site drainage
off-site drainage

Landscaping and open space
structural landscaping
general landscaping

open space
amenity open space
footpath
cycleway

tree/shrub planting
tree/shrub protection
fence provision

riverside walk
dockside walk
riverside access
lifting bridge
boat moorings

riverside park
new park entrance
car-park refurbishment
woodland conservation
woodlands planting
water feature
conservation

maintenance payments

Parking
parking spaces
public car-parking
car-park provision
commuted car-parking

Community facilities
buildings: on-site; off-site
buildings: contributions

play areas
play equipment

Child-care
crèche

Employment and training
management centre

Affordable housing
affordable housing plots
plots with service provision
affordable housing quotas

Nature conservation

Building restoration

Public transport
bus service provision
rail service provision
taxi rank

Refurbishment
building refurbishment
rebuilding wall

Public toilets

Serviced sites

Other
archaeological
disabled car-park relocation
demolition
noise attenuation
ensuring site stability
bridge
provision of market area
LA contributions
developer contributions

APPENDIX 2: INDEX OF LEGAL CASES

References to legal cases appear in bold in the text

Abbreviations used:

AC	Appeal Cases
ALL E R	All England Law Reports
JPL	Journal of Planning and Environment Law
P&CR	Property Planning and Compensation Reports
SC	Scottish Courts
SCt	Supreme Court
US	United States
WLR	Weekly Law Report

Barber [1991]: Barber v Secretary of State for the Environment [1991] JPL 559

Bolton [1991]: Bolton MDC v Secretary of State for the Environment [1991] JPL 241

Bradford [1986]: Bradford MDC v Secretary of State for the Environment (1986) 53 P&CR 55

Brighton [1979]: Brighton Borough Council v Secretary of State for the Environment [1979] JPL 173

British Airports Authority [1979]: British Airports Authority v Secretary of State for Scotland [1979] SC 200

British Railways Board [1994]: British Railways Board v Secretary of State for the Environment [1994] JPL 32

Brittania [1978]: Brittania (Cheltenham) Ltd v Secretary of State for the Environment [1978] JPL 554

Charles Church [1990]: R v Wealden DC *ex parte* Charles Church (1990) 59 P&CR 150

REFERENCES

Alder, J. (1990) Planning agreements and planning powers, *Journal of Planning and Environmental Law*, 880–9.

Alterman, R. (ed.) (1988) *Private Supply of Public Services: Evaluation of Real Estate Exactions, Linkages and Alternative Land Policies*, New University Press, New York.

Ambrose, P. (1986) *Whatever Happened to Planning?*, Methuen, London.

Amin, A. and Dieterich, M. (eds) (1991) *Towards a New Europe*, Edward Elgar, Aldershot, Hants.

Ashworth, S. (1993) Plymouth and After II, *Journal of Planning and Environment Law*, 1105–10.

Backwell, J. and Dickens, P. (1978) *Town Planning, Mass Loyalty and the Restructuring of Capital: The Origins of the 1947 Planning Legislation Revisited*, Urban and Regional Studies Working Paper No 11, University of Sussex.

Bailey, S. (1990) Charges for local infrastructure, *Town Planning Review*, **61**(4), 427–53.

Ball, M. (1983) *Housing Policy and Economic Power*, Methuen, London.

Ball, M. (1986) The built environment and the urban question, *Society and Space*, **4**, 447–64.

Barlow, J. and Chambers, D. (1992) *Planning Agreements and Affordable Housing Provision*, Department of Urban and Regional Research, University of Sussex.

Barlow, J. and Duncan, S. (1994) *Success and Failure in Housing Provision*, Pergamon, Oxford.

Barlow, J. and King, A. (1992) The State, the market and competitive strategy: the house building industry in Britain, France and Sweden, *Environment and Planning A*, **24**, 381–400.

Barras, R. (1987) Technical change and the urban development cycle, *Urban Studies*, **24**(1), 5–30.

Barrett, S., Boddy, M. and Steward, M. (1978) *The Implementation of the Community Land Act*, SAUS Occasional Paper School of Advanced Urban Studies, Bristol.

Barton Willmore Planning Partnership (1991) *Planning Gain and the Berkshire County Council Guide*, Barton Willmore, Reading, Berks.

Beck, U. (1992) *The Risk Society*, Sage, London.

Berkshire County Council (1989) *Infrastructure, Services and Amenity Requirements for New Developments in Berkshire*, Berkshire CC, Reading.

Birmingham City Council (1990) *Unitary Development Plan: Consultation Draft*, Birmingham City Council.

Booth, P. (1991) Preparing land for development in France: the role of the amenageur – Lotisseur, *Journal of Property Research*, **8**(3), 239–51.

Bowers, J. (1992) The economics of planning gain: a re-appraisal, *Urban Studies*, **29**(8), 1329–40.

Bramley, G. (1993) Land use planning and the housing market: the impact on housebuilding and houseprices, *Urban Studies*, **25**, 1021–51.

Brindley, T., Rydin, R. and Stoker, G. (1989) *Remaking Planning*, Unwin Hyman, London.

Bryant, C. R., Rushworm, L. H. and McLellan (1992) *The City's Countryside*, Longman, London.

Burrows, J. (1978) Vacant urban land, *The Planner*, **64**(1), 7–9.

Cadman, D. and Austin-Crowe, L. (1978) *Property Development*, E & FN Spon, London.

Callies, D. L. and Grant, M. (1991) Planning for growth and planning gain: an anglo-american comparison of development conditions, impact fees and development agreements, *The Urban Lawyer*, **23**(2), 221–48.

Choudhury, A. and Lichfield, N. (1993) Evaluation for transport policies and programmes, *The Planner*, **79**(8), 13–16.

Clarke, L. (1992) *Building Capitalism: Historical Change and the Labour Process in the Production of the Built Environment*, Routledge, London.

Cowell, R. (1993) *'Take and give': managing the impacts of development with environmental compensation*, UKCEED Discussion Paper No. 10, UKCEED, Cambridge.

Cowling, T. and Steeling, G. (1973) *Subregional Planning Studies: Evaluation*, Pergamon Press, Oxford.

Cullingworth, J. B. (1975) *Reconstruction and Land Use Planning 1934–1947: Environmental History*, Vol. 1, HMSO, London.

Cullingworth, J. B. (1988) *Town and Country Planning in Britain*, 10th edn, Unwin Hyman, London.

Cullingworth, J. B. (1993) *The Political Culture of Planning*, Routledge, London.

Cullingworth, J. B. (1980) *Environmental Planning 1939–1969, Vol. IV, Land Values, Compensation and Betterment*, HMSO, London.

Curry, N. (1991) Viewpoint: selling planning permission, *Town Planning Review*, **62**(3), v–viii.

Davies, H. W. E., Edwards, D. and Rowley, A. R. (1986) The relationship between development plans, development control and appeals, *The Planner*, **72**(10), 11–15.

Davies, H. W. E., Edwards, D., Hooper, A. and Punter, J. (1989) *Planning Control in Western Europe*, HMSO, London.

Davies, K, (1984) *Law of Compulsory Purchase and Compensation*, 4th edn, Butterworths, London.

Davis, J. and Healey, P. (1983) *Wokingham: The Implementation of Strategic Planning Policy in a Growth Area*, Oxford Working Paper No. 74, Department of Town Planning, Oxford Polytechnic.

Delafons, J. (1991a) Planning in the USA: paying for development, *The Planner*, **77**(20), 8–9.

Delafons, J. (1991b) *Development Impacts Fees and Other Devices*, University of California, Berkeley.

Delaney, C. J. and Hayward, D. (1994) Development contributions in Australia: unresolved issues, *Journal of Property Research*, **11**, 51–63.

Department of the Environment (DoE) (1972) *Report of the Working Party on Local Authority/Private Enterprise Partnership Schemes*, Sheaf Report, HMSO, London and Circular 102/72 (attached).

Department of the Environment (DoE) (1978) *Circular 44/78 Private Sector Land Requirement and Supply*, HMSO, London.

Department of the Environment (DoE) (1983) *Circular 22/83: Planning Gain*, HMSO, London.

Department of the Environment (DoE) (1985) *Circular 14/85: Development and Environment*, HMSO, London.

Department of the Environment (DoE) (1986) *The Future of Development Plans*, HMSO, London.

Department of the Environment (DoE) (1988a) *Planning Policy Guidance: West Midlands Strategic Guidance*, HMSO, London.

Department of the Environment (DoE) (1991a) *Circular 7/91: Planning and Affordable Housing*, HMSO, London.

Department of the Environment (DoE) (1991b) *Circular 16/91: Planning Obligations*, HMSO, London.

Department of the Environment (DoE) (1991c) *Planning Policy Guidance*

17: Sport and Recreation, HMSO, London.

Department of the Environment (DoE) (1992a) *Planning Policy Guidance 1: General Policy and Principles (revised version),* HMSO, London.

Department of the Environment (DoE) (1992b) *Planning Policy Guidance 12: Development Plans and Regional Guidance*, HMSO, London.

Department of the Environment (DoE) (1992c) *Planning Policy Guidance 3: Housing*, HMSO, London.

Department of the Environment (DoE) (1993a) *Planning Policy Guidance 6: Town Centres and Retail Development*, HMSO, London.

Department of the Environment (DoE) (1993b) *The UK Strategy for Sustainable Development*, Consultation paper, DoE, London.

Department of Transport (DTp) (1989) *Circular 1/89 Development in the Vicinity of Trunk Roads: Agreements under Section 278 of the Highways Act 1980*, HMSO, London.

Department of Transport (DTp) (1991) *Circular 6/91 Development in the Vicinity of Trunk Roads: Agreements under Section 278 of the Highways Act 1980*, HMSO, London.

Department of Transport (DTp) (1992) *Developers' Contributions to Highway Works: Consultation Document*, Department of Transport, London.

Durman, R. and Rowan-Robinson, J. (1991) *Section 50 Agreements: Final Report*, Scottish Office.

Dyos, H. (1961) *Victorian Suburb: A Study of the Growth of Camberwell,* Leicester University Press, Leicester.

Elson, M. (1990a) *Negotiating the Future: Planning Gain in the 1990s,* ARC Ltd.

Elson, M. (1990b) Recreational and community provision in new settlements, *The Planner*, **76**(36), 10–12.

Elson, M. and Payne, D. (ed.) (1993) *Planning Obligation for Sport and Recreation: A Guide for Negotiation and Action*, Sports Council, London.

Ennis, F., Healey, P. and Purdue, M. (1993) *Frameworks for Negotiating Development: Towards a Systematic Approach to Development Obligations*, Research Report, Department of Town and Country Planning, University of Newcastle upon Tyne.

Ennis, F. (1994) Planning obligations in development plans, *Land Use Policy*, **11**(3), 195–207.

Evans, A. (1982) *Externalities, Rent-seeking and Town Planning*, Discussion papers in Urban and Regional Economics No. 10, Department of Economics, University of Reading.

Fainstein, S. (1994) *The City Builders*, Blackwell, Oxford.

Feagin, J. (1983) *Free Enterprise City*, Rutgers, New Brunswick.

Ferguson, B. (1991) How impact fees affect residential development, paper to *ACSP/AESOP Joint Conference*, Oxford, July.

Fothergill, S., Monk, S. and Perry (1987) *Property and Industrial Development*, Hutchinson, London.

Francis, J. (1993) *The Politics of Regulation*, Blackwell, Oxford.

Gerald Eve, Chartered Surveyors and the Department of Land Economy Cambridge (1992) *The Relationship of House Prices and Land Supply,* HMSO, London.

Glasson, B. and Booth, P. (1992) Negotiation and delay in the development control process: case studies in Yorkshire and Humberside, *Town Planning Review*, **63**(1), 63–78.

Glasson, J., Therivel, R. and Chadwick, A. (1994) *Introduction to Environmental Impact Assessment,* UCL Press, London.

Goodchild, B. and Henneberry, J. (1994) *Impact Fees for Planning*, RICS, London.

Gore, T. and Nicholson, D. (1991) Models of the land development process: a critical review, *Environmental and Planning A*, **123**, 705–30.

Grant, M. (1978) Developers' contributions and planning gain: ethics and legalities, *Journal of Planning and Environmental Law,* 8–15.

Grant, M. (1979) Britain's Community Land Act: a post-mortem, *Urban Law and Policy*, **2**(2), 359–75.

Grant, M. (1986) Planning and land taxation, *Journal of Planning and Environmental Law,* 4–19, 92–106.

Grant, M. (1991) Betterment again, JPEL Occasional Paper No. 18, *The Planning Balance in the 1990s*, Sweet & Maxwell, London.

Grimley, J. R. Eve in association with Thames Polytechnic and Alsop Wilkinson (1992) *The Use of Planning Agreements,* HMSO, London.

Grove-White, R. (1991) Land-use law and environment, *Journal of Law and Society*, **18**(1), 32–47.

Hall, P., Gracey, H., Drewett, R. and Thomas, R. (1973) *The Containment of Urban England*, Allen & Unwin, London.

Hambleton, R. and Thomas, H. (eds) (1995) *Urban Policy Evaluation,* Paul Chapman, London.

Harlow District Council (1991) *Local District Plan: Deposit Version,* HDC, Harlow, Essex.

Harvey, D. (1985) *The Urbanisation of Capital*, Blackwell, Oxford.

Harvey, J. (1987) *Urban Land Economics*, Macmillan, London.

Healey, P. (1983) *Local Plans in British Land Use Planning*, Pergamon Press, Oxford.

Healey, P. (1988) The British planning system and managing the urban environment, *Town Planning Review*, **59**(4).

Healey, P. (1991a) Models of the development process: a review, *Journal of Property Research*, **8**(3), 210–38.

Healey, P. (1991b) *The treatment of planning gain in the 'new' local plans*, Working paper no. 14, Department of Town and Country Planning, University of Newcastle.

Healey, P. (1992a) An institutional model of the development process, *Journal of Property Research*, **9**, 33–44.

Healey, P. (1992b) Development plans and markets, *Planning Practice and Research*, **7**(2), 13–20.

Healey, P. (1993) The communicative work of development plans, *Environment and Planning B: Planning and Design*, **20**(1), 83–194.

Healey, P. (1994a) Development plans: new approaches to making frameworks for land use regulation, *European Planning Studies*, **2**(1), 39–57.

Healey, P. (1994b) Urban policy and property development: the institutional relations of property development in an old industrial region, *Environment and Planning A*, **26**, 177–98.

Healey, P. (1994c) Trends in development plan making in England, in Healey (ed.), *Tendencies in Development Plan Making in Europe*, Working paper no. 42, Department of Town and Country Planning, University of Newcastle upon Tyne.

Healey, P., McNamara, P., Doak, J. and Elson, M. (1988) *Land Use Planning and the Mediation of Urban Change,* Cambridge University Press, Cambridge.

Healey, P. and Barrett, S. (1990) Structure and agency in land and property development processes, *Urban Studies*, **27**(1), 89–104.

Healey, P., Ennis, F. and Purdue, M. (1992a) Planning gain and the 'new' local plans, *Town and Country Planning*, **61**(2), 39–43.

Healey, P., Purdue, M. and Ennis, F. (1992b) Rationales for 'planning gain', *Policy Studies*, **13**(2), 18–30.

Healey, P., Purdue, M. and Ennis, F. (1993a) *Gains from Planning?*, Joseph Rowntree Foundation, York.

Healey, P., Ennis, F. and Purdue, M. (1993b) Development impacts and obligations, *The Planner*, **79**(7), 11–14.

Healey, P., Cameron, S., Davoudi, S., Graham, S. and Madani Pour, A. (eds) (1995) *Managing Cities*, John Wiley, London.

Healey, P. and Shaw, T. (1993) Planning policies, plans and sustainability, *Regional Studies*, **27**(8), 769–76.

Heap, D. (1975) *The Land and the Development: or the Turmoil and the Torment*, Stevens & Sons, London.

Heap, D. and Ward, J. (1980) Planning bargaining – the pros and the cons: or how much can the system stand?, *Journal of Planning and Environmental Law*, 631–7.

Henry, D. (1983) *Planning by Agreement in a Berkshire District*, Oxford working paper no. 69, Oxford Polytechnic Department of Town Planning.

Henry, D. (1984) Planning by agreement, *Journal of Planning and Environmental Law*, 395–400.

Jacobs, M. (1991) *The Green Economy*, Pluto Press, London.

Jowell, J. (1977) Bargaining and development control, *Journal of Planning and Environmental Law*, 414–33.

Jowell, J. and Grant, M. (1983) Guide-lines for planning gain, *Journal of Planning and Environmental Law*, July, 427–31.

Kennedy-Skipton, H. (1994) *Property Development and Urban Regeneration: Policy-led Office Development in Glasgow/Clydebank and Manchester, Salford*, unpublished PhD thesis, University of Strathclyde.

Keogh, G. (1981) *Land Use Planning and the Production of Market Information* Discussion paper in Urban and Regional Economics, University of Reading.

Keogh, G. (1982) *Planning Gain: an Economic Analysis*, Department of Economics Working Paper, Reading University.

Kirwan, R. (1989) Finance for Urban Public Infrastructure, *Urban Studies*, **26**, 285–300.

KPMG Peat Marwick Management Consultants (1990) *Planning Gain*, KPMG, London.

Krabben, E. and Lambooy, J. (1993) A theoretical framework for the functioning of the Dutch property market, *Urban Studies*, **30**(8), 1382–95.

Labour Party (1994) *In Trust for Tomorrow: Report of the Labour Party Policy Commission on the Environment,* Labour Party, London.

Lichfield, N. (1989) From planning gain to community benefit, *Journal of Planning and Environmental Law*, February, 68–81.

Lichfield, N. (1992) From planning obligations to community impact analysis, *Journal of Planning and Environmental Law*, 1103–18.

Lichfield, N. and Darin-Drabkin, H. (1980) *Land Policy and Urban Growth*, Allen & Unwin, London.

Logan, J. and Molotch, H. (1987) *Urban Fortunes: The Political Economy of Place*, University of California Press, Berkeley.

Loughlin, M. (1978) Bargaining as a development tool, *Journal of Planning and Environmental Law*, 290–5.

Loughlin, M. (1980) Planning control and the property market, *Urban Law and Policy*, **1**, 1–22.

Loughlin, M. (1981) Planning gain: law, policy and practice, *Oxford Journal of Legal Studies*, 61–97.

Loughlin, M. (1982) Planning gain: another viewpoint, *Journal of Planning and Environmental Law*, 352–8.

MacDonald, R. (1991) *The Use of Planning Agreements by District Councils: Report of Research Findings*, Working paper, Oxford Polytechnic, Oxford.

McKay, D. and Cox, A. (1979) *The Politics of Urban Change*, Croom Helm, London.

McLoughlin, B. (1973) *Control and Urban Planning*, Faber & Faber, London.

Macmillan, H. (1979) *Tides of Fortune*, Macmillan, London.

Marriott, O. (1967) *The Property Boom*, Abingdon Publishing, London.

Massey, D. and Catalano, A. (1978) *Capital and Land*, Edward Arnold, London.

Morley, S. (1980) *Positive planning and direct development by local authorities*, Planning Studies No. 9, Polytechnic of Central London, London.

Nabarro, R. and Key, T. (1992) Current trends in commercial property investment and development, in Healey, P., Davoudi, S., O'Toole, M., Tavsanoglu, T. and Usher D. (eds), *Rebuilding the City: Property-led Urban Regeneration*, E and F N Spon, London, 44–59.

Needham, B., Koenders and Krujt, B. (1993) *Urban Land and Property Markets: The Netherlands*, UCL Press, London.

Newcastle City Council (1993) *Unitary Development Plan: Deposit Draft*, Newcastle CC, Newcastle upon Tyne.

Nicholas, J. C., Nelson, A. C. and Juergensmeyer, J. C. (1991) *A Practitioners Guide to Development Impact Fees*, Planners, Press, Chicago.

OFWAT (1992) *1991 Report of the Director General*, London, HMSO.

Owens, S. (1994) Land limits and sustainability: a conceptual framework and some dilemmas for the planning system, *Transactions of the Institute of British Geographers*, **14**, 434–56.

Pears, S. (1989) *Planning Gain and Urban Regeneration* (unpublished M.Phil), Department of Town and Country Planning, University of Newcastle upon Tyne.

Property Advisory Group (1980) *The Structure and Activity of the Development Industry,* HMSO, London.

Property Advisory Group (1981) *Planning Gain,* Department of the Environment, London.

Pryke, M. (1991) An international city going 'global': spatial change in the city of London, *Environment and Planning D: Society and Space,* **8**(2), 156–61.

Purdue, M. (1994) The impact of Section 54A, *Journal of Planning and Environment Law,* 399–407.

Purdue, M., Young, E. and Rowan-Robinson, J. (1989) *Planning Law and Procedure,* Butterworths, London.

Purdue, M., Healey, P. and Ennis, F. (1992) Planning gain and the grant of planning permission: is the US test of the 'rational nexus' the appropriate solution, *Journal of Environmental and Planning Law,* November, 1012–24.

Ravetz, A. (1980) *Remaking Cities,* Croom Helm, London.

Rodriguez-Bachiller, A., Thomas, M. and Ward, S. (1992) The English planning lottery: some insights from a more regulated system, *Town Planning Review,* **63**, 387–402.

Rowan-Robinson, J. and Lloyd, G. (1988) *Land Development and the Infrastructure Lottery,* T and T Clerk, Edinburgh.

Rowan-Robinson, J. (1992) Conditions or agreements, *Journal of Planning and Environmental Law,* 1003–13.

Rowan-Robinson, J. (1994) Planning decisions and planning agreements, *Conveyancer,* 31–40.

Ryan, J. C. (1991) Impact fees: a new funding source for local growth, *Journal of Planning Literature,* **5**(4), 401–7.

Rydin, Y. (1993) *The British Planning System: An introduction,* Macmillan, London.

Secretaries of State (1990) *This Common Inheritance,* HMSO, London.

Simkins, D. (1991) Planning gain: the developers' viewpoint, paper to Seminar on Planning Gain, London, September.

Skaburskis, A. (1988) Criteria for compensating for the impacts of large projects: the Impact of British Columbia's Revelstoke Dam on local government services, *Journal of Policy Analysis and Management,* **7**(4), 668–86.

Skaburskis, A. (1990) The burden of development impact fees, *Land Development Studies,* **7**, 173–85.

Skaburskis, A. (1991) The design of development cost charge schedules, *Journal of Property Research,* **8**(1), 83–98.

Solihull Metropolitan Borough Council (1990) *Unitary Development Plan: Deposit Draft*, SMBC, Solihull.

Stach, P. (1987) Zoning: to plan or to protect, *Journal of Planning Literature*, **2**(4), 371–82.

Thornley, A. (1991) *Urban Planning Under Thatcherism*, Routledge, London.

Uthwatt Committee (1942) *(Final Report) Expert Committee on Compensation and Betterment*, Cmnd 6386, HMSO, London.

Wakeford, R. (1990) *American Development Control: Parallels and Paradoxes from an English Perspective*, HMSO, London.

Weiss, M. (1987) *The Rise of the Community Builders*, Columbia University Press, New Brunswick.

Whatmore, S. and Boucher, S. (1992) *Planning Gain? An Assessment of its Contribution to Conservation and Amenity in the Countryside*, Research Report, Department of Geography, University of Bristol.

Whatmore, S. and Boucher, S. (1993) Bargaining with nature: the discourse and practice of environmental planning gain, *Transactions of the Institute of British Geographers*, **18**(2), 166–78.

Williams, G., Bell, G. and Russell, L. (1991) *Evaluating the Low-Cost Rural Housing Initiative*, HMSO, London.

Willis, K. (1980) Planning agreements and planning gain, *Planning Outlook*, **24**(2), 55–62.

Wood, W. (1947) *Planning and the Law: A Guide to the Town and Country Planning Act*.

Young, G. (1992) *Keynote address in Hart, G. (ed.), Development Plans: Master or Servant*, JPEL occasional paper no. 18, Sweet & Maxwell, London.

INDEX